Lua Programming Gems

Lua Programming Gems

edited by
Luiz Henrique de Figueiredo
Waldemar Celes
Roberto Ierusalimschy

Lua.org

Rio de Janeiro
2008

Lua Programming Gems

edited by Luiz Henrique de Figueiredo, Waldemar Celes, Roberto Ierusalimschy.

ISBN 978-85-903798-4-3.

Book cover by Pedro de Mazza Cerqueira. Lua logo design by Alexandre Nako. Typesetting by the editors using LaTeX.

Book web site: http://www.lua.org/gems/

Contents

III   Algorithms and Data Structures

IV   Game Programming

V   Embedding and Extending

Preface

It gives us great pleasure to publish this collection of Lua gems. Not only does it record some of the existing wisdom and practice on how to program well in Lua, but it also reflects the maturity of the Lua community. It is gratifying to see that Lua has motivated other people to learn it well and to share their knowledge with other users. In well-written articles that go much beyond the brief informal exchange of tips in the mailing list or the wiki, the authors share their mastery of all aspects of Lua programming, elementary and advanced.

Producing this book has required several steps. In response to a call for contributions, we received over 70 abstracts, selected 43, and received full versions for 28 of these. The authors received our comments and suggestions to prepare the final version of their articles. The whole process took two years, much longer than we had imagined. The selection of abstracts proved to be surprisingly difficult. Many potentially good submissions could not be accepted due to space limitations. Despite the long time it took and the amount of work it required (or because of it!), we are very happy to have this collection of articles on Lua contributed by members of our community. We trust the book was worth waiting for.

We thank all the authors for their hard work on the articles and everyone that submitted abstracts in the first phase. We also thank the whole Lua community for its friendliness and expertise. The active participation of our users has been to us a constant source of motivation for improving Lua. Finally, we give our warm thanks to Cameron Laird and Mark Hamburg for writing forewords to this book.

Additional material and errata will appear in the book web site:

http://www.lua.org/gems/

The Lua team
Rio de Janeiro, November 2008

Foreword

by Cameron Laird

When I need a programming language that's as easy as possible to embed, I choose Lua. Lua isn't just supple, free, portable, and compact, though; it's also powerful — and to get the most out of it, I'm glad I have *Lua Programming Gems*.

I need to explain that I mean something specific by that. Most of my reading is on the 'Net: I look up references, I read tutorials for unfamiliar material, I moderate a half-dozen Wikis, and I chat about specific techniques with colleagues on-line. My consumption of books has nose-dived. *Lua Programming Gems* is a book worth reading, though: its individual chapters get across ideas that simply aren't explained anywhere else.

Lua Programming Gems emphasizes practicality in a way I like. While the six authors in Part III certainly employ classroom concepts correctly in their examinations of "Algorithms and Data Structures", they do it all with working Lua code. The same pattern is apparent throughout *Lua Programming Gems*: it's filled with ideas likely to help me in my next programming project.

If you're new to Lua, you might be anxious about what you'll find. You can see that Lua offers definite advantages, but how hard is it to pick up what's undeniably a minority language? *Lua Programming Gems* will ease your concerns: the authors write clearly, modestly, and even deftly. The very first chapter, for example, tackles difficult material, including dynamically-allocated per-thread storage. The tone is consistent throughout the book. Rather than show off their expertise or indulge in private jokes, habits common for authors from other domains, the *Lua Programming Gems* authors focus on the specific details and examples that best teach their chosen topics. They make it inviting to dig deeper in Lua than you might do on your own.

Among the highlights of *Lua Programming Gems* for me: Part IV gives insight into "Game Programming", an area where I'll probably never work, although many of the techniques apply more broadly; Part V on "Embedding and Extending" is crucial for much of the programming I like; and Chapter 13, "Exceptions in Lua", is a particular interest of mine.

Do you want to "program well in Lua"? The Lua team set that as a goal when it first announced its plans for *Lua Programming Gems*. The final result fulfills that goal; you'll like it.

Lua and Lightroom

Mark Hamburg
Founder, Adobe Photoshop Lightroom

When we started work on the project that would become Adobe Photoshop Lightroom, we knew we wanted to make scriptability an important part of our story, so early on we reviewed the usual suspects. What drew us to Lua was its combination of simplicity, power, ease of embedding, and relatively high-performance. Having a straightforward license helped too when it came time to talk to Adobe's lawyers. Personally, as an old Scheme fan, I was drawn to its first-class closure support. I also found the coroutine system intriguing. The relative minimalism also resonated with a back-to-basics attitude that had us weaning ourselves away from intensive C++ usage and back toward C.

Still, it was hard to position Lua as anything other than an obscure choice. We could cite heavy use in the games community and we had set out with a mission of learning something from game developers, but if asked what materials one could turn to learn Lua or where we would find experienced Lua programmers, the answers were limited. For the former, we had the well-written reference manual, some good material on the Lua users wiki, and an intelligent forum on the Lua mailing list. This was good material, but there wasn't a lot of it. For the latter question, our answer was essentially "Any programmer worth hiring ought to be able to learn Lua quickly." This was a situation we were prepared to deal with and the arrival of *Programming in Lua* certainly helped, but it was easy to understand why it might be off putting to someone looking in from the outside.

Why this matters is that along with Lua's simplicity come some issues that make people with backgrounds in other languages stumble. The beauty of a small core is that there is a real opportunity for mastery. This is one of C's great strengths as well. That small core, however, comes at a price. For example, Lua has no syntax for exception handling. C doesn't either but having one seems almost required in modern languages. Lua has a syntax for object-oriented message sends, but the actual implementation of an object system or class system is a roll-your-own affair in Lua. As a result, one sees such issues raised repeatedly on the Lua users list as people new to the language start using it and then ask "But what about ____ ?"

Programming in Lua provides answers to some of these questions but those answers are necessarily terse. *Lua Programming Gems* dives deeper on these issues and many more. It shows ways to deal with threading — an issue we went through a few iterations on in Lightroom — and gives extended examples of how to hook Lua into your application. You may not always like the answers. For example, the object system presented here is quite minimalist. In the spirit of Lua, however, you remain free to roll your own using or not using the ideas presented here. The value comes in seeing the well worked examples together with a discussion of motivations and comparisons to other approaches. If this book had been around during Lightroom's development, we probably would have happily adopted some of the techniques it presents while simply taking inspiration from others. As it was, we largely had to find our own way and while that was rewarding in itself, the Lua community and particularly new Lua users can be happy to now have a field guide that maps out some of the trails.

The broader lesson from Lightroom that I would like to leave Lua users with is that you should let it pervade your work. Lua is sometimes described as being a language for gluing pieces together, but as we discovered that glue can extend quite deep. We started out looking for a scripting language for a native code application. Then we started thinking it would be nice to allow Lua to exist as a peer to native code. In the end, we ended up with a system where native code provides the foundation, but it is effectively a second-class citizen in the application as a whole. Large portions of Lightroom ended up getting written in Lua including the object-relational mapping layer for the database and the layout system for views. Lua defines the structure of the application and its extensibility mechanisms. As a result, we had an application that was smaller by far than some of its competitors, easy to change, largely cross-platform in its implementation, and suffered essentially no compile-link cycle. The reason things work out this way is that Lua is both very expressive compared to most native languages and sufficiently efficient that you can let it do a lot more of the work than one might be tempted to in other scripting languages. At the same time, the boundary between native code and Lua is sufficiently clean and efficient that when we needed to do things in native code, it wasn't a huge burden to expose that functionality to Lua nor to access functionality written in Lua.

So, my advice to Lua users and potential users is to think seriously about how widely you can let Lua spread through your work, be grateful for books like this one and *Programming in Lua* and be even more grateful for the work that the Lua team has done and their generosity in sharing it with the world.

Contributors

Following the Brazilian tradition, the contributors are listed in alphabetical order of first name.

André Carregal was introduced to Lua in 1994 during his MSc in Computer Science, which was supervised by Roberto Ierusalimschy. He has been working with web development using Lua since 1996. He currently coordinates the Kepler project and the LuaForge site while working as a consultant for Lua-related projects.

Ben Sunshine-Hill is a PhD student at the University of Pennsylvania, studying computer graphics. He did his undergraduate studies at the University of Southern California and received an MSc from the University of California, Los Angeles. He has been a game developer at several mobile and mainstream game development studios, and has previously published work on real-time rendering methods.

Diego Nehab was introduced to Lua in 1996, while working for Tecgraf in PUC-Rio. Over the years, he has been involved in a variety of Lua-related projects, including the IupLua, CDLua, IMLua, and LuaSQL libraries. He is best known as the author of the LuaThreads and LuaSocket libraries. Diego received a BEng in Computer Engineering and an MSc in Programming Languages from PUC-Rio, under the supervision of Roberto Ierusalimschy. He later received an MSc and a PhD in Computer Graphics from Princeton University. His research now focuses on high-quality shape acquisition and on real-time rendering techniques.

Doug Currie develops award-winning medical devices with Sunrise Labs, Inc. in Auburn, New Hampshire, USA. Over a thirty-year career, Doug has led electronics, mechanical, and software teams developing high-tech products with particular emphasis on reliability and adaptability. Some of these products, based on a massively parallel computing architecture Doug invented, are used in national transportation and world-class manufacturing operations. With a special interest in little languages, Doug has also contributed technically to open source projects such as Moscow ML, Hibernate, Gambit Scheme, and SICStus Prolog. Doug holds an S.B. degree in Electrical Engineering and Computer Science from the Massachusetts Institute of Technology.

Eduardo Ochs is a mathematician, or sort of; his interest on simplification of proofs led him to Non-Standard Analysis, and from there he drifted to Logic, Type Theory and Categorical Semantics. In parallel with his "normal" academic life he has been a contributor to the GNU Project since 1999, and his main focus areas in Free Software are little languages and programmable textual interfaces. He keeps a big, messy homepage at http://angg.twu.net/; all the html pages in it are generated with "BlogMe", another extensible little language built on top of Lua.

Gavin Wraith is Emeritus Reader in Mathematics, Sussex University, UK. Joined Sussex University in 1963, retired in 1999. Founding chairman of the Sussex University Computer Science department in 1985.

Jérôme Vuarand is a young software engineer specialized in AI and working in the video games industry. He discovered Lua while looking for an embeddable scripting language, just when Lua 5.1 was released, and he fell in love both for the language itself and its new package system. His initial motivation was to move away from legacy in-house script engines, but he's now using it as a general programming language in all his personal projects, from mobile robotics to modern game engines entirely written in Lua.

John Belmonte is a software engineer currently residing in New York City. He happened upon Lua as a video game developer in 2000 and was among the first to embed it into a home console title. Since then he has been active in the Lua community through chartering lua-users.org, participating in workshops, and contributing to the language's evolution.

Julio M. Fernández-Díaz has a PhD degree in Mining Engineering (1989). He is Professor of Applied Physics at the University of Oviedo in Spain and researches mainly in the field of atmospheric aerosols. His interests lie in developing physical and mathematical simulations on computers. His first 'computer' was an HP25 calculator in 1977. As a programmer, he uses Fortran, C, Lua, Tcl/Tk and Postscript, usually as part of his research.

Konstantin Sokharev professionally develops video games since 2001, successfully completed two RPG/RTS projects for PC, one for PocketPC/Palm. He currently holds a post of technical director at IceHill llc. developing Action-RTS title "Empire Above All" and several unannounced projects.

Luis Eduardo Ximenes Carvalho has a BSc (1997) in Civil Engineering from the Federal University of Ceará (UFC), an MSc (2000) in Transportation

Engineering from the Federal University of Rio de Janeiro (UFRJ), and an MSc (2002) in Computer Science from UFC, all in Brazil. He is currently a PhD candidate in the Division of Applied Math at Brown University, where his research comprises applications of Bayesian statistics to computational biology. He also has interest in logistics and optimization, scientific computing, graph theory, and programming languages, especially Lua.

Matthew Burke is an Assistant Professor of Computer Science at The George Washington University in Washington, D.C. Lua has replaced Forth as his favorite language in which to program while riding the subway, and he does so using whatever device is serving as his PDA du jour. He is also developing a curriculum for introductory Computer Science which uses Lua. When not programming, he likes to travel with his wife and son. He was the organizer of the Lua Workshop 2008.

Nicolas Peri is co-founder and technical director of the French company Stone-Trip, creator of the 3D game development platform ShiVa. He is in charge, among other things, of the ShiVa scripting engine, which is based on Lua. Before that, he worked as engine developer for other gaming companies, including Kalisto Entertainment and UbiSoft Tiwak.

Patrick Rapin studied at the Swiss Federal Institute of Technology at Lausanne (EPFL). He is now a software engineer working for Olivetti Engineering at Yverdon-les-Bains, developing printer firmware, image processing algorithms, and printer test tools.

Pedro Miller Rabinovitch, a PUC-Rio graduate, has worked with Lua at Tecgraf and Cipher Technology, and is currently a game developer at Jagex.

Rafael Moreira Savelli graduated in Computer Engineering at PUC-Rio. He worked for Tecgraf in PUC-Rio for over four years. He is now studying for an MSc at UFF and working in the Visgraf laboratory at IMPA.

Ralph Hempel is a Professional Engineer in Ontario, Canada and specializes in designing embedded systems. After learning to program on an HP41C, he never lost his fascination with small languages and hacking consumer products. He wrote pbForth for the LEGO MINDSTORMS RCX and then ported Lua to the NXT. When he's not wrangling embedded systems, Ralph enjoys mountain biking in the summer, snowboarding in the winter, and ice hockey all year long.

Ralph Steggink joined Océ in 2001. With a degree in both chemistry and computer science, he now develops controller software for printers. Together with Wim Couwenberg he prototyped revolutionary concepts using Lua. These currently find their way into several Océ products. He is an enthusiastic volleyball player and trainer.

Reuben Thomas is a freelance singer and computer scientist living in London. He took a BA in Mathematics with Computer Science from Cambridge University, as well as a doctorate in virtual machines. These days his computing interests center on contributions to a multitude of open source projects, with particular emphasis on improving the quality of mature software, and on automatic document processing. He is mostly employed as a classical baritone.

Robert Oates is a professional game programmer specializing in gameplay systems, artificial intelligence, and machine learning.

Roberto de Beauclair Seixas works with Research and Development at the Institute of Pure and Applied Mathematics (IMPA) in Rio de Janeiro, as member of the Vision and Computer Graphics Laboratory (Visgraf). He got his PhD in Computer Science at PUC-Rio, where he works with the Computer Graphics Technology Group (Tecgraf). From 1982 to 1998, he worked in the Computer Science Department at the National Laboratory for Scientific Computation (LNCC). His research interests include Scientific Visualization, Volume Rendering, Computer Graphics, High Performance Computing, Geometric Modeling, Military Warfare Simulations, GIS, and Medical Images.

Roberto Ierusalimschy is an Associate Professor at the Catholic University in Rio de Janeiro. He is the leading architect of Lua and the author of the book "Programming in Lua".

Sérgio Alvares Maffra is a MSc and Computer Engineer from PUC-Rio. He's been working with Lua at Tecgraf as a software developer for over a decade now.

Steve Gargolinski spent his early programming days hacking together small games built with code snippets from a QuickBasic programming manual. He has since evolved into a professional game developer, working as a member of the technical teams that produced the Zoo Tycoon 2 series, Star Trek: Legacy, and the upcoming Empire Earth III. Steve is currently working for Blue Fang Games as an AI Programmer. His interests include baseball, abstract strategy, practical AI, and walking in the woods.

Tobias Sülzenbrück and Christoph Beckmann are bachelor students of media systems at the Bauhaus-University of Weimar. Tobias fields of interests range from web development up to graphics programming. He has implemented a multi-agent system for simulating construction processes in Lua. Christoph is also interested in web development and is active in the research field of computer-supported cooperative work.

Tomás Guisasola works with Lua since 1995 when he developed with Roberto Ierusalimschy (his MSc advisor) the first implementation of the hooks mechanism and the debug facilities. Since then he worked mainly with CGILua as the platform for some administrative systems at PUC-Rio and also contributed with the Kepler team in the development of LuaLDAP, LuaXMLRPC, LuaSOAP, LuaDoc, and LuaSQL.

Vadim Groznov began programming at the age of fourteen, was involved in database programming for a long time, and took part in the creation of a custom scripting language. He professionally develops video games since 2002. His extensive experience of system programming allowed for the design and realisation of complex architectural solutions for game tools at IceHill llc.

Wim Couwenberg holds a PhD in mathematics and is employed at the R&D department of the European printing and document company Océ, based in The Netherlands, where he organised the international Lua Workshop 2006. He has been using Lua in projects ranging from simple data processing scripts to entire networked applications.

Yuri Takhteyev is a doctoral student at the UC Berkeley School of Information studying the role of space in software development communities.

Han Zhao is a shareware programmer in Beijing, P.R. China. Before that he worked for a mobile-phone design house. Now he uses Lua and C++ for everyday programming: an isometric role-playing game engine, an action game, and a shareware product. He also maintains a bit-operation lib LuaBit on LuaForge.

Part I

Programming Techniques

1

Lua Per-Thread Library Context

Doug Currie

Libraries written in C for use with Lua sometimes have a context that can be modified by the Lua program. For example, in the decNumber library, the Lua program may select the rounding mode and precision for arithmetic operations. The decNumber library user expects the context to be applied during library operations, and remain fixed until explicitly changed.

There are many other examples of library context. Libraries may need to maintain a per-thread global variable, like the POSIX library's errno. The C standard libraries have a current input file and current output file that are implied for many operations.

It would be wrong for a context setting in one Lua thread to affect the setting in another Lua thread. The other thread would get an unexpected rounding error, or an unexpected errno value, for example. Each thread should have its own context so that the library functions it uses operate the same way independent of the activities of other threads.

Lua does not provide a per-thread variables mechanism directly, though there are many ways to create this affect. The solution presented in this gem is to use the mechanism provided by LUA_ENVIRONINDEX. All functions in the library share a common closure. In this closure is a table used to map the thread's identity, i.e., L to a context. Since only the functions in the library have access to the common closure, there is no chance of interference from other libraries. The mechanism is fast, and can be made even faster with caching.

This gem presents the solution in a straightforward implementation, and adds userdata context functions, caching, and performance measurement in incremental steps.

There are other design alternatives to a per-thread context. The C library API can be revised to eliminate the global context. One way is by forcing the caller to provide a context argument with every API call. Alternatively, the API may require a context argument with data constructor calls, storing the context somewhere in the newly allocated data. Subsequent API calls using this data reference the context through the data. There are trade-offs with these alternatives.

Requiring a context with every API call is regular and applicative (sometimes called "functional") — the functions in the API can be idempotent. These are nice features, but while they make reasoning about your program easier in theory, they give up much in convenience. This method also simply pushes the problem of where to keep the per-thread context from the library into the library's client, the application.

Saving a context with every data structure may make reasoning about your program even harder, and makes sharing data among threads problematic. So, in addition to having dubious benefit, it shares many of the drawbacks of requiring a context with every API call.

One key benefit of a per-thread context is that Lua operators may use the context when operating on data managed by the library.

For example, the decNumber library uses userdata to implement arbitrary precision decimal numbers, and uses a metatable to support using Lua operators with these decimal numbers. The decNumber context has several user settable arithmetic parameters such as the number of significant digits, and the rounding mode. So, with a per-thread decNumber library context, the expression for computing compound interest with decimal numbers is simply:

```
((rate/100+1)^years)*start
```

but, if every decNumber function had to have the context supplied, it might look like this:

```
decNumber.multiply(CONTEXT,
  decNumber.expt(CONTEXT,
    decNumber.add(CONTEXT, 1,
        decNumber.divide(CONTEXT, rate, 100)),
    years),
  start)
```

I suspect you'd prefer the Lua operators to the API with context.

Implementation alternatives

So, how do we implement a per-thread library context?

The Lua 5.1 Reference Manual describes a "thread environment" that is accessible using LUA_GLOBALSINDEX. But all threads share the same global table as their thread environment by default. This prevents the thread environment's use as a per-thread storage mechanism for a library. It would depend on mechanisms to create a new thread environment at thread creation time, and these mechanisms are outside the library's control.

Libraries compiled and built together with the Lua sources can use the LUAI_EXTRASPACE mechanism to allocate some per-thread storage. To use this trick you must recompile the whole Lua library with a proper definition for LUAI_EXTRASPACE. If two or more libraries use this trick, their use of LUAI_EXTRASPACE must be coordinated. Clearly this approach doesn't work for dynamically loaded libraries and stock Lua.

What's needed is dynamically allocated per-thread storage.

With help from Lua users on the Lua mailing list, several implementation alternatives were explored. The first one was using the Lua registry to connect each thread to a userdata representing the context. The thread itself could be used as the registry key. The drawback to this approach is that it is not scalable. If two libraries use this mechanism then they will overwrite each others' contexts in the registry.

A fix to the registry approach is to use another level of indirection. Each library could create a table in the registry, keyed using a light userdata in the library's address space, and then this table would be used to associate the threads to the contexts. While this approach would work, the extra level of indirection and the double table lookup were unsatisfying.

Using LUA_ENVIRONINDEX **for library private storage**

Lua 5.1 also provides a little documented mechanism using a pseudo-index called LUA_ENVIRONINDEX. The Lua 5.1 Reference Manual (§3.3) simply says that "the environment of the running C function is always at pseudo-index LUA_ENVIRONINDEX".

What is the environment of a running C function?

Digging into the Lua 5.1 source code, we find uses of LUA_ENVIRONINDEX in liolib.c and loadlib.c where the function environment mechanism is used create a table shared privately among all the functions of a library. How does this work?

When a C function closure is created with lua_pushcclosure, which is used by luaL_register when registering a library's C functions for example, the current C function environment is saved in the new C function's closure as its C environment. The function lua_replace may be used to set the current C function environment to a newly allocated table. This table will then be shared by all subsequently created C function closures.

A function's environment may also be set using lua_setfenv—but this is not nearly as useful for our purposes! It would mean iterating over all the functions in the library after they were created by luaL_register duplicating a lot of effort.

So, for example, registering your library's functions could be done with:

```
/* make library private storage in new c function environment */
lua_newtable (L);
lua_replace (L, LUA_ENVIRONINDEX);
/* create library global table and register its functions */
luaL_register (L, LIBRARY_NAME, lib_luaL_reg_array);
```

The library private storage is now available to all the functions in
lib_luaL_reg_array by using pseudo-index LUA_ENVIRONINDEX with any Lua API
function that takes an index argument. So, for example, accessing the library
private storage from functions in lib_luaL_reg_array can be accomplished with:

```
lua_pushliteral (L, "somevalue");    /* value to store */
lua_setfield (L, LUA_ENVIRONINDEX, "somekey");  /* key */
```

to store a value in library private storage, and

```
lua_getfield (L, LUA_ENVIRONINDEX, "somekey");
```

to retrieve it.

Using library private storage to implement per-thread private storage

Now that we have library private storage, how do we use it to implement per-
thread library private storage? The simple answer is to use the current thread
as a key for the library private storage table. Then each Lua thread in the
system will have one value in our library private storage.

Our example accessing the library private storage from functions in
lib_luaL_reg_array becomes:

```
lua_pushthread (L);          /* key */
lua_pushvalue (L, index);  /* value */
lua_rawset (L, LUA_ENVIRONINDEX);
```

to save the thread's value, and

```
lua_pushthread (L);          /* key */
lua_rawget (L, LUA_ENVIRONINDEX);
```

to retrieve the thread's value.

If multiple values must be stored for each thread, we can make the thread's
value a table or userdata and store several values in it.

There is one further thing we must do to make this mechanism a good Lua
citizen. By using threads as our library private storage table keys, we are
preventing Lua from ever garbage collecting the threads that use our library.
The solution is making our library private storage table a weak table on its
keys. Registering our library's functions becomes:

```
lua_newtable (L);           /* make environment "private storage" */
lua_createtable (L, 0, 1);          /* its metatable, which is */
lua_pushliteral (L, "__mode");      /* used to make environment */
lua_pushliteral (L, "k");               /* weak in the keys */
lua_rawset (L, -3);                 /* metatable.__mode = "k" */
lua_setmetatable (L, -2);     /* set the environment metatable */
lua_replace (L, LUA_ENVIRONINDEX);   /* the new c function env */
/* create library global table and register its functions */
luaL_register (L, LIBRARY_NAME, lib_luaL_reg_array);
```

One may wonder if using lua_pushlightuserdata(L,L) might be faster than lua_pushthread(L) as the key for accessing our private storage. There are two problems with using lua_pushlightuserdata(L,L):

- Lua offers no guarantee that the thread will not be relocated by the garbage collector; if it is relocated, the value L will change from one library invocation to another, and our key is useless to identify the thread private data;

- Our private storage table would never be garbage collected since Lua cannot determine if our light userdata is garbage, so the table entries will remain in the table until we explicitly remove them.

Fortunately, lua_pushthread(L) is quite fast, convenient, and avoids both problems.

Using per-thread private storage for per-thread library context

Now that we have per-thread library-private storage we are ready to implement per-thread library context. For this implementation we will use userdata for the per-thread context. This supports adding as many fields of context for each thread as necessary while having only one value in the thread private storage for each thread.

For Lua decNumber, a wrapper for the IBM decNumber library, the context is simply the decContext structure defined by the underlying decNumber library. The examples in subsequent sections will use Lua decNumber code. To use these techniques in your own code, simply substitute your own context structure for the decContext structure.

The mechanism has just a few pieces:

- The weak key table implementation of per-thread library private storage, above;

- Functions to create and type-check a context userdata;

- Functions to get and set the current thread's context;

- A function to push current thread's context to return it to Lua code.

The functions to create and type-check a context userdata will be familiar to Lua library authors. The creation function simply allocates storage, and sets the userdata metatable to a unique metatable that is used for runtime type checking, along with providing the table of callable methods for the context. The metatable is created at library load time, and I won't bore you with the details since this is a standard Lua library technique — the details are available in the decNumber library, for example, at LuaForge.

The functions to get and set the current thread's context are the heart of the matter. The getter function uses a helper function to push current thread's context as a helper. The reason for this will become clearer in the next section on caching.

```
/*  ldn_set_context has no stack effect
*/
static void ldn_set_context (lua_State *L, int index)
{
    /* make value at index the context for this thread */
    if (index < 0) index -= 1;
    lua_pushthread (L);        /* key */
    lua_pushvalue (L, index); /* value */
    lua_rawset (L, LUA_ENVIRONINDEX);
}


static decContext *ldn_push_context (lua_State *L)
{
    decContext *dc;
    lua_pushthread (L);        /* key */
    lua_rawget (L, LUA_ENVIRONINDEX);

    if (lua_isnil (L, -1))
    {
        /* nothing in the thread local state, so make a new context */
        lua_pop (L, 1);
        dc = ldn_make_context (L);
        dc = decContextDefault (dc, LDN_CONTEXT_DEFAULT); /* init */
        /* make it the context for this thread */
        ldn_set_context (L, -1, dc);
    }
    else
    {
        dc = ldn_check_context (L, -1);
    }
    return dc; /* and leaves context on Lua stack */
}
```

```
static decContext *ldn_get_context (lua_State *L)
{
    decContext *dc;
    dc = ldn_push_context (L);
    lua_pop (L, 1);
    return dc;
}
```

Caching per-thread library context

While the implementation of per-thread library context using library private storage is quite fast, there is room for improvement. We can avoid the table lookup in the library private storage if we cache the last lookup. This will be beneficial in a couple common cases:

- The library is only used from only one thread;

- The library is used several times between thread yields.

First we will develop a caching approach, and then explore its benefits, measuring its performance advantage, and discuss some potential drawbacks.

The caching technique is quite straightforward: we simply record the thread (L) and context on each lookup in the library private storage. Each reference to the thread context first checks if the reference is from the last thread to perform a lookup, and if so returns the cached value avoiding the second and subsequent lookups.

This implementation depends on threads and userdata not being moved by the garbage collector. Fortunately, this is true for present Lua implementations, and those in the foreseeable future since the Lua authors "have no intention of allowing userdata addresses to change during GC" (http://lua-users.org/lists/lua-1/2006-04/msg00384.html).

Lua doesn't provide a way to push a userdata from the C library; the pointer returned by lua_touserdata or luaL_checkudata is incremented past the Lua userdata header. The userdata header structure is opaque to the C library. Most of the time the library doesn't care about this; it just wants a pointer to the context and doesn't need to put it on the Lua stack. In these cases the cache works fine. In other rare cases, the C library must push the context to pass it as an argument to Lua code or return it to the Lua library caller. In these situations the cache is simply bypassed.

Another optimization is that ldn_set_context now takes the decContext as an argument. This avoids having to convert the context value on the stack to a userdata pointer for storage into the cache. The caller generally has this pointer in hand at the time of the call.

Our C code is uses preprocessor macros to enable and disable caching so we can build with either implementation. Here are the updated functions:

```
#if LDN_ENABLE_CACHE
static lua_State *L_of_context_cache;
static decContext *context_cache;
#endif

/* the value on stack at index must be
   the decContext userdata corresponding to dc
   ldn_set_context must have no stack effect
*/
static void ldn_set_context (lua_State *L, int index, decContext *dc)
{
    /* make value at index the context for this thread */
    if (index < 0) index -= 1;
    lua_pushthread (L);          /* key */
    lua_pushvalue (L, index); /* value */
    lua_rawset (L, LUA_ENVIRONINDEX);
#if LDN_ENABLE_CACHE
    /* and cache */
    L_of_context_cache = L;
    context_cache = dc;
#endif
}


/*
 * either we need a decContext on the Lua stack, so we must bypass the
 * cache, or we have a cache miss
 */
static decContext *ldn_push_context (lua_State *L)
{
    decContext *dc;
    lua_pushthread (L);          /* key */
    lua_rawget (L, LUA_ENVIRONINDEX);

    if (lua_isnil (L, -1))
    {
        /* nothing in the thread local state, so make a new context */
        lua_pop (L, 1);
        dc = ldn_make_context (L);
        dc = decContextDefault (dc, LDN_CONTEXT_DEFAULT);
        /* make it the context for this thread */
        ldn_set_context (L, -1, dc);
    }
```

```
    else
    {
        dc = ldn_check_context (L, -1);
#if LDN_ENABLE_CACHE
        /* and cache */
        L_of_context_cache = L;
        context_cache = dc;
#endif
    }
    return dc; /* leaves context on Lua stack */
}

static decContext *ldn_get_context (lua_State *L)
{
    decContext *dc;
#if LDN_ENABLE_CACHE
    /* try the cache first */
    if (L_of_context_cache == L)
    {
        dc = context_cache;
    }
    else
#endif
    {
        /* go to the per-thread storage next */
        dc = ldn_push_context (L);
        lua_pop (L, 1);
    }
    return dc;
}
```

Note: There is an unlikely but possible failure mode for this cache implementation. The following things must all happen:

- A thread X uses the per-thread library context;

- It is the last thread to reference the per-thread library context before a garbage collection;

- The thread X is garbage collected;

- A new thread Y is created *and* is allocated at the exact same memory address as X;

- The new thread X is the first to reference the per-thread library context after the garbage collection.

At this point, thread Y will use the (possibly freed) userdata context of thread X leading to, at worst, a crash. Even if the userdata context has not been freed yet, it is not the context of the new thread, which presumably should be a newly initialized context. So, for example, thread Y could use a rounding mode and precision set by thread X rather than the defaults, or could use file handles thread X established for I/O rather than the standard I/O handles.

The root cause of the problem is that we are holding a reference to the thread and userdata context that is not reachable from Lua's root set. Of course, if it was reachable, we'd have the same memory leak that we fixed using a weak table for the per-thread library context.

Can this failure mode be eliminated?

Adding a __gc method to the context userdata that invalidates the per-thread library context cache is probably a good place to start; that will prevent access to freed memory. This is not a general solution to the problem, though, since the context may not have been collected yet. The context may not be garbage if it can be shared by multiple threads (in decNumber it can be shared). Furthermore, even if the context is not shared, it is not guaranteed to be collected on the same collection cycle as the thread, so there is still a potential problem with using the wrong context, that of the freed thread (thread X's context rather than thread Y's).

Unfortunately, Lua does not have a gc hook that is called after every collection; otherwise a hook function could simply invalidate the per-thread library context cache after every collection. One can emulate this hook by allocating a sacrificial userdata with a __gc method that invalidates the cache, and immediately popping it from the stack. It's __gc method would also create another identical userdata so that the cache is flushed every collection cycle.

This is a bit tricky, and dependent on non-specified behavior of the garbage collector. The Lua garbage collector offers no guarantee that either (a) garbage is collected in any particular order relative to becoming untraceable, or (b) all garbage is collected on every cycle. There are garbage collectors that collect in some arbitrary order, e.g., memory address order, and/or only a portion of the free memory on each collection cycle. The Caml Light GC works that way, for example. So, if the thread is collected but not the sacrificial userdata on the same cycle, the trick (now a bad kludge) doesn't work.

However the trick works with the present Lua 5.1 garbage collector, and probably with most future implementations. As the sacrificial userdata is already dead when the cycle starts, it will surely be collected. Even if the Lua implementers introduce generational garbage collection, this userdata will never move to older generations.

Another solution to eliminating the failure mode is to require that each new thread calls an initialization function in the library that, perhaps among other things, invalidates the cache. Since this depends on actions of library users to prevent the failure mode, it is not ideal. However, if your library needs per-thread initialization for other reasons, it may be a reasonable fix.

In summary, to avoid the highly unlikely caching failure mode, you should use a __gc method of the context userdata that invalidates the per-thread library context, and either require library users in each new thread to call an initialization function that invalidates the cache, or create a sacrificial userdata that invalidates the cache and regenerates a garbage copy of itself. In the latter case, if a future Lua has an incompatible garbage collector, look for its new post collection hook instead!

Of course, the failure mode does not exist if the non-cached implementation of per-thread library context is used. Whether it is worth the effort to implement a totally safe cache depends on the expected performance benefit. That is examined in the next section.

Testing and performance measurement

The Lua decNumber library is delivered with extensive test suite, both the IBM decTest suite as well as Lua implementation specific tests. There are over 30,000 test cases. Among these tests are some performance measurements of Lua decNumber with and without caching of the per-thread library context. There are specific tests of correctness of the per-thread context using two Lua threads, and implementation of cache hit and miss counters.

The performance measurement is done with an included Lua library providing access to the Windows high resolution QueryPerformanceCounter API. Please experiment with these tools on your system.

Two test cases were studied to determine if per-thread library context caching is beneficial: a minimal arithmetic loop (one decNumber add and assignment to a local), and a more complex calculation involving decNumber division, remainder, square root, and exponentiation. Both cases were timed in single threaded mode — this is the best case for caching since all but the first context access will hit.

The testing method was simple: Time N iterations of an empty loop and N iterations of each calculation. Repeat this several times and discard the obvious outliers (best and worst). Subtract the empty loop time from the calculation loop times. Compare the cache and non-cache results:

- For the simple arithmetic loop, caching gave a bit over a 21% reduction in compute time. In other words, the arithmetic loop run with the context-cache-enabled library ran in 79% of the time of the no-context-cache library.

- For the complex calculation loop, caching gave a bit over a 0.6% reduction in compute time. Lua table lookup is quite fast compared with this calculation!

So, as you'd expect, the benefits of caching the library context will depend a lot on the time complexity of your library functions.

Conclusion

Caching the per-thread library context provides a small increase in performance. The caching failure mode identified above is highly unlikely, but catastrophic. The solutions to avoid the failure are either Lua implementation dependent, or put a per-thread initialization obligation on library users. Fortunately, the non-cache version of per-thread library context performs quite well. Unless you need the small performance gain, or until Lua implements a gc hook, the cache may be more trouble than it's worth. If you need the performance, use a solution to avoid the failure that's best for your application.

Lua's LUA_ENVIRONINDEX mechanism has several interesting uses. It was a joy to discover, and seems to be just the right approach for per-thread library context. The mechanism is so easy to implement that every library with context should use per-thread library context.

2

Lua Performance Tips

Roberto Ierusalimschy

In Lua, as in any other programming language, we should always follow the two maxims of program optimization:

Rule #1: *Don't do it.*

Rule #2: *Don't do it yet.* (for experts only)

Those rules are particularly relevant when programming in Lua. Lua is famous for its performance, and it deserves its reputation among scripting languages.

Nevertheless, we all know that performance is a key ingredient of programming. It is not by chance that problems with exponential time complexity are called *intractable*. A too late result is a useless result. So, every good programmer should always balance the costs from spending resources to optimize a piece of code against the gains of saving resources when running that code.

The first question regarding optimization a good programmer always asks is: "Does the program needs to be optimized?" If the answer is positive (but only then), the second question should be: "Where?"

To answer both questions we need some instrumentation. We should not try to optimize software without proper measurements. The difference between experienced programmers and novices is *not* that experienced programmers are better at spotting where a program may be wasting its time: The difference is that experienced programmers know they are not good at that task.

A few years ago, Noemi Rodriguez and I developed a prototype for a CORBA ORB (Object Request Broker) in Lua, which later evolved into OiL (*Orb in Lua*). As a first prototype, the implementation aimed at simplicity. To avoid the need for extra C libraries, the prototype serialized integers using a few arithmetic operations to isolate each byte (conversion to base 256). It did not support floating-point values. Because CORBA handles strings as sequences of characters, our ORB first converted Lua strings into a sequence (that is, a Lua table) of characters and then handled the result like any other sequence.

When we finished that first prototype, we compared its performance against a professional ORB implemented in C++. We expected our ORB to be somewhat slower, as it was implemented in Lua, but we were disappointed by how much slower it was. At first, we just laid the blame on Lua. Later, we suspected that the culprit could be all those operations needed to serialize each number. So, we decided to run the program under a profiler. We used a very simple profiler, not unlike the one described in Chapter 23 of *Programming in Lua*. The profiler results shocked us. Against our gut feelings, the serialization of numbers had no measurable impact on the performance, among other reasons because there were not that many numbers to serialize. The serialization of strings, however, was responsible for a huge part of the total time. Practically every CORBA message has several strings, even when we are not manipulating strings explicitly: object references, method names, and some other internal values are all coded as strings. And the serialization of each string was an expensive operation, because it needed to create a new table, fill it with each individual character, and then serialize the resulting sequence, which involved serializing each character one by one. Once we reimplemented the serialization of strings as a special case (instead of using the generic code for sequences), we got a respectable speed up. With just a few extra lines of code, the performance of your implementation was comparable to the C++ implementation.[1]

So, we should always measure when optimizing a program for performance. Measure before, to know where to optimize. And measure after, to know whether the "optimization" actually improved our code.

Once you decide that you really must optimize your Lua code, this text may help you about how to optimize it, mainly by showing what is slow and what is fast in Lua. I will not discuss here general techniques for optimization, such as better algorithms. Of course you should know and use those techniques, but there are several other places where you can learn them. In this article I will discuss only techniques that are particular to Lua. Along the article, I will constantly measure the time and space performance of small programs. Unless stated otherwise, I do all measures on a Pentium IV 2.9 GHz with 1 GB of main memory, running Ubuntu 7.10, Lua 5.1.1. Frequently I give actual measures (e.g., 7 seconds), but what is relevant is the relationship between different measures. When I say that a program is "$X\%$ times faster" than another it means that it runs in $X\%$ less time. (A program 100% faster would take no time to run.) When I say that a program is "$X\%$ times slower" than another I mean that the other is $X\%$ faster. (A program 50% slower means that it takes twice the time.)

---

[1]Of course our implementation was still slower, but not by an order of magnitude.

Basic facts

Before running any code, Lua translates (precompiles) the source into an internal format. This format is a sequence of instructions for a virtual machine, similar to machine code for a real CPU. This internal format is then interpreted by C code that is essentially a *while* loop with a large *switch* inside, one case for each instruction.

Perhaps you have already read somewhere that, since version 5.0, Lua uses a register-based virtual machine. The "registers" of this virtual machine do not correspond to real registers in the CPU, because this correspondence would be not portable and quite limited in the number of registers available. Instead, Lua uses a stack (implemented as an array plus some indices) to accommodate its registers. Each active function has an *activation record*, which is a stack slice wherein the function stores its registers. So, each function has its own registers[2]. Each function may use up to 250 registers, because each instruction has only 8 bits to refer to a register.

Given that large number of registers, the Lua precompiler is able to store all local variables in registers. The result is that access to local variables is very fast in Lua. For instance, if a and b are local variables, a Lua statement like a = a + b generates one single instruction: ADD 0 0 1 (assuming that a and b are in registers 0 and 1, respectively). For comparison, if both a and b were globals, the code for that addition would be like this:

```
GETGLOBAL       0 0       ; a
GETGLOBAL       1 1       ; b
ADD             0 0 1
SETGLOBAL       0 0       ; a
```

So, it is easy to justify one of the most important rules to improve the performance of Lua programs: *use locals!*

If you need to squeeze performance out of your program, there are several places where you can use locals besides the obvious ones. For instance, if you call a function within a long loop, you can assign the function to a local variable. For instance, the code

```
for i = 1, 1000000 do
  local x = math.sin(i)
end
```

runs 30% slower than this one:

```
local sin = math.sin
for i = 1, 1000000 do
  local x = sin(i)
end
```

---

[2]This is similar to the *register windows* found in some CPUs.

Access to external locals (that is, variables that are local to an enclosing function) is not as fast as access to local variables, but it is still faster than access to globals. Consider the next fragment:

```
function foo (x)
  for i = 1, 1000000 do
    x = x + math.sin(i)
  end
  return x
end
```

```
print(foo(10))
```

We can optimize it by declaring sin once, outside function foo:

```
local sin = math.sin
function foo (x)
  for i = 1, 1000000 do
    x = x + sin(i)
  end
  return x
end
```

```
print(foo(10))
```

This second code runs 30% faster than the original one.

Although the Lua compiler is quite efficient when compared with compilers for other languages, compilation is a heavy task. So, you should avoid compiling code in your program (e.g., function loadstring) whenever possible. Unless you must run code that is really dynamic, such as code entered by an end user, you seldom need to compile dynamic code.

As an example, consider the next code, which creates a table with functions to return constant values from 1 to 100000:

```
local lim = 10000
local a = {}
for i = 1, lim do
  a[i] = loadstring(string.format("return %d", i))
end
print(a[10]())    --> 10
```

This code runs in 1.4 seconds.

With closures, we avoid the dynamic compilation. The next code creates the same 100000 functions in $\frac{1}{10}$ of the time (0.14 seconds):

```
function fk (k)
  return function () return k end
end
```

```
local lim = 100000
local a = {}
for i = 1, lim do  a[i] = fk(i)  end
print(a[10]())    --> 10
```

About tables

Usually, you do not need to know anything about how Lua implement tables to use them. Actually, Lua goes to great lengths to make sure that implementation details do not surface to the user. However, these details show themselves through the performance of table operations. So, to optimize programs that use tables (that is, practically any Lua program), it is good to know a little about how Lua implements tables.

The implementation of tables in Lua involves some clever algorithms. Every table in Lua has two parts: the *array* part and the *hash* part. The array part stores entries with integer keys in the range 1 to n, for some particular n. (We will discuss how this n is computed in a moment.) All other entries (including integer keys outside that range) go to the hash part.

As the name implies, the hash part uses a hash algorithm to store and find its keys. It uses what is called an *open address* table, which means that all entries are stored in the hash array itself. A hash function gives the primary index of a key; if there is a collision (that is, if two keys are hashed to the same position), the keys are linked in a list, with each element occupying one array entry.

When Lua needs to insert a new key into a table and the hash array is full, Lua does a *rehash*. The first step in the rehash is to decide the sizes of the new array part and the new hash part. So, Lua traverses all entries, counting and classifying them, and then chooses as the size of the array part the largest power of 2 such that more than half the elements of the array part are filled. The hash size is then the smallest power of 2 that can accommodate all the remaining entries (that is, those that did not fit into the array part).

When Lua creates an empty table, both parts have size 0 and, therefore, there are no arrays allocated for them. Let us see what happens when we run the following code:

```
local a = {}
for i = 1, 3 do
  a[i] = true
end
```

It starts by creating an empty table a. In the first loop iteration, the assignment a[1]=true triggers a rehash; Lua then sets the size of the array part of the table to 1 and keeps the hash part empty. In the second loop iteration, the assignment a[2]=true triggers another rehash, so that now the array part of the table has size 2. Finally, the third iteration triggers yet another rehash, growing the size of the array part to 4.

A code like

```
a = {}
a.x = 1; a.y = 2; a.z = 3
```

does something similar, except that it grows the hash part of the table.

For large tables, this initial overhead is amortized over the entire creation: While a table with three elements needs three rehashings, a table with one million elements needs only twenty. But when you create thousands of small tables, the combined overhead can be significant.

Older versions of Lua created empty tables with some pre-allocated slots (four, if I remember correctly), to avoid this overhead when initializing small tables. However, this approach wastes memory. For instance, if you create millions of points (represented as tables with only two entries) and each one uses twice the memory it really needs, you may pay a high price. That is why currently Lua creates empty tables with no pre-allocated slots.

If you are programming in C, you can avoid those rehashings with the Lua API function `lua_createtable`. It receives two arguments after the omnipresent `lua_State`: the initial size of the array part and the initial size of the hash part of the new table.[3] By giving appropriate sizes to the new table, it is easy to avoid those initial rehashes. Beware, however, that Lua can only shrink a table when rehashing it. So, if your initial sizes are larger than needed, Lua may never correct your waste of space.

When programming in Lua, you may use constructors to avoid those initial rehashings. When you write {true, true, true}, Lua knows beforehand that the table will need three slots in its array part, so Lua creates the table with that size. Similarly, if you write {x = 1, y = 2, z = 3}, Lua will create a table with four slots in its hash part. As an example, the next loop runs in 2.0 seconds:

```
for i = 1, 1000000 do
  local a = {}
  a[1] = 1; a[2] = 2; a[3] = 3
end
```

If we create the tables with the right size, we reduce the run time to 0.7 seconds:

```
for i = 1, 1000000 do
  local a = {true, true, true}
  a[1] = 1; a[2] = 2; a[3] = 3
end
```

If you write something like {[1] = true, [2] = true, [3] = true}, however, Lua is not smart enough to detect that the given expressions (literal numbers, in this case) describe array indices, so it creates a table with four slots in its *hash part*, wasting memory and CPU time.

---

[3]Although the rehash algorithm always sets the array size to a power of two, the array size can be any value. The hash size, however, must be a power of two, so the second argument is always rounded to the smaller power of two not smaller than the original value.

The size of both parts of a table are recomputed only when the table rehashes, which happens only when the table is completely full and Lua needs to insert a new element. As a consequence, if you traverse a table erasing all its fields (that is, setting them all to nil), the table does not shrink. However, if you insert some new elements, then eventually the table will have to resize. Usually this is not a problem: if you keep erasing elements and inserting new ones (as is typical in many programs), the table size remains stable. However, you should not expect to recover memory by erasing the fields of a large table: It is better to free the table itself.

A dirty trick to force a rehash is to insert enough nil elements into the table. See the next example:

```
a = {}
lim = 10000000
for i = 1, lim do a[i] = i end              --  create a huge table
print(collectgarbage("count"))              --> 196626
for i = 1, lim do a[i] = nil end            --  erase all its elements
print(collectgarbage("count"))              --> 196626
for i = lim + 1, 2*lim do a[i] = nil end    --  create many nil elements
print(collectgarbage("count"))              --> 17
```

I do not recommend this trick except in exceptional circumstances: It is slow and there is no easy way to know how many elements are "enough".

You may wonder why Lua does not shrink tables when we insert nils. First, to avoid testing what we are inserting into a table; a check for nil assignments would slow down all assignments. Second, and more important, to allow nil assignments when traversing a table. Consider the next loop:

```
for k, v in pairs(t) do
  if some_property(v) then
    t[k] = nil     -- erase that element
  end
end
```

If Lua rehashed the table after a nil assignment, it would havoc the traversal.

If you want to erase all elements from a table, a simple traversal is the correct way to do it:

```
for k in pairs(t) do
  t[k] = nil
end
```

A "smart" alternative would be this loop:

```
while true do
  local k = next(t)
  if not k then break end
  t[k] = nil
end
```

However, this loop is very slow for large tables. Function next, when called without a previous key, returns the "first" element of a table (in some random order). To do that, next traverses the table arrays from the beginning, looking for a non-nil element. As the loop sets the first elements to nil, next takes longer and longer to find the first non-nil element. As a result, the "smart" loop takes 20 seconds to erase a table with 100,000 elements; the traversal loop using pairs takes 0.04 seconds.

About strings

As with tables, it is good to know how Lua implements strings to use them more efficiently.

The way Lua implements strings differs in two important ways from what is done in most other scripting languages. First, all strings in Lua are *internalized*; this means that Lua keeps a single copy of any string. Whenever a new string appears, Lua checks whether it already has a copy of that string and, if so, reuses that copy. Internalization makes operations like string comparison and table indexing very fast, but it slows down string creation.

Second, variables in Lua never hold strings, but only references to them. This implementation speeds up several string manipulations. For instance, in Perl, when you write something like $x = $y, where $y contains a string, the assignment copies the string contents from the $y buffer into the $x buffer. If the string is long, this becomes an expensive operation. In Lua, this assignment involves only copying a pointer to the actual string.

This implementation with references, however, slows down a particular form of string concatenation. In Perl, the operations $s = $s . "x" and $s .= "x" are quite different. In the first one, you get a copy of $s and adds "x" to its end. In the second one, the "x" is simply appended to the internal buffer kept by the $s variable. So, the second form is independent from the string size (assuming the buffer has space for the extra text). If you have these commands inside loops, their difference is the difference between a linear and a quadratic algorithm. For instance, the next loop takes almost five minutes to read a 5MByte file:

```
$x = "";
while (<>) {
  $x = $x . $_;
}
```

If we change $x = $x . $_ to $x .= $_, this time goes down to 0.1 seconds! Lua does not offer the second, faster option, because its variables do not have buffers associated to them. So, we must use an explicit buffer: a table with the string pieces does the job. The next loop reads that same 5MByte file in 0.28 seconds. Not as fast as Perl, but quite good.

```
local t = {}
for line in io.lines() do
  t[#t + 1] = line
end
s = table.concat(t, "\n")
```

Reduce, reuse, recycle

When dealing with Lua resources, we should apply the same three R's promoted for the Earth's resources.

Reduce is the simplest alternative. There are several ways to avoid the need for new objects. For instance, if your program uses too many tables, you may consider a change in its data representation. As a simple example, consider that your program manipulates polylines. The most natural representation for a polyline in Lua is as a list of points, like this:

```
polyline = { { x = 10.3, y = 98.5 },
             { x = 10.3, y = 18.3 },
             { x = 15.0, y = 98.5 },
             ...
           }
```

Although natural, this representation is not very economic for large polylines, as it needs a table for each single point. A first alternative is to change the records into arrays, which use less memory:

```
polyline = { { 10.3, 98.5 },
             { 10.3, 18.3 },
             { 15.0, 98.5 },
             ...
           }
```

For a polyline with one million points, this change reduces the use of memory from 95 KBytes to 65 KBytes. Of course, you pay a price in readability: `p[i].x` is easier to understand than `p[i][1]`.

A yet more economic alternative is to use one list for the x coordinates and another one for the y coordinates:

```
polyline = { x = { 10.3, 10.3, 15.0, ...},
             y = { 98.5, 18.3, 98.5, ...}
           }
```

The original `p[i].x` now is `p.x[i]`. With this representation, a one-million-point polyline uses only 24 KBytes of memory.

A good place to look for chances of reducing garbage creation is in loops. For instance, if a constant table is created inside a loop, you can move it out the loop, or even out of the function enclosing its creation. Compare:

```
function foo (...)
  for i = 1, n do
    local t = {1, 2, 3, "hi"}
    -- do something without changing 't'
    ...
  end
end

local t = {1, 2, 3, "hi"}    -- create 't' once and for all
function foo (...)
  for i = 1, n do
    -- do something without changing 't'
    ...
  end
end
```

The same trick may be used for closures, as long as you do not move them out
of the scope of the variables they need. For instance, consider the following
function:

```
function changenumbers (limit, delta)
  for line in io.lines() do
    line = string.gsub(line, "%d+", function (num)
            num = tonumber(num)
            if num >= limit then return tostring(num + delta) end
            -- else return nothing, keeping the original number
          end)
    io.write(line, "\n")
  end
end
```

We can avoid the creation of a new closure for each line by moving the inner
function outside the loop:

```
function changenumbers (limit, delta)
  local function aux (num)
    num = tonumber(num)
    if num >= limit then return tostring(num + delta) end
  end
  for line in io.lines() do
    line = string.gsub(line, "%d+", aux)
    io.write(line, "\n")
  end
end
```

However, we cannot move aux outside function changenumbers, because there
aux cannot access limit and delta.

For many kinds of string processing, we can reduce the need for new strings by working with indices over existing strings. For instance, the `string.find` function returns the position where it found the pattern, instead of the match. By returning indices, it avoids creating a new (sub)string for each successful match. When necessary, the programmer can get the match substring by calling `string.sub`.[4]

When we cannot avoid the use of new objects, we still may avoid creating these new objects through reuse. For strings reuse is not necessary, because Lua does the job for us: it always *internalizes* all strings it uses, therefore reusing them whenever possible. For tables, however, reuse may be quite effective. As a common case, let us return to the situation where we are creating new tables inside a loop. This time, however, the table contents are not constant. Nevertheless, frequently we still can reuse the same table in all iterations, simply changing its contents. Consider this chunk:

```
local t = {}
for i = 1970, 2000 do
  t[i] = os.time({year = i, month = 6, day = 14})
end
```

The next one is equivalent, but it reuses the table:

```
local t = {}
local aux = {year = nil, month = 6, day = 14}
for i = 1970, 2000 do
  aux.year = i
  t[i] = os.time(aux)
end
```

A particularly effective way to achieve reuse is through *memoizing*. The basic idea is quite simple: store the result of some computation for a given input so that, when the same input is given again, the program simply reuses that previous result.

LPeg, a new package for pattern matching in Lua, does an interesting use of memoizing. LPeg compiles each pattern into an internal representation, which is a "program" for a parsing machine that performs the matching. This compilation is quite expensive, when compared with matching itself. So, LPeg memoizes the results from its compilations to reuse them. A simple table associates the string describing a pattern to its corresponding internal representation.

A common problem with memoizing is that the cost in space to store previous results may outweigh the gains of reusing those results. To solve this problem in Lua, we can use a weak table to keep the results, so that unused results are eventually removed from the table.

In Lua, with higher-order functions, we can define a generic memoization function:

---

[4]It would be a good idea for the standard library to have a function to compare substrings, so that we could check specific values inside a string without having to extract that value from the string (thereby creating a new string).

```
function memoize (f)
  local mem = {}                        -- memoizing table
  setmetatable(mem, {__mode = "kv"})    -- make it weak
  return function (x)           -- new version of 'f', with memoizing
    local r = mem[x]
    if r == nil then     -- no previous result?
      r = f(x)           -- calls original function
      mem[x] = r         -- store result for reuse
    end
    return r
  end
end
```

Given any function f, memoize(f) returns a new function that returns the same results as f but memoizes them. For instance, we can redefine loadstring with a memoizing version:

```
loadstring = memoize(loadstring)
```

We use this new function exactly like the old one, but if there are many repeated strings among those we are loading, we can have a substantial performance gain.

If your program creates and frees too many coroutines, recycling may be an option to improve its performance. The current API for coroutines does not offer direct support for reusing a coroutine, but we can circumvent this limitation. Consider the next coroutine:

```
co = coroutine.create(function (f)
      while f do
        f = coroutine.yield(f())
      end
    end
```

This coroutine accepts a job (a function to run), runs it, and when it finishes it waits for a next job.

Most recycling in Lua is done automatically by the garbage collector. Lua uses an incremental garbage collector. That means that the collector performs its task in small steps (incrementally) interleaved with the program execution. The pace of these steps is proportional to memory allocation: for each amount of memory allocated by Lua, the garbage collector does some proportional work. The faster the program consumes memory, the faster the collector tries to recycle it.

If we apply the principles of reduce and reuse to our program, usually the collector will not have too much work to do. But sometimes we cannot avoid the creation of large amounts of garbage and the collector may become too heavy. The garbage collector in Lua is tuned for average programs, so that it performs reasonably well in most applications. However, sometimes we can improve the performance of a program by better tunning the collector for that particular case.

We can control the garbage collector through function `collectgarbage`, in Lua, or `lua_gc`, in C. Both offer basically the same functionality, although with different interfaces. For this discussion I will use the Lua interface, but often this kind of manipulation is better done in C.

Function `collectgarbage` provides several functionalities: it may stop and restart the collector, force a full collection cycle, force a collection step, get the total memory in use by Lua, and change two parameters that affect the pace of the collector. All of them have their uses when tunning a memory-hungry program.

Stopping the collector "forever" may be an option for some kinds of batch programs, which create several data structures, produce some output based on those structures, and exit (e.g., compilers). For those programs, trying to collect garbage may be a waste of time, as there is little garbage to be collected and all memory will be released when the program finishes.

For non-batch programs, stopping the collector forever is not an option. Nevertheless, those programs may benefit from stopping the collector during some time-critical periods. If necessary, the program may get full control of the garbage collector by keeping it stopped at all times, only allowing it to run by explicitly forcing a step or a full collection. For instance, several event-driven platforms offer an option to set an *idle function*, which is called when there are no other events to handle. This is a perfect time to do garbage collection. (In Lua 5.1, each time you force some collection when the collector is stopped, it automatically restarts. So, to keep it stopped, you must call `collectgarbage("stop")` immediately after forcing some collection.)

Finally, as a last resort, you may try to change the collector parameters. The collector has two parameters controlling its pace. The first one, called *pause*, controls how long the collector waits between finishing a collection cycle and starting the next one. The second parameter, called *stepmul* (from *step multiplier*), controls how much work the collector does in each step. Roughly, smaller pauses and larger step multipliers increase the collector's speed.

The effect of these parameters on the overall performance of a program is hard to predict. A faster collector clearly wastes more CPU cycles per se; however, it may reduce the total memory in use by a program, which in turn may reduce paging. Only careful experimentation can give you the best values for those parameters.

Final remarks

As we discussed in the introduction, optimization is a tricky business. There are several points to consider, starting with whether the program needs any optimization at all. If it has real performance problems, then we must focus on where and how to optimize it.

The techniques we discussed here are neither the only nor the most important ones. We focused here on techniques that are peculiar to Lua, as there are
several sources for more general techniques.

Before we finish, I would like to mention two options that are at the border-
line of improving performance of Lua programs, as both involve changes outside
the scope of the Lua code. The first one is to use LuaJIT, a Lua just-in-time
compiler developed by Mike Pall. He has been doing a superb job and LuaJIT
is probably the fastest JIT for a dynamic language nowadays. The drawbacks
are that it runs only on x86 architectures and that you need a non-standard Lua
interpreter (LuaJIT) to run your programs. The advantage is that you can run
your program 5 times faster with no changes at all to the code.

The second option is to move parts of your code to C. After all, one of Lua
hallmarks is its ability to interface with C code. The important point in this case
is to choose the correct level of granularity for the C code. On the one hand, if you
move only very simple functions into C, the communication overhead between
Lua and C may kill any gains from the improved performance of those functions.
On the other hand, if you move too large functions into C, you loose flexibility.

Finally, keep in mind that those two options are somewhat incompatible. The
more C code your program has, the less LuaJIT can optimize it.

3

Vardump: The Power of Seeing What's Behind

Tobias Sülzenbrück and Christoph Beckmann

A universal debugging tool is popular in other programming languages, such as the scripting language PHP. When coming to writing code it seems as an advantage for us to work with a quite usable built-in function called `vardump` to quickly overview variable contents. There the contents are structured in order by their appearance in arrays or by their data types which makes it easier to read the variables and refer to them.

This means in detail that when programming you may want to supervise your data. This abstract description of the problem covers nearly all issues when dealing with complex program structures or when having trouble because some variables or classes get out of hand. For instance, you are implementing a non-trivial algorithm and while testing certain functionality you will print out variables to control single values.

But what to do with complex data structures? You will need a tool that is capable of dealing with custom-made structures. For instance, a nested table containing data should be printed out. Instead of reinventing a special output function for your problem, it is likely better to use an generic function that covers all possible data types. This fact becomes more important in dynamically typed languages like Lua. (In the beginning of experiencing Lua we hardly missed such a functionality as described above.)

In this gem, we introduce a universal debugging tool for Lua. This solution covers many demands that programmers have in their development workflow.

Here is a simple example of vardump in action. It prints out the variable foo that contains the string *"Hello World"*.

```
> foo = "Hello World"
> vardump(foo)
(string) Hello World
```

Implementation

As shown in Listing 1, vardump is a Lua function with three parameters: one for the resulting data value and two others reserved for the recursive function invocation through itself.

First the *key* parameter is checked for adding a line prefix. This is used when printing tables to also print out the index of the table cell. Second, depending on the table depth (i.e., the current iteration step when printing a table), spaces are added in front of each line to enhance the readability. When calling vardump with a simple data type, such as a string, the afore mentioned additions to lines have no influence on those. As said before, this is only interesting when printing out tables, because the Lua print function automatically adds a line break.

Next the value is checked against some basic types. This includes *tables*, *functions*, *threads*, *userdata*, and all other types the data in vardump can have. When the resulting type is a simple data type, it is displayed with the Lua print function. The data type is printed in brackets in front of the value. Functions, threads, userdata, and nil values are printed without their data types at the beginning of the line. E.g. the vardump of a function will print out its memory address, as the standard print function will do.

Tables are the universal structure in Lua and they need special handling in vardump. As tables may contain other tables it is essential to get all information out of them, no matter how deep the nesting is. The output of vardump for a set of nested tables is shown in Listing 2.

The function begins with obtaining the current iteration depth. From the depth value, the amount of fore-standing spaces in determined. A table can contain other tables or the special *metatable*. If so, the current value is replaced by the contents of the metatable. Next, vardump is invoked recursively for each pair in the table. The new value and the corresponding key are two of the arguments for the call. The third parameter is the current depth, as mentioned for adding spaces at the beginning of the line.

Conclusion

The functionality of vardump is powerful and a must for any developer. vardump gives you the transparency you need for every variable you use. One improvement for extending vardump to adapt it to your workflow might be another argument that describes the maximum iteration depth for tables — this is very useful when handling large, deeply nested tables.

```
function vardump(value, depth, key)
  local linePrefix = ""
  local spaces = ""

  if key ~= nil then
    linePrefix = "["..key.."] = "
  end

  if depth == nil then
    depth = 0
  else
    depth = depth + 1
    for i=1, depth do spaces = spaces .. "  " end
  end

  if type(value) == 'table' then
    mTable = getmetatable(value)
    if mTable == nil then
      print(spaces ..linePrefix.."(table) ")
    else
      print(spaces .."(metatable) ")
        value = mTable
    end
    for tableKey, tableValue in pairs(value) do
      vardump(tableValue, depth, tableKey)
    end
  elseif type(value) == 'function'
      or type(value) == 'thread'
      or type(value) == 'userdata'
      or value        == nil
  then
    print(spaces..tostring(value))
  else
    print(spaces..linePrefix.."("..type(value)..") "..tostring(value))
  end
end
```

Listing 1. The `vardump` function.

```
> foo = {"zero",1,2,3,{1,{1,2,3,4,{1,2,{1,"cool",2},4},6},3,vardump,5,6},
        5,{Mary = 10, Paul = "10"},"last value"}
> vardump(foo)
(table)
   [1] = (string) zero
   [2] = (number) 1
   [3] = (number) 2
   [4] = (number) 3
   [5] = (table)
     [1] = (number) 1
     [2] = (table)
        [1] = (number) 1
        [2] = (number) 2
        [3] = (number) 3
        [4] = (number) 4
        [5] = (table)
           [1] = (number) 1
           [2] = (number) 2
           [3] = (table)
              [1] = (number) 1
              [2] = (string) cool
              [3] = (number) 2
           [4] = (number) 4
        [6] = (number) 6
     [3] = (number) 3
     function: 0x304650
     [5] = (number) 5
     [6] = (number) 6
   [6] = (number) 5
   [7] = (table)
     [Mary] = (number) 10
     [Paul] = (string) 10
   [8] = (string) last value
```

Listing 2. Output of `vardump` for nested tables.

4

Serialization with Pluto

Ben Sunshine-Hill

Serialization refers to the process of taking a piece or set of data from a running program and writing it to a one-dimensional datastream (such as could be stored in a string or a file), with the goal of restoring that data later from the datastream. The most common use of serialization is implementing a "save" feature. In this instance, the serialized data is the data in a spreadsheet application, or the state of the gameboard in a chess game. A closely related use is the creation of "rollback points", useful in simulations and databases, which allows the application to revert to an earlier state. The idea of rollback points is particularly interesting as it relates to coroutines, because the state of the application is contained not only in the data of the program, but in the execution state of all extant coroutines. A similar situation can easily be encountered in a save-game feature in video games, particularly where the state of a character's AI is embodied in a coroutine.

The plot, therefore, thickens: like many problems in computer science, serialization starts out sounding trivial, and becomes more complex as the full scope of the problem is examined. An additional level of complexity arises when one begins to consider the practical aspects of serialization as opposed to treating it as an exercise in theory. Indeed, the creation of a serialization system that is both correct and useful is a remarkably involved task. Because of this, premade serialization libraries are a convenient way to reduce development time while ensuring a robust, efficient result. In the ideal case, the complexities of deciding on a file format and keeping the loading and saving code in sync are swept away in favor of a simple "serialize this". Pluto is one such system, which handles the complexities of serialization and presents as simple an interface as possible (but no simpler).

The complexities of serialization

This section covers some of the theoretical aspects of serialization. If the phrase "depth-first graph traversal" makes your eyes glaze over, you can skip to the next section.

Much of the complexity of serialization arises from the fact that a single piece of "data" is rarely confined to a single object. The string `"foo"` is a single object, as is the string `"bar"`, but the table `{foo = "bar"}` consists of three objects: the table, the key, and the value. And we must deal with more than simple associative mappings: the table `{{"foo"},{"bar","baz",{"qux","quux"}}}` consists of four tables and five strings (not counting the implicit integer keys). The real problems, though, begin to arise when the data is structured not as a tree but as a generalized graph. Consider the data returned by the following function:

```
function creategraph()
  local a = {}
  local b = {}
  a.foo = b
  b.foo = a
  return a
end
```

The returned object is a table, which has as its single value a table, which has as its single value the first table. This structure cannot be represented declaratively, because of the cyclic links. Likewise, during deserialization the structure cannot be rebuilt without visiting at least one of the tables twice: If the first table is rebuilt first, it cannot refer to a fully rebuilt second table; and vice versa.

The solution employed by most serialization libraries, including Pluto, is to layer a new container over the objects. The data returned by `creategraph` above could be equivalently generated by the function in Listing 1. The array `objs` is first filled with every object in the data, each one initially "empty" but referenceable. The objects are then filled, one by one, with the other objects which they reference, and the root objects (the initial set of objects explicitly chosen to be serialized) are returned. It should be clear from the above code that the ordering of the objects in `obj` can be arbitrary: as long as all objects are created before all objects are filled, the creation and filling of individual objects can be performed in any order.

In practice, these two phases may be interleaved. The algorithm is closely based on a depth-first graph traversal, and is as follows. During serialization, maintain a table of written objects and the integer indices assigned to them. To write an object, check whether that object has already been written. If it has, output the integer index assigned to the object when it was first written.

```
function creategraph2()
  local objs = {}

  local insert = function(tableindex, keyindex, valueindex)
    local table = objs[tableindex]
    local key = objs[keyindex]
    local value = objs[valueindex]
    table[key] = value
  end

  -- creation
  objs[1] = {}
  objs[2] = {}
  objs[3] = "foo"

  -- filling
  insert(1, 3, 2)
  insert(2, 3, 1)

  return objs[1]
end
```

Listing 1.

Otherwise, assign a new integer index to the object and output that index, and output the object's data. For other objects that it references, recursively write those objects. During deserialization, maintain an array of integer indices and the objects to which they refer. when an object is encountered, read whether that object has been encountered before. If it has, simply return the object with the given index. Otherwise, create a new object of the specified type within the array at the specified index, and then read the object's data (recursively invoking the routine to read objects which have been referenced), finally returning the fully created object.

The correctness of these algorithms may easily be proven: Assuming that integer indices are assigned incrementally, it may be shown that during serialization no object completes being written unless all other objects with lower indices already been assigned these indices. Likewise, it may be shown that during deserialization no object begins being written unless all other objects with lower indices have already been created, and that all created objects are fully initialized by the time deserialization completes.

Using Pluto

Pluto is implemented as a Lua module in C, which must be built for a particular version of the Lua interpreter (due to its direct manipulation of Lua's data structures). It can serialize every Lua type except for C functions, which would not be possible without architectural support. (Such a feature would usually be undesirable anyway; C functions can be registered as permanent objects, as described later.) In particular, Pluto correctly supports shared upvalues, a necessary feature for certain OO systems.

In its simplest form, Pluto can be used as follows:

```
require("pluto")

obj = "Hello, world!"
encoded = pluto.persist({}, obj)
outfile = io.open("test.plh", "wb")
outfile:write(encoded)
outfile:close()

-- then, later...

infile = io.open("test.plh", "rb")
encoded = io.read("*a")
infile.close()
obj = pluto.unpersist({}, encoded)
print(obj) -- prints "Hello, world!"
```

This example barely leverages Pluto's capabilities: obj could be replaced with an object contained within a complex, interconnected mass of data, and all of that data would be saved and reloaded correctly.

Custom serialization routines

Not all objects can be blindly serialized without regard to the semantics of the data. At certain times, special procedures are necessary to serialize data in such a manner that it will be useful when deserialized. The most obvious example of this in Lua is userdata. Because Lua has no idea what the content of the userdata represents, writing that data out as a bytestream may not be a sensible thing to do, and restoring the data from the bytestream may not be a safe thing to do. For instance, if the userdata consists of a pointer to an array of integers, that pointer will be dangling if the object is deserialized on a subsequent run of the program. If such data is to be persisted, the programmer will need to supply a custom routine to serialize the userdata using a format of their own devising (which would then be inlined by the library into the bytestream), and a matching routine to deserialize it later. Pluto accomplishes this with a __persist metamethod, which is called by Pluto when the object is encountered. This metamethod takes the object as its sole argument, and is expected to return a function which will, when run, produce the original object. Upvalues are generally necessary to accomplish this. Suppose, for instance, that we had a userdata-based 2D vertex type, produced by the constructor function vertex2d(x,y), which we needed to serialize:

```
require("pluto")

function persistvertex2d(v)
  local x = v.x
  local y = v.y
  return function()
    return vertex2d(x, y)
  end
end

-- obj's metatable's __persist method is set to persistvertex2d
obj = vertex2d(3, 4)

encoded = pluto.persist({}, obj)
```

In this example, persistvertex2d takes a vertex as its argument, and returns a closure which, when called, returns the original vertex. The key here, however, is that the inner function does not refer to v at all, only to locally-declared variables. When this closure is persisted in lieu of the original vertex, it will pull in x and y to use later in reconstruction. Note also that the inner function does not refer to the C function vertex2d, only to the string containing its name. If we did not wish to look up the constructor via the global table, we could instead refer to the vertex2d function as a permanent object.

Permanent objects

When one examines the space of situations where custom serialization routines are necessary, two distinct patterns emerge. In one pattern, it is fully possible to serialize the state of the object into a file as long as the system knows how. In the other pattern, however, the state of the object extends past the scope of the serialized data. A userdata, for instance, may be a handle to a database, for instance, or to a hardware function used to access the system time.

One can invent different custom serialization routines for these, of course, but they all tend to involve the same thing: fixing up references during deserialization with preexisting objects. In the case of the system time function, for instance, it is likely that during deserialization such a routine will have already been loaded by a module, just as it was before the creation of the data which was originally serialized. Ideally, therefore, during serialization the system would not even attempt to save this routine to disk, but instead describe the routine in some way (likely through a unique identifier). During deserialization, the same routine in its new instantiation would be connected with the same identifier, and the objects being loaded would have their references fixed-up to reference this new routine. Some convention would be used to ensure that the new object would be equivalent to the old one, such as giving the function's "canonical name" in the global namespace as its identifier.

Pluto supports this fixup behavior with a "permanents table". During serialization, a table of permanents is passed in (the empty first argument in the examples above), with the keys being the permanent objects and the values being the identifiers for the objects. The identifiers are serialized in the normal way, and can be of any type, although in practice only integers and strings are used. During deserialization, the reverse is passed in, with the keys being the identifiers and the values being the permanent objects. In the example shown in Listing 2, `canvas` is a userdata created by the Canvas Draw library, which refers to the hardware screen; for obvious reasons, it cannot be serialized, and is instead fixed up via an entry in the permanents table.

One common situation in which the permanents table is required is that of serializing coroutines. When a coroutine has yielded by calling `coroutine.yield`, that C function is still referenced by the coroutine's callstack. If Pluto tried to serialize the callstack, it would fail to serialize that value. Therefore, in order to serialize a running coroutine it is necessary to have `coroutine.yield` in the permanents table.

Limitations of Pluto

There are certain guarantees which Pluto does not currently provide. None of these are fundamental limitations of the technology, but rather implementation decisions which keep the library's design simple. If any of these features would be particularly useful to Pluto's users, they could be added to a future release.

First, Pluto does not handle byte ordering issues. It is assumed that the memory representations of numbers will be the same between serialization and deserialization. This makes Pluto of limited use in network protocols for cross-platform applications, and for other situations where a differently endian architecture will be deserializing data.

Secondly, Pluto is not hardened against invalid bytestreams. Untrusted bytestreams should not be deserialized in security-critical situations, as they could crash the application or even enable code-injection attacks.

Finally, Pluto uses an inefficient algorithm for deserializing certain types of upvalues, requiring a traversal of the entire garbage collection list. This has not caused any known significant slowdowns, but applications with extremely large working sets could conceivably experience problems.

Other approaches to general-purpose serialization

In this section, I will examine two other serialization possiblities available to the Lua programmer, covering both the concepts behind their implementation and the practicalities of choosing each one for a serialization system. Although Pluto is a robust and general-purpose library, these approaches have advantages of their own.

```
require("pluto")

nativecanvas = cd.CreateCanvas(cd.NATIVEWINDOW, nil)

permanents = {[nativecanvas] = "CD canvas"}

drawingagent = {
  canvas = nativecanvas,
  drawblueline = function(this, x1, y1, x2, y2)
    this.canvas.SetForeground(cd.BLUE)
    this.canvas.Line(x1, y1, x2, y2)
  end,
  drawredline = function(this, x1, y1, x2, y2)
    this.canvas.SetForeground(cd.RED)
    this.canvas.Line(x1, y1, x2, y2)
  end}

encoded = pluto.persist(permanents, drawingagent)

outfile = io.open("test.plh", "wb")
outfile:write(encoded)
outfile:close()

-- Then, later (on a different run of the program)...

nativecanvas = cd.CreateCanvas(cd.NATIVEWINDOW, nil)

permanents = {["CD canvas"] = nativecanvas}

infile = io.open("test.plh", "rb")
encoded = io.read("*a")
infile.close()

drawingagent = pluto.unpersist(permanents, encoded)
```

Listing 2.

LuaPickle

The first approach is found in the "Lua Pickle" library available on the lua-users.org wiki. This library is implemented entirely in Lua and outputs plain text files, making it fully cross-platform. Elegantly, it outputs data as a Lua program, which is simply executed to deserialize the data. The ease with which this is possible reflects Lua's pedigree as a data-description language.

LuaPickle does not support custom serialization routines or permanent objects. That is not a result of any fundamental limitations of the technology, though, and could be added to the library without too much effort. The pure-Lua approach, however, does limit the number of built-in types which may be serialized. Userdata, coroutines, and functions are all unsupported, as the built-in Lua libraries do not provide adequate introspection facilities for them.

As the library requires no nonstandard native code, it is the easiest of the three to integrate with an existing program. If you are certain you will never need to serialize any of the unsupported data types, its convenience is unmatched.

lper

lper is a melding of the Lua virtual machine with LPSM, an off-the-shelf persistent memory manager. By maintaining the VM's entire memory space in a disk-backed virtual memory region (a surprisingly straightforward task, thanks to Lua's support for custom memory allocation routines), the entire Lua universe may be written and read. The simplicity of this approach is admirable: after all the worrying about upvalues and userdata, this type-agnostic system can serialize it all, in a manner reminiscent of Alexander's cutting of the Gordian Knot. If this approach is sufficient for your needs, it's difficult to beat for simplicity, power, and ease of use.

There are definite tradeoffs, however. The chief issue is that the entire Lua universe must be saved. This severely limits its usefulness for saving games or documents, unless an effort is made to segregate the data into a separate VM instantiation (which presents its own set of difficulties relating to data sharing). lper is therefore best suited for long-running, processor-intensive simulations. In such a situation, lper could be used for creating rollback points, where potentially most of the system state must be saved regardless. It is also necessary to ensure that references to memory not allocated by Lua (such as registered C functions) remain invariant across invocations. Custom serialization routines are also unsupported. Finally, lper is an experimental library, which has not been fully tested and is limited to POSIX environments due to the requirements of LPSM.

Conclusion

Serialization is an important task for many applications, and often a complicated one, particularly if it is not planned for from the outset. At the same time, it is undeniably prosaic. The implementation of a robust serialization system is a task to be deferred to third-party solutions whenever possible, to allow the programmer to concentrate on application-specific tasks. If you are planning out the technology to be used for an application, or if you need to graft serialization or persistence onto an existing project, Pluto can minimize the pain involved in integrating serialization.

5

Abstractions for LuaSQL

Tomás Guisasola Gorham

This article shows how to build an abstraction layer over LuaSQL to ease the most common uses of the library made by application developers. The reader is expected to know Lua and the basics of LuaSQL: how to install, open a connection, and execute SQL statements. We will show some common uses of LuaSQL's API, extracted from our own experience, and try to develop, step by step, a set of abstractions to simplify them, aiming at a higher level programming style.

We will begin by showing an example from which we point out common pieces of code that are found in many programs. The following four sections will detail those constructions, showing some forms of generalization and abstraction that should help make the whole program easier to write, maintain and understand. Finally, a complete abstraction is obtained in the form of a library that encapsulates the main of LuaSQL.

Common uses

Listing 1 shows an example of a common use of LuaSQL library, which includes almost all the points we plan to examine. These points are marked with numbers between parentheses.

The example starts by loading a LuaSQL driver and opening the connection. This initialization phase is marked by number (1). Then the example builds an SQL statement (2), sends it to the database and checks for errors (3), and finally

43

```lua
-- Initialization (1)
require"luasql.postgres"
local env = luasql.postgres ()
local conn = assert (env:connect ("lpg"))

-- Building SQL statement (2)
local course_list = { "Music", "Literature", }
local c_list = "'"..table.concat (course_list, "','").."'"
local year = 2007
local stmt = string.format ([[
    select a.id, a.name
        from alumn a inner join course c on (a.course_id = c.id)
        where c.name in (%s) and adm_year = %s]], c_list, year)

-- SQL execution and error handling (3)
local cur, err = conn:execute (stmt)
if not cur then
    error (err.." SQL = {"..stmt.."}")
end

-- Iteration loop (4)
local id, name = cur:fetch ()
while id do
    print (id, name)
    id, name = cur:fetch ()
end

-- Closing (5)
cur:close()
conn:close()
env:close()
```

Listing 1. An ordinary complete sample of LuaSQL use, where the typical phases are marked by numbers between parentheses.

retrieves the results set (4).[1] These phases will be analyzed in the following sections.

Defining a module

As mentioned above, we will develop a Lua module to group all the abstractions together. We shall use a table to encapsulate the actual LuaSQL connection and add functions/methods to its metatable. The programmer can access the actual LuaSQL object to perform other operations such as turn the auto-commit mode on or off, or call the `commit` and the `rollback` methods. Let us start with a constructor of this new type of object, which will be also responsible for opening the connection to the database, and a closing function. This will constitute the file `database.lua`.

```
local assert, require, setmetatable = assert, require, setmetatable
module"database"
local mt = { __index = _M, } -- _M is the module itself
function connect (dbname, user, pass, driver)
   local luasql = require("luasql."..driver)
   local env = assert (luasql[driver] ())
   local obj = { conn = assert (env:connect (dbname, user, pass)) }
   setmetatable (obj, mt)
   return obj
end

function close (obj)
   setmetatable (obj, nil)
   return obj.conn:close ()
end
```

We will also write a test file. It will be useful for testing, but also as a set of use samples.

```
local database = require"database"
local db = database.connect ("lpg", nil, nil, "postgres")
```

From now on, we will develop the following two files in parallel: the module file (`database.lua`) and the test file. Sometimes we will enhance a piece of code that had been developed earlier and thus it will be replaced by the new implementation.

---

[1]The code that retrieves the results set can be more compact like this:

```
for id, name in cur.fetch, cur do print (id, name) end
```

I chose the more verbose version mainly because I could not found any use of this compact form in a search in the Internet, at least by the time of this writing. Anyway, my point is that legibility could be improved in both forms.

Error handling

LuaSQL handles errors just like the standard Lua libraries: an error is raised only if the arguments do not follow the types defined by the API. Errors generated by the database client, such as incorrect SQL syntax, unknown identifiers, or even violation of database restrictions, are informed in the conventional way, by returning `false` and an error message. This behavior provides the programmer with the freedom to check for errors *only when they show up*. Although it is tedious to write down an if-test everywhere, the fact is that they are not usually written anywhere! However, a simple function can do this for us. Let us add the following definition to our module:

```
function assertexec (self, stmt)
   local cur, msg = self.conn:execute (stmt)
   return cur or error ((msg or '')..." SQL = { "..stmt.." }", 2)
end
```

To test it, let us create a test database and insert some rows into it, not forgetting to check if it raises errors properly:

```
assert (pcall (db.assertexec, db, "wrong SQL statement") == false)
db:assertexec[[create table people (
   id     integer,
   name   varchar (100),
   sex    char(1),
   tel    varchar (10)
)]]
```

```
-- Adding content to the table
db:assertexec"insert into people values (1, 'John Doe', 'M', '12')"
db:assertexec"insert into people values (2, 'Jane Doe', 'F', '01')"
db:assertexec"insert into people values (3, 'O\\'Neill', 'M', '98')"
```

Now we can try a query and make sure it executes correctly:

```
local stmt = "select * from people where name = 'John Doe'"
assert (pcall (db.assertexec, db, stmt))
```

Since it is a frequent mistake to forget the quotes around a string, we should add a test to make sure the system always raises an error in this situation:

```
local stmt = "select * from people where name = John Doe"
assert (not pcall (db.assertexec, db, stmt))
```

Result set iterator

Now we will try to generalize the iteration loop, by adding an iterator factory to our module:

```
function select (self, stmt)
   local cur = self:assertexec ("select "..stmt)
   return function ()
      return cur:fetch ()
   end
end
```

With this new function, the iteration loop can be replaced by a *for-construction*. Besides its conciseness, the for-construction avoids the need for two calls to the fetch method, one before the loop starts and the other at the end of its body. The following code should be added to the test file in order to test the new function:

```
for name, sex in db:select"name, sex from people" do
   print (name, sex)
end
```

If only one row is needed, we can make it simpler:

```
local n, t = db:select"name, tel from people where id = 1"()
assert (n == "John Doe")
assert (t == "12")
```

This implementation covers the most common uses, but it restricts the call to fetch, preventing the return of a table with the values of all columns in a row. In order to add flexibility and keep the module easy and practical to use, we can add an optional parameter to our iterator function to indicate whether we want a table. Additionally, we could use this parameter to indicate the *modestring* used by fetch in the construction of the table:

```
function select (self, stmt, modestring)
   local cur = self:assertexec ("select "..stmt)
   return function ()
      local t
      if modestring then t = {} end
      return cur:fetch (t, modestring)
   end
end
```

When called with this third argument, the iterator will create a new table to store the values of the row and return this table. There is no restriction anymore, but there are two drawbacks: we must specify a modestring to obtain a table with the values, and we cannot reuse that table. I consider both of minor importance: this is the price of convenience. Besides, one can use the raw LuaSQL connection object if necessary.

SQL statement constructors

Our final subject is the creation of SQL statements. This task is completely different from everything done to our module so far. One might prefer to develop a separate module for that, but we will put everything together for concision. Our main goal is to provide both practicality and robustness. Practicality can be achieved with a small set of functions covering the most common SQL statements: delete, insert, update and select. Robustness — at this level — has to be assured by properly quoting and escaping the sentences, preventing common mistakes and also reducing tedious work — which is another common cause of error.

Infrastructure

As we have mentioned, a common mistake is to forget to quote a string, but a more common one is to forget to escape a quote inside a quoted string. These arguments should be enough to force us to define functions for escaping and quoting a given string. Until LuaSQL 2.1 there was no support for these operations[2] thus both had to be done in Lua. These operations should be included in the assembly of the SQL statements but we should also be cautious about their use, so that we do not escape or quote the same string twice.

Nevertheless sometimes we do not want a quoted string, for example when using a select as the value of a column (a sub-select), or when using a pre-defined database value such as NULL or CURRENT_TIMESTAMP. Consequently it is important to let the user differentiate these situations in a convenient way.

Since all SQL expressions could be represented between parentheses — and, in fact, the case of sub-select have to be done this way —, we decided that *parenthesized strings would not be quoted*. Thus, we can write the quote function in order to quote only strings that are not enclosed by parentheses[3]:

```
function escape (s) return (string.gsub (s, "'", "\\%1")) end
function quote (s)
    if string.find (s, "^%(.*%)$") then
        return s
    else
        return "'"..escape(s).."'"
    end
end
```

Insert

Now let us consider a change to our test file, establishing that every value retrieved from the database be checked. A reasonable way to do that is by defining a Lua table with all the values we want. Then, an automatic routine could store this data on the database and another routine could retrieve and check the values, item by item, comparing them to the original data.

---

[2]The escape function was added to LuaSQL 2.2 as a consequence of writing this article.

[3]Some systems require that a single quote be escaped with two single quotes instead of a backslash, as shown in the code.

In order for this to work, we need an `insert` method in our database connection. Basically, an insert SQL statement contains three "arguments": a table name, an optional list of columns and a list of values. The natural way to provide lists in Lua is using a table as an array. Better yet, since we want *two corresponding* lists we can use the same table to provide both pieces of information: the list of columns is the list of table keys, and the list of values is the list of values associated with these keys. Therefore, our new method only needs to inform the name of the table to act on and a table with the column-value pairs, as in:

```
db:insert ("people", { id=1, name="John Doe", sex="M", tel="12", })
```

The function that builds the two lists may be added to our infrastructure as displayed below:

```
function twolists (tab)
    local k, v = {}, {}
    local i = 0
    for key, val in pairs (tab) do
        i = i+1
        k[i] = key
        v[i] = quote (val)
    end
    return table.concat (k, ','), table.concat (v, ',')
end
```

The `twolists` function can also be used to build parts of other SQL statements as will be shown later.

Hence, the implementation of the `insert` method can be:

```
function insert (self, tablename, contents)
    return self:assertexec (string.format (
        "insert into %s (%s) values (%s)",
        tablename, twolists (contents)))
end
```

Our test script can be rewritten to automatically populate the database with data from a table, by using the following code:

```
-- Set of data
data = {
    { name = "John Doe", sex = "M", tel = "12", },
    { name = "Jane Doe", sex = "F", tel = "01", },
    { name = "O'Neill",  sex = "M", tel = "98", },
}
-- Adding content to the table
for i, row in ipairs (data) do
    row.id = i
    db:insert ("people", row)
end
```

Select revisited

We can add the same facility to assemble the SQL statement of our result
set iterator. The second argument, that is, the statement, can be replaced by
a string with a list of columns, followed by the table name, the conditional
expression and any other text. In this way, the iterator will be responsible for
adding some words to guarantee the correct syntax of the statement:

```
function select (self, columns, tabname, cond, other, modestring)
    -- Assemble the SQL statement
    tabname = tabname and (" from "..tabname) or ""
    cond    = cond and (" where "..cond) or ""
    other   = other or ""
    local stmt = string.format ("select %s%s%s %s",
        columns, tabname, cond, other)
    -- Do the query
    local cur = self:assertexec (stmt)
    return function ()
        local t
        if modestring then t = {} end
        return cur:fetch (t, modestring)
    end
end
```

Sometimes it is important to hide the internals of the implementation. In
this case, however, I believe it is better to expose it. In other words, it is
important for the programmer to know that the arguments will be joined to form
the final SQL statement, because he is able to use this to his own advantage.
The programmer can exploit the fact that the list of columns is not just a list
of columns and add more text to enhance the SQL statement being built, like
renaming a column, adding two or more columns with a string separator and
others. The same applies to all of the arguments[4]. Now we can automatically
check each column of each row against the original data:

```
for row in db:select ("*", "people", nil, "order by id", "a") do
    row.id = tonumber(row.id)
    for col, val in pairs (data[row.id]) do
        assert (row[col] == val)
    end
end
```

A subtle point to note is the release of open cursors, which are confidently
left to the garbage collector. LuaSQL's implementation of fetch[5] already closes

---

[4]In fact, this new implementation can be used just like the others with the raw SQL statement
(removing the "select" word from the beginning) as in: db:select"* from people order by id".

[5]This behavior — closing the cursor when there are no more rows — is in part a consequence of
writing this article and was planned to be added to LuaSQL version 2.2, which should have been
released by the time this article is published.

the cursor when there is no more rows to return, but if the iterator is not called to the end, the cursor remains open. In some systems, with severe restrictions, this practice could make the system get out of resources, therefore the select iterator have to be used with care. The most effective way to avoid this situation is to create queries that return the exact number of rows needed, so that the loop will call `fetch` until there is no more rows and the cursor will be closed. Nevertheless, the raw LuaSQL connection is accessible via the `conn` field and the usual `execute-fetch` loop could be used.

Delete

The `delete` method should be simple, following the same guidelines used for the `insert` method: the name of the table and a condition.

```
function delete (self, tablename, cond)
   cond = cond and (" where "..cond) or ""
   local stmt = string.format ("delete from %s%s", tablename, cond)
   return self:assertexec (stmt)
end
```

As with the `select` method, the `tablename` argument can be the complete SQL statement including the condition[6], so the last argument is optional.

Update

While the *insert* command requires two comma-separated lists (for column names and column values), the *update* command requires a single comma-separated list of pairs in the form *column-name = column-value*. Since the where clause also requires a similar list of pairs, we will define a function to cover both uses by accepting an optional separator. By providing the string " AND " as the separator, the function can be used to form a typical condition to the where clause.

```
function pairslist (tab, sep)
   sep = sep or ','
   local l = {}
   for key, val in pairs (tab) do
      l[#l+1] = string.format ("%s=%s", key, quote (val))
   end
   table.sort (l)
   return table.concat (l, sep)
end
```

Since Lua does not guarantee the order of the traversal of a table, I added a call to `table.sort` so that `pairslist` always produces the same string for the same contents of a table. This predictability makes it easier to test the function.

---

[6]As in db:delete"table where status='invalid'".

```
local pl = db.pairslist ({ a="I'm a quoted text", b=2, }, " AND ")
assert (pl == [[a='I\'m a quoted text' AND b='2']])
```

Now we can define the update method:

```
function update (self, tabname, contents, cond)
    cond = cond and (" where "..cond) or ""
    local values = contents and pairslist(contents) or ""
    local stmt = string.format ("update %s set %s%s",
        tabname, values, cond)
    return self:assertexec (stmt)
end
```

Since the `pairslist` function is exported from our module, the programmer can use it to assemble the where clause for the select iterator or for the update or delete commands.

We should add some lines to test these functions:

```
assert (db:select ("tel", "people", "id=3")() == data[3].tel)
assert (db:update ("people", { tel = 87, sex = "F", }, "id=3") == 1)
assert (db:select ("tel", "people", "id=3")() == "87")
assert (db:delete ("people", "id=3") == 1)
assert (db:select ("tel", "people", "id=3")() == nil)
```

Finally, to clean up the test, we drop the table created:

```
db:assertexec"drop table people"
```

Extensions

Here we explore the facility to extend this library by showing a pair of examples and proposing others. LuaSQL is not supposed to be extended directly and for security reasons it has to be that way. On the other hand, our library is easily extendable, such as most Lua libraries.

Complete result set

The easiest way to extend our library is by adding a function to it. A useful function is one that builds the entire result set as an array of rows. It could be simple as:

```
function selectall (self, columns, tabname, cond, other, modestring)
    modestring = modestring or 'a'
    local r = {}
    for row in self:select (columns, tabname, cond, other, modestring) do
        r[#r+1] = row
    end
    return r
end
```

A test for the new function could be:

```
rs = db:selectall ("*", "people", nil, "order by id")
assert (rs[1].name == "John Doe")
assert (rs[2].name == "Jane Doe")
assert (rs[3].name == "O'Neill")
```

Logging SQL execution

A more elaborated extension can be the redefinition of one of its functions. An interesting facility that could be exploited is the redefinition of `assertexec` to trace SQL execution. This could be used to provide a log of all or part of the SQL statements executed by an application without the need to change the whole application. A log could help debugging or even be used to fine-tune the software. A possible redefinition could be as follows. The debug library is used to obtain names for the functions on the call stack.

```
-- Redefinition of 'assertexec' to log SQL statements
local old_exec = database.assertexec
local fh = io.open ("sql.log", "w")
database.assertexec = function (self, stmt)
    local f2 = debug.getinfo (2, "n").name or "?" -- function name
    local f3 = debug.getinfo (3, "n").name or "?" -- function name
    local s = stmt:gsub("%%", "%%"):gsub("[\r\n]", ""):gsub("\t", " ")
    fh:write ("("..f3.."->"..f2.."):"..s.."\n")
    return old_exec (self, stmt)
end
```

Moreover, the redefinition of `assertexec` could also be used to provide other features, such as a query rewriting tool for SQL statements or a proxy just like the recent MySQL Proxy[7].

Of course, such an example does not depend on the existence of `assertexec`, but the fact that this wrapper already encapsulates the `execute` method eases this task. LuaSQL does not provide access to the objects' metatables for security reasons, thus there is no way to redefine `execute`. The only solution I can think of is to create a wrapper, as we are doing, to intercept the statements sent to the database driver.

Other ideas

An even more sophisticated (and also useful) extension is the implementation of a pool or a cache of database connections encapsulated by the `connect` method. In both cases, careful must be taken on the release of open transactions and also on the sharing policy.

A cache of database connections should improve the efficiency of an application that repeatedly connects to the same database, does some stuff and release

---

[7]http://forge.mysql.com/wiki/MySQL_Proxy

the connection, by avoiding the destruction and recreation of these connections. Since the connections will not be really closed, open transactions have to be terminated either by a *commit* or a *rollback* operation. Therefore, the close method should be redefined to do a *commit*. The *rollback* operation, on the other hand, have to be executed in case an error occur, a situation that is not so easy to handle.

An interesting case is a long-term application such as a server. A Web server, for instance, could offer a pool of connections for its request-attendants, to optimize the database access. But it has to take care of the forgotten connections since it is not uncommon to an attendant to trust in a general clean up at the end of its execution and simply not close anything! Since our connections are encapsulated by tables, which don't have finalizers, the garbage collector won't help us. Hence, the solution would have to keep a list of used connections to later proceed with a *commit* or a *rollback*, according to the execution status of the attendant.

Discussion

Our implementation is now complete, although it can receive some additions. The test case should be much better developed but as the goal here was to show how to do it, I left this task to be done as an exercise.

I think the main functions should check their arguments' types whenever possible, using features such as the luaL_check* set of functions in the Lua auxiliary library. However, these C functions are not exported to Lua and implementing them in Lua can cause a significant performance penalty. In fact, this could be the subject for another gem.

A last but not less important point regards my decisions on the API style and its organization. I chose the arguments of the SQL constructors guided by our own usage and, I have to confess, changed them a little while writing this document. Take the result set iterator, for instance: it could receive five lengthy arguments which can make the call difficult to understand. To reduce this problem, the function could have been implemented to receive a table with the arguments in particular fields, as the following example:

```
db:select{
    columns = "col1, col2, col3, col4",
    from = "tablename t inner join othertable o",
    having = "t.fk = o.id and t.col3 > 10",
    groupby = "...",
}
```

The drawbacks of this approach are the growth of the library size and the possibility of having to deal with differences between the accepted SQL syntax of the databases or even limit the use of particular extensions.

The functions I grouped as "infrastructure" (escape, quote, twolists and pairslist) could be generalized and stored in pre-existing packages, such as string and `table`. Additionally, I packaged all SQL constructors into another file which helped reuse the *select* constructor to build sub-selects. I do not think there is any canonical way to decide whether to put a function in a new module or inside a pre-existing one.

Conclusion

To illustrate the point we have made, let us rewrite the first example in the article using the tools developed:

```
-- Initialization (1)
local database = require"database"
local db = database.connect("lpg", "tomas", nil, "postgres")

-- Building SQL statement (2)
local _, course_list = db.twolists{ "Music", "Literature", }
local year = 2007
local cond = string.format([[c.name in (%s) and adm_year = %s]],
    course_list, year)
local tab = "alumn a inner join course c on (a.course_id = c.id)"

-- SQL execution and error handling (3) and Iteration loop (4)
for id, name in db:select("a.id, a.name", tab, cond) do
    print(id, name)
end
```

There is a huge difference from the previous version to this one. The former explicitly checked for errors, while in the new one, this is performed automatically by the library functions. The iteration loop is now a concise for-construct without repeated calls to the `fetch` method. In addition, the SQL statement construction is now much better supported, which helps build correct and more legible code in a convenient way.

Finally, this library settles a new ground over which other abstractions could be defined. Some applications are already constructed on top of it and so are other libraries. An example is a module that provides facilities to the definition of classes and objects directly associated with database tables and rows. It takes advantage of the homogeneity of the API (insert and update methods) and also of the SQL statements creation (table of fields becomes a where clause).

6

Boostrapping a Forth in 40 Lines of Lua Code

Eduardo Ochs

The core of a conventional Forth system is composed of two main programs: an outer interpreter, which interprets textual scripts, and an inner interpreter, which runs bytecodes. The outer interpreter switches between an "immediate mode", where words as executed as soon as they are read, and a "compile mode", where the words being read are assembled into bytecodes to define new words.

In Forth all variables are accessible from all parts of the system. Several important words use that to affect the parsing: they read parts of the input text themselves, process that somehow, and advance the input pointer—and with that they effectively implement other languages, with arbitrary syntax, on top of the basic language of the outer interpreter.

Due mostly to cultural reasons, Forths tend to be built starting from very low-level pieces: first the inner interpreter, in Assembly or C, then the basic libraries and the outer interpreter, in Forth bytecodes or (rarely) in C. We take another approach. If we consider that Lua is more accessible to us than C or Assembly—and thus for us Lua is "more basic"—then it is more natural to start from the outer interpreter, and the dictionary only has to have the definition for one word, one that means "interpret everything that follows, up to a given delimiter, as Lua code, and execute that". An outer interpreter like that fits in less than 40 lines of Lua code, and it can be used to bootstrap a whole Forth-like language.

Introduction

The real point of this article is to propose a certain way of implementing a Forth virtual machine; let's call this new way "mode-based". The main loop of a mode-based Forth is just this:

```
while mode ~= "stop" do modes[mode]() end
```

In our mode-based Forth, which is implemented in Lua and that we will refer to as "miniforth", new modes can be added dynamically very easily. We will start with a virtual machine that "knows" only one mode — "interpret", which corresponds to less than half of the "outer interpreter" of traditional Forths — and with a dictionary that initially contains just one word, which means "read the rest of the line and interpret that as Lua code". That minimal virtual machine fits in 40 lines of Lua, and is enough to bootstrap the whole system.

But, "Why Forth?", the reader will ask. "Forth is old and weird, why shouldn't we stick to modern civilized languages, and ignore Forth? What do you still like in Forth?". My feeling here is that Forth is one of the two quintessential extensible languages, the other one being Lisp. Lisp is very easy to extend and to modify, but only within certain limits: its syntax, given by 'read', is hard to change(1). If we want to implement a little language (as in [1]) with a free-from syntax on top of Lisp, and we know Forth, we might wonder that perhaps the right tool for that would have to have characteristics from both Lisp and Forth. And this is where Lua comes in — as a base language for building extensible languages.

Disclaimer: I'm using the term "Forth" in a loose sense throughout this article. I will say more about this in the last section.

Forth via examples

Any "normal" Forth has an interactive interface where the user types a line, then hits the "return" key, and then the Forth executes that line, word by word, and displays some output; our miniforth does not have an interactive interface, but most ideas still carry on. Here's a very simple program; the text on the left of '-->' is the user input, the text on the right is the output from the Forth system. Note that "words" are sequences on non-whitespace characters, delimited by whitespace.

```
5 DUP * .   -->  25 ok
```

This program can be "read aloud" as this: "Put 5 on the stack; run 'DUP', i.e., duplicate the element on the top of the stack; multiply the two elements on the top of the stack, replacing them by their product; print the element at the top of the stack and remove it from the stack."

Here's a program that defines two new functions ("words", in the Forth jargon):

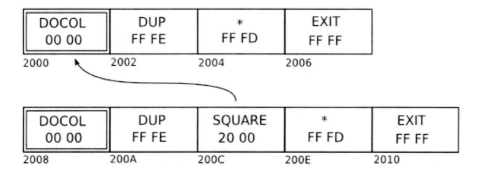

Figure 1. A 16-bit Forth with primitives. Forth instructions with very high values are primitives.

```
: SQUARE DUP * ;          -->  ok
: CUBE DUP SQUARE * ;     -->  ok
5 CUBE .                  -->  125 ok
```

It can be read aloud as this: Define two new words: SQUARE: run DUP, then multiply; CUBE: run DUP, then run SQUARE, then multiply. Now put 5 on the stack, CUBE it, and print the result.

The words SQUARE and CUBE are represented in the memory as some kind of bytecode; different Forths use different kinds of bytecodes. Here we are more interested in "indirect threaded" Forths (see [3]) that store the dictionary in a separate region of the memory. Some possible representations would be like in Figures 1, 2, and 3; in these box diagrams all numbers are in hexadecimal, and we are assuming a big-endian machine for simplicity. Figure 4 shows the "bytecode" representation that we will use in miniforth. It is not exactly a bytecode, as the memory cells can hold arbitrary Lua objects, not just bytes, but we will call it a "bytecode" anyway, by abuse of language.

Here's a trace of what happens when we run CUBE in miniforth:

```
RS={ 5 }       mode=head    DS={ 5 }       head="DOCOL"
RS={ 7 }       mode=forth   DS={ 5 }       instr="DUP"
RS={ 8 }       mode=forth   DS={ 5 5 }     instr=1
RS={ 8 1 }     mode=head    DS={ 5 5 }     head="DOCOL"
RS={ 8 3 }     mode=forth   DS={ 5 5 }     instr="DUP"
RS={ 8 4 }     mode=forth   DS={ 5 5 5 }   instr="*"
RS={ 8 5 }     mode=forth   DS={ 5 25 }    instr="EXIT"
RS={ 9 }       mode=forth   DS={ 5 25 }    instr="*"
RS={ 10 }      mode=forth   DS={ 125 }     instr="EXIT"
```

Note that we don't have a separate variable for the instruction pointer (IP); we use the top of the return stack (RS) as IP. The rightmost part of our traces always describes what is going to be executed, while the rest describes the current state. So, in the sixth line in the trace above we have RS = { 8, 4 }, and we are going to execute the instruction in memory[4], i.e., "*", in mode "forth".

(DUP)
(*)
(EXIT)
DOCOL
DUP
*
EXIT
DOCOL
DUP
SQUARE
*
EXIT

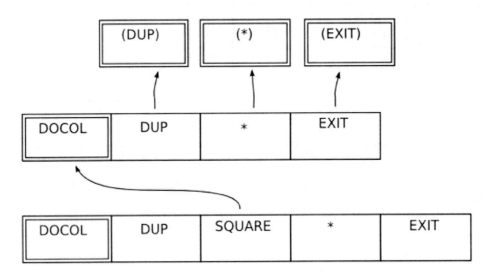

Figure 2. A 16-bit Forth with no primitives. All Forth instructions point to heads (double boxes); each head points to a routine in 8086 machine code.

DO COL
DUP
*
EXIT
2000 SQUARE
2001
2002
2004
DO COL
DUP
SQUARE 20 00
*
EXIT
2005 CUBE
2006
2007
2009
200B

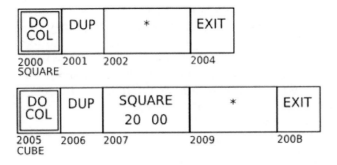

Figure 3. An imaginary 16-bit Forth with 1-byte heads and variable-length Forth instructions.

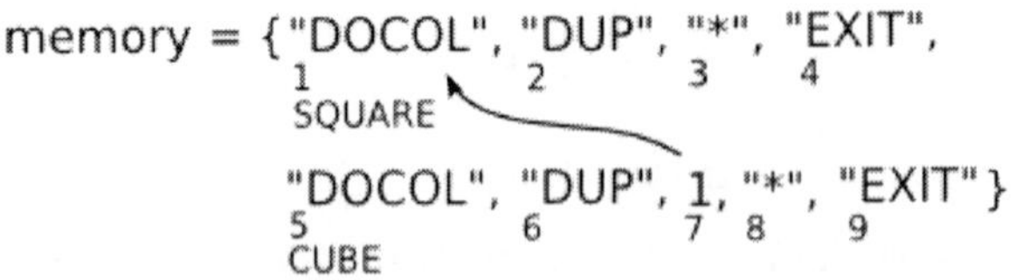

memory = {"DOCOL", "DUP", "*", "EXIT",
1 2 3 4
SQUARE
"DOCOL", "DUP", 1, "*", "EXIT"}
5 6 7 8 9
CUBE

Figure 4. Miniforth. Heads and Forth primitives are represented by strings in the memory cells. Forth non-primitives are represented by numbers.

Bootstrapping miniforth

The program in Listing 1 is all that we need to bootstrap miniforth. It defines the main loop (run), one mode (interpret), the dictionary (_F), and one word in the dictionary: %L, meaning "evaluate the rest of the current line as Lua code".

The program below is a first program in miniforth. It starts with only "%L" defined and it defines several new words: what to do on end-of-line, on end-of-text, and "[L", which evaluates blocks of Lua code that may span more than one line; then it creates a data stack DS and defines the words "DUP", "*", "5", and ".", which operate on it.

```
subj = [=[
%L _F["\n"] = function () end
%L _F[""]   = function () mode = "stop" end
%L _F["[L"] = function () eval(parsebypattern("^(.-)%sL]()")) end
[L
  DS = { n = 0 }
  push = function (stack, x)
                    stack.n = stack.n + 1; stack[stack.n] = x end
  pop  = function (stack)
                    local x = stack[stack.n]; stack[stack.n] = nil;
                    stack.n = stack.n - 1; return x end
  _F["5"]   = function () push(DS, 5) end
  _F["DUP"] = function () push(DS, DS[DS.n]) end
  _F["*"]   = function () push(DS, pop(DS) * pop(DS)) end
  _F["."]   = function () io.write(" "..pop(DS)) end
L]
]=]


-- Now run it. There's no visible output.
pos = 1
mode = "interpret"
run()
-- At this point the dictionary (_F) has eight words.
```

After running this program the system is already powerful enough to run simple Forth programs like, for example,

```
5 DUP * .
```

Note that to "run" this Forth program what we need to do is:

```
subj = "5 DUP * ."; pos = 1; mode = "interpret"; run()
```

It is as if we were setting the memory (here the subj) and the registers of a primitive machine by hand, and then pressing its "run" button. Clearly, that interface could be made better, but here we have other priorities.

```
-- Global variables that hold the input:
subj = "5 DUP * ."      -- what we are interpreting (example)
pos  = 1                -- where we are (1 = "at the beginning")

-- Low-level functions to read things from "pos" and advance "pos".
-- Note: the "pat" argument in "parsebypattern" is a pattern with
-- one "real" capture and then an empty capture.
parsebypattern = function (pat)
    local capture, newpos = string.match(subj, pat, pos)
    if newpos then pos = newpos; return capture end
  end
parsespaces = function () return parsebypattern("^([ \t]*)()") end
parseword = function () return parsebypattern("^([^ \t\n]+)()") end
parsenewline = function () return parsebypattern("^(\n)()") end
parserestofline = function () return parsebypattern("^([^\n]*)()") end
parsewordornewline = function () return parseword() or parsenewline() end

-- A "word" is a sequence of one or more non-whitespace characters.
-- The outer interpreter reads one word at a time and executes it.
-- Note that 'getwordornewline() or ""' returns a word, or a newline, or "".
getword = function () parsespaces(); return parseword() end
getwordornewline = function () parsespaces(); return parsewordornewline() end

-- The dictionary. Entries whose values are functions are primitives.
_F = {}
_F["%L"] = function () eval(parserestofline()) end

-- The "processor". It can be in any of several "modes".
-- Its initial behavior is to run modes[mode]() - i.e.,
-- modes.interpret() - until 'mode' becomes "stop".
mode  = "interpret"
modes = {}
run = function () while mode ~= "stop" do modes[mode]() end end

-- Initially the processor knows only this mode, "interpret"...
-- Note that "word" is a global variable.
interpretprimitive = function ()
    if type(_F[word]) == "function" then _F[word](); return true end
  end
interpretnonprimitive = function () return false end    -- stub
interpretnumber       = function () return false end    -- stub
p_s_i = function () end  -- print state, for "interpret" (stub)
modes.interpret = function ()
    word = getwordornewline() or ""
    p_s_i()
    local _ = interpretprimitive() or interpretnonprimitive() or
              interpretnumber() or error("Can't interpret: "..word)
  end
```

Listing 1.

The programs above don't have support for non-primitives; this will have to be added later. Look at Figure 4: non-primitives, like "SQUARE", are represented in the bytecode as numbers (addresses of heads in the memory[]) and we have not introduced either the memory or the states "head" or "forth" yet.

Note that the names of non-primitives do not appear in the memory, only in the dictionary, _F. For convenience in such memory diagrams we will draw the names of non-primitives below their corresponding heads. For instance, in Figure 4, we have _F["SQUARE"] = 1 and _F["CUBE"] = 5.

Modes

When the inner interpret runs — i.e., when the mode is "head" or "forth"; see Figure 5 —, at each step the processor reads the contents of the memory at IP and processes it. When the outer interpreter runs, at each step it reads a word from subj starting at pos, and processes it. There's a parallel between these behaviors...

I have never seen any references to "modes" in the literature about Forth. In the usual descriptions of inner interpreters for Forth, the "head" mode is not something separate; it is just a transitory state that is part of the semantics of executing a Forth word. Also, the "interpret" and "compile" modes do not exist: the outer interpreter is implemented as a Forth word containing a loop; it reads one word at a time, and depending on the value of a state variable, it either "interprets" or "compiles" that word. So, in a sense, "interpret" and "compile" are "virtual modes"...

Let me explain how I arrived at this idea of "modes" — and what I was trying to do that led me there.

Some words interfere with the variables of the outer interpreter. For example, ":" reads the word the pos is pointing at (for example, SQUARE), adds a definition for that word (SQUARE) to the dictionary, and advances pos. When the control returns to modes.interpret(), the variable pos is pointing to the position after SQUARE — modes.interpret() never tries to process the word SQUARE. Obviously, this can be used to implement new languages, with arbitrary syntax, on top of Forth.

Some words interfere with the variables of the inner interpreter — they modify the return stack. Let's use a more colorful terminology: we will speak of words that "eat text" and of words that "eat bytecode". As we have seen, ":" is a word that eats text; numerical literals are implemented in Forth code using a word, LIT, that eats bytecode. In the program below,

```
: DOZENS 12 * ;    -->  ok
5 DOZENS . 60      -->  ok
```

the word DOZENS is represented in bytecode in miniforth as:

```
memory = {"DOCOL", "LIT", 12, "*", "EXIT"}
      -- 1         2      3    4    5
      -- DOZENS
```

When the `LIT` in `DOZENS` executes, it reads the 12 that comes after it, and places it on the data stack; then it changes the return stack so that in the next step of the main loop the IP will be 4, not 3. Here is a trace of its execution; note that there is a new mode, "lit". The effect of "executing" the 12 in `memory[3]` in mode "lit" is to put the 12 in DS.

```
RS={ 1 }  mode=head   DS={ 5 }      head="DOCOL"
RS={ 2 }  mode=forth  DS={ 5 }      instr="LIT"
RS={ 3 }  mode=lit    DS={ 5 }      data=12
RS={ 4 }  mode=forth  DS={ 5 12 }   instr="*"
RS={ 5 }  mode=forth  DS={ 60 }     instr="EXIT"
```

The code in Lua for the primitive `LIT` and for the mode "lit" can be synthesized from the trace. By analyzing what happens between steps 2 and 3, and 3 and 4, we see that `LIT` and "lit" must be:

```
_F["LIT"] = function () mode = "lit" end
modes.lit = function ()
    push(DS, memory[RS[RS.n]])
    RS[RS.n] = RS[RS.n] + 1
    mode = "forth"
  end
```

so from this point on we will consider that the traces give enough information, and we will not show the corresponding code.

Note that different modes read what they will execute from different places: "head", "forth", and "lit" read from `memory[RS[RS.n]]` (they eat bytecode), whereas "interpret" and "compile" read from `subj`, starting at `pos` (they eat text). Our focus here will be on modes and words that eat bytecode.

Virtual modes

How can we create words that eat bytecode, like `LIT`, in Forth? In the program below, the word `TESTLITS` call first `LIT`, then `VLIT`; `VLIT` should behave similarly to `LIT`, but `LIT` is a primitive and `VLIT` is not.

```
memory = {"DOCOL", "R>P", "PCELL", "P>R", "EXIT",
      --   1        2       3        4      5
      --   VLIT <---------------+
      --                        |
          "DOCOL", "LIT", 123, 1, 234, "EXIT",}
      --   6        7      8    9  10    11
      --   TESTLITS
```

Here is a trace of TESTLITS:

```
t=0  RS={ 6 }      mode=head   PS={  }   DS={  }           head="DOCOL"
t=1  RS={ 7 }      mode=forth  PS={  }   DS={  }           instr="LIT"
t=2  RS={ 8 }      mode=lit    PS={  }   DS={  }           data=123
t=3  RS={ 9 }      mode=forth  PS={  }   DS={ 123 }        instr=1
t=4  RS={ 10 1 }   mode=head   PS={  }   DS={ 123 }        head="DOCOL"
t=5  RS={ 10 2 }   mode=forth  PS={  }   DS={ 123 }        instr="R>P"
t=6  RS={ 3 }      mode=forth  PS={ 10 } DS={ 123 }        instr="PCELL"
t=7  RS={ 4 }      mode=pcell  PS={ 10 } DS={ 123 }        pdata=234
t=8  RS={ 4 }      mode=forth  PS={ 11 } DS={ 123 234 }    instr="P>R"
t=9  RS={ 11 5 }   mode=forth  PS={  }   DS={ 123 234 }    instr="EXIT"
t=10 RS={ 11 }     mode=forth  PS={  }   DS={ 123 234 }    instr="EXIT"
```

This is a full solution, so start by ignoring the cells 2, 3, and 4 of the memory, and the lines t=5 to t=8 of the trace. From t=5 to t=9 what we need to do is

```
push(DS, memory[RS[RS.n - 1]])
RS[RS.n - 1] = RS[RS.n - 1] + 1
```

where the −1 is a magic number: roughly, the number of "call frames" in the stack between the call to VLIT and the code that will read its literal data, negated. In other situations this could be −2, −3, ... One way to get rid of that magic number is to create a new stack — the "parsing stack" (PS) — and to have "parsing words" that parse bytecode from the position that the top of PS points to; then a word like VLIT becomes a variation of a word, PCELL, that reads a cell from memory[PS[PS.n]] and advances PS[PS.n]. The code for VLIT given above shows how that is done — we wrap PCELL as "R>P PCELL P>R" — and from the trace we can infer how to define these words.

Note that the transition from t=2 to t=3 corresponds to the transition from t=4 to t=10; the mode being "lit" corresponds to having the address of the head of VLIT at the top of RS, and the mode being "head"; using this idea we can implement virtual modes in Forth. Better yet: it all becomes a bit simpler if we regard the mode as being an invisible element that is always above the top of RS. So, an imaginary mode "vlit" would be translated, or expanded, into a 1 (the head of VLIT), plus a mode "head"; or another word, similar to VLIT, would just switch the mode to "vlit", and the action of that word would be to expand it into the head of VLIT, plus the mode "head".

A bytecode for polynomials

A polynomial with fixed numerical coefficients can be represented in memory as first the number of these coefficients, then the value of each of them; for example, $P(x) = 2x^3 + 3x^2 + 4x + 5.5$ is represented as $\{\ldots, 4, 2, 3, 4, 5.5, \ldots\}$. We will call this representation — number of coefficients, then coefficients — the "data of the polynomial". Let's start with a primitive, PPOLY, that works like

PCELL, in the sense that it reads the data of the polynomial from the memory, starting at the position PS[PS.n], and advancing PS[PS.n] at each step. This PPOLY takes a value from the top of the data stack —it will be 10 in our examples— and replaces it with the result of applying P on it, —P(10)—, which is 2345.5 for the example above.

By defining POLY from PPOLY, as we defined VLIT from PCELL

```
: POLY R>P PPOLY P>R ;
```

we get a word that eats bytecode; a call to POLY should be followed by data of a polynomial, just like LIT is followed by a number. And we can also do something else: we can create new heads, DOPOLY and DOADDR, and represent polynomials as two heads followed by the data of the polynomial. The program and trace below test this idea.

```
memory = {"DOPOLY", "DOADDR", 4, 2, 3, 4, 5.5,
      --   1            2          3  4  5  6   7
      --   P(X)         &P(X)
      --   ^--------------------+
      --                        |
           "DOCOL",    "LIT", 10, 1, "EXIT"}
      --   8           9      10 11 12
      --   TESTDOPOLY: put 10 on the stack and call P(X)
```

```
RS={ 8 }           mode=head    PS={ }    DS={ }      head="DOCOL"
RS={ 9 }           mode=forth   PS={ }    DS={ }      instr="LIT"
RS={ 10 }          mode=lit     PS={ }    DS={ }      data=10
RS={ 11 }          mode=forth   PS={ }    DS={ 10 }   instr=1
RS={ 12 1 }        mode=head    PS={ }    DS={ 10 }   head="DOPOLY"
RS={ 12 forth }    mode=ppolyn  PS={ 3 }  DS={ 10 }   n=4
RS={ 12 forth }    mode=ppolyc  PS={ 4 }  DS={ 10 }   n=4 acc=0 coef=2
RS={ 12 forth }    mode=ppolyc  PS={ 5 }  DS={ 10 }   n=3 acc=2 coef=3
RS={ 12 forth }    mode=ppolyc  PS={ 6 }  DS={ 10 }   n=2 acc=23 coef=4
RS={ 12 forth }    mode=ppolyc  PS={ 7 }  DS={ 10 }   n=1 acc=234 coef=5.5
RS={ 12 forth }    mode=ppolye  PS={ 8 }  DS={ 10 }   acc=2345.5
RS={ 12 }          mode=forth   PS={ 8 }  DS={ 2345.5 }  instr="EXIT"
```

The trace above does not show what &P(X) does; the effect of running &P(X) is to put the address of the beginning of data of the polynomial, namely, 3, into the data stack. Note how a polynomial—which in most other languages would be a piece of passive data—in Forth is represented as two programs, P(X) and &P(X), that share their data. Compare that with the situation of closures in Lua—two closures created by the same mother function, and referring to variables that were local to that mother function, share upvalues.

A bytecode language for propositional calculus

Here is another example. Let's write '=>' for "implies", and '&' for "and". Then (Q=>R)=>((P&Q)=>(P&R)) is a "formula", or a "proposition", in Propositional Calculus; incidentally, it is a tautology, i.e., always true.

In some situations, for example, if we want to find a proof for that proposition, or if we want to evaluate its truth value for some assignment of truth values to P, Q, and R, we need to refer to subformulas of that formula. If we represent the formula in bytecode using Polish Notation (not Reverse Polish Notation! Can you see why?) then this becomes trivial:

```
memory = { "=>", "=>", "Q", "R", "=>", "&", "P", "Q", "&", "P", "R" }
   --    1     2    3    4    5    6    7    8    9    10    11
```

Subformulas can now be referred to by numbers: the position in the memory where they start. We can write a word to parse a proposition starting at some position in the memory; if that position contains a binary connective like '=>' or '&', then that word calls itself twice to parse the subformulas at the "left" and at the "right" of the connective. If the word memoizes the resulting structure by storing it in a table named formulas, then re-parsing the formula that starts at the position, say, 6, becomes very quick: the result is formulas[6], and the pointer should be advanced to formulas[6].next. Here are the contents of that table after parsing the formula that starts at memory[1].

```
 1: { addr=1, cc="=>", l=2,  r=5,  next=12, name="((Q=>R)=>((P&Q)=>(P&R)))" }
 2: { addr=2, cc="=>", l=3,  r=4,  next=5,  name="(Q=>R)" }
 3: { addr=3,                      next=4,  name="Q" }
 4: { addr=4,                      next=5,  name="R" }
 5: { addr=5, cc="=>", l=6,  r=9,  next=12, name="((P&Q)=>(P&R))" }
 6: { addr=6, cc="&",  l=7,  r=8,  next=9,  name="(P&Q)" }
 7: { addr=7,                      next=8,  name="P" }
 8: { addr=8,                      next=9,  name="Q" }
 9: { addr=9, cc="&",  l=10, r=11, next=12, name="(P&R)" }
10: { addr=10,                     next=11, name="P" }
11: { addr=11,                     next=12, name="R" }
```

(Meta)Lua on miniforth

The parser for the language for Propositional Calculus in the last section had to be recursive, but it didn't need backtracking to work. Here is a language that is evidently useful — even if at this context it looks like an academic exercise — and whose parser needs a bit of backtracking, or at least lookahead. Consider the following program in Lua:

```
foo = function ()
    local storage
    return function () return storage end,
           function (x)   storage = x end
    end
```

It can be represented in bytecode in miniforth as:

```
memory = {
  "foo", "=", "function", "(", ")",
      "local", "storage",
      "return", "function", "(", ")", "return", "storage", "end", ",",
                "function", "(", "x", ")", "storage", "=", "x", "end",
    "end",
  "<eof>" }
```

One way of "executing" this bytecode made of string tokens could be to produce in another region of the memory a representation in Lua of the bytecode language that the Lua VM executes; another would be to convert that to another sequence of string tokens — like what MetaLua [5] does. Anyway, there's nothing special with our choice of Lua here — Lua just happens to be a simple language that we can suppose that the reader knows well, but it could have been any language. And as these parsers and transformers would be written in Lua, they would be easy to modify.

Why Forth?

Caveat lector: there is no single definition for what "Forth" is... Around 1994 the community had a big split, with some people working to create an ANSI Standard for Forth, and the creator of the language and some other people going in another direction, and not only creating new Forths that went against ideas of the Standard, but also stating that ANS Forth "was not Forth". I can only write this section clearly and make it brief if I choose a very biased terminology; also, I'm not going to be historically precise, either — I will simplify and distort the story a bit to get my points across. You have been warned!

Forth was very popular in certain circles at a time when computers were much less powerful than those of today. Some of the reasons for that popularity were easy to quantify: compactness of programs, speed, proximity to machine code, simplicity of the core of the language, i.e., of the inner and the outer interpreters. None of these things matter so much anymore: computers got bigger and faster, their assembly languages became much more complex, and we've learned to take for granted several concepts and facilities — malloc and free, high-level data structures, BNF — and now we feel that it is "simpler" to send characters through stdout than poking bytes at the video memory. Our notion of simplicity has changed.

In the mid-90s came the ANS-Forth Standard, and with it a way to write Forth source that would run without changes in Forths with different memory models, on different CPU architectures. At about the same time the creator of the language, Chuck Moore, started to distance himself from the rest of the community, to work on Forths that were more and more minimalistic, and on specialized processors that ran Forth natively.

My experience with (non-Chuck-Moore-) Forth systems written before and after the ANS Standard was that in the pre-ANS ones the format of the bytecode was stated clearly, and users were expected to understand it; in Forths written after the Standard the bytecode was not something so mundane anymore—it became a technical detail, hidden under abstractions.

Old Forths were fun to use. When I was a teenager I spent hundreds of evenings playing with Forths on an IBM-PC: first FIG-Forth and MVP-Forth, then HS-Forth, a commercial Forth whose memory model (8086 machine code, dictionary and Forth definitions in different memory segments, indirect-threaded, no primitives, multiple heads) inspired some of the ideas in this article. At one point I spent some weeks writing a program that constructed a "shadow image" of the Forth segment, with a letter or a number for each byte in a head, a '.' for each byte in a Forth instruction, '_' and '$' for bytes in literal numbers and strings, '<' and '>' for the bytes that were addresses in backward or forward jumps (i.e., the two bytes following each call to BRANCH or 0BRANCH)—and spaces for the unknown bytes, as I didn't have the source for the whole core system, and some words were tricky to decompile... Then I printed the result, in five pages, each with a grid of 64x64 characters, and addresses at the borders; that gave me a map of all the bytes in words in the core system that were not defined in assembly language.

I've met many people over the years who have been Forth enthusiasts in the past, and we often end up discussing what made Forth so thrilling to use at that time—and what we can do to adapt its ideas to the computers of today. My personal impression is that Forth's main points were not the ones that I listed at the beginning of this section, and that I said that were easy to quantify; rather, what was most important was that nothing was hidden, there were no complex data structures around with "don't-look-at-this" parts (think on garbage collection in Lua, for example, and Lua's tables—beginners need to be convinced to see these things abstractly, as the concrete details of the implementation are hard), and everything—code, data, dictionaries, stacks—were just linear sequences of bytes, that could be read and modified directly if we wished to. We had total freedom, defining new words was quick, and experiments were quick to make; that gave us a sense of power that was totally different from, say, the one that a Python user feels today because he has huge libraries at his fingertips.

A Forth-like language built on top of Lua should be easier to integrate with the rest of the system than a "real" Forth written in C. Also, it's much easier to add new syntaxes and bytecode languages to a mode-based Forth than to a conventional one. And we are not forced to store only numbers in the memory; we can store also strings—I've used strings for primitives and heads here because this makes programs more readable—, or any other Lua objects, if we need to.

I do not intend to claim that miniforth is compact—in terms of memory usage—or efficient, or useful for practical applications. But the natural ways for doing things in Forth were different from the ways that are natural in today's systems; and I believe that miniforth can be used to give to people glimpses into interesting ways of thinking that have practically disappeared, and that have become hard to communicate.

Conclusion

After a draft of this article had been written, Marc Simpson engaged in a long series of discussions with me about Forths, Lisp, SmallTalk, several approaches to minimality, etc., and at one point, over the course of one hectic weekend in December, 2007, he implemented a usable (rather than just experimental) dialect of Forth — based mainly on Frank Sergeant's Pygmy Forth and Chuck Moore's cmForth, and borrowing some ideas from this article — on top of Ruby ("RubyForth"), and later ported his system to Python and C. A port of it to Lua is underway.

I thank Marc Simpson and Yuri Takhteyev for helpful discussions.

References

[1] Jon Bentley: *More Programming Pearls*, Addison-Wesley, 1990 (chapter 9: *Little Languages*).

[2] James T. Callahan: HS-Forth (program and manual). Harvard Softworks, 1986–1993.

[3] Anton Ertl: Threaded Code. `http://www.complang.tuwien.ac.at/forth/threaded-code.html`

[4] Brad Rodriguez: A BNF Parser in Forth. `http://www.zetetics.com/bj/papers/bnfparse.htm`

[5] Fabien Fleutot: MetaLua. `http://metalua.luaforge.net/`

[6] Kein-Hong Man: A No-Frills Introduction to Lua 5.1 VM Instructions. `http://luaforge.net/docman/view.php/83/98`

7

Effecting Large-Scale Change (with little trauma) using Metatables

Sérgio Alvares Maffra & Pedro Miller Rabinovitch

Introduction

In real-world conditions, software maintenance becomes as important as software development. Environments change, business partners choose different strategies, technology evolves — and devolves. Distributed systems become centralized, and centralized ones get scattered around. In particular, requirements have a peculiar way of being significantly altered once a project approaches completion... or the day after it has been deployed.

It becomes more and more important to be able to quickly adapt to these changing conditions. In the following sections we'll discuss the application of a particularly powerful feature of Lua to this end. We'll start by presenting a short review of metamethods along with a couple of simple examples. We will then show how Lua's metatables were used to dramatically change the performance profile of an application with little effort. Finally, we conclude showing a few examples where metatables can help developers change the key features of a system even if it's already in a late development phase or even in production.

Metamethods and environments

Metatables offer an unique way to intercept and change language events in specific objects. By specifying code to be executed when simple operations are attempted on specific objects, developers can provide a scripting environment where values behave the way they're expected to, which is particularly useful where non-programmers are concerned (e.g., AI scripting or other problem domain specific scripting). However, much more interesting applications are available. The index and newindex metamethods, in particular, are specially useful since they allow one to check for variable resolution and provide missing values on the fly in a just-in-time fashion. This, of course, is perfect for default values and inheritance (as described in detail in *Programming in Lua*) and lazy evaluation procedures, where values are computed as required, but always accessed in a transparent and consistent manner.

The index metamethod is called every time a table is indexed and there's no appropriate value set for the relevant key. Listing 1 shows an example of index being used to calculate values on the fly as the cache (or look-up) table is indexed. The first time the user attempts to index the table where there's no value set, the metamethod is called. After the computing is done, the metamethod sets the value at the table, memoizing it for the next time it's needed. When the same key of the table is indexed again further down the line, the value is already there, and the method is not called.

The newindex metamethod works in an analogue fashion — it is called every time the table has a new value being set. This means that we can watch a table for change and record every time one of its values is updated by an operation, as long as we keep the relevant fields of the table empty (typically by using a proxy table).

The mechanisms above become even more useful because of Lua's environment functions, getfenv and setfenv. These functions allow us to change the global environment of any given executing routine. The call getfenv(0), in particular, returns a reference to the table that contains all global variables in our program at the current context, and which will be inherited when we require other modules. Since it's a table, we can set metamethods on it, and watch as global variables are accessed and updated should we so desire.

Our sample problem

Consider an application heavily based in Lua. As development progresses, the number of Lua files in the project increases, and the dependency graph grows more and more complex at each iteration. At a certain point, the application starts taking a long time to compile at run time, since all the modules are loaded right at the beginning of the execution in a long series of requires or dofiles. This series of module loading instructions also presume a certain order, since dependency issues must not be ignored. At first, this is taken in stride — the target equipment that will run the application is well-known and established as

```
local tableOfHeavyData = {}

setmetatable( tableOfHeavyData,
  {
    __index = function( tbl, key )
      -- calculate the required value
      local data = performHeavyComputing( key )
      -- cache response in the table
      tbl[key] = data
      return data
    end
  }
)

-- do serious computing
function performHeavyComputing( x )
  print( "computing the value of "..x )
  return x * x -- dude. Heavy.
end

print( "value for 2 is "..tableOfHeavyData[2] )
for i = 1, 3 do
  print( "value for "..i.." is "..tableOfHeavyData[i] )
end

--[[ Output:
computing the value of 2
value for 2 is 4
computing the value of 1
value for 1 is 1
value for 2 is 4
computing the value of 3
value for 3 is 9
--]]
```

Listing 1. An example of the `index` metamethod.

being of "high performance". Lines such as "we'll just tell them to buy more RAM" are heard and management is confident of the project success. Boat catalogs are browsed.

This is all well and good until requirements change. Perhaps the code will have to run on a less powerful platform, such as portable devices. Perhaps the client can't afford the extra budget for better equipment. Or perhaps the testing cycle just got way too long, since each time the application is run, everything is loaded into memory in one big shot.

Now we have a problem. Our hypothetical application is bloated; its modules and libraries are not well separated; the libraries it depends on are taking much more cycles than expected; what is one to do? Picture modules named pic.lua that define functions with naming conventions as diverse as pic_open, PICdecode, and pngPICformat. Add a couple of list_of_pictures or images tables. Multiply that by, say, 30 or 40 functions defined in each of 20+ modules. Throwing a couple of interns at the problem probably won't give the best results.

We had such a problem in an actual application we developed — in our case, the graphical interface library which the application depended on went through a large change and started taking a lot longer to create dialogs. The change was for the better as far as the GUI presentation was concerned, of course. But running it, even if one was just trying to check on the latest changes, was taking way too long. Granted, our application was not the nightmarish vision we presented above, but we're making a point here.

Well, if your development is in a language as powerful as Lua, you can solve your problems[1] in about an hour with the judicious use of metamethods and the replacement of a couple of system functions. We will present a solution as we analyze a sample implementation in the following section.

Resolution through "Origins"

The new release of the GUI library used in our application was expected with great anxiety at the time. We had been eagerly waiting for it for about a year. We couldn't wait to use the new features (and get rid of the old bugs!). Unfortunately, what should have been a joyful occasion, became a great disappointment. Moreover, we had a big problem in our hands. Sooner or later, we would have to upgrade to the latest release, since there was no support for the old ones.

A deeper investigation showed us that the GUI library was taking a lot longer to create dialogs due to the new widget placement algorithm. In our application all dialogs were created at startup, what explained the humongous loading time we were experiencing. Fortunately, the solution was, actually, quite simple: the dialogs should be individually created when needed and not all at once at startup. Given that our application is composed of quite a few hundred source files, this solution fits well in the "easier said than done" category. At first glance,

---

[1]Actually, you can solve a couple of your problems. The memory and processing issue will be solved, but the perverse naming conventions are more into the realm of physical punishment.

```
-- generated in 06/19/07 21:09:16 by origins
origins.data = {
  ["alpha_create"] = "libAlpha",
  ["gamma_function1"] = "libGamma",
  ["alpha_function2"] = "libAlpha",
  ["alpha_global"] = "libAlpha",
  ["alpha_function1"] = "libAlpha",
  ["beta_name"] = "libBeta",
  ["alpha_constant1"] = "libAlpha",
  ["beta_constant1"] = "libBeta",
  ["alpha_name"] = "libAlpha",
  ["beta_function1"] = "libBeta",
  ["beta_table"] = "libBeta",
  ["gamma_name"] = "libGamma",
  ["beta_create"] = "libBeta",
}
```

Listing 2. A sample data file

that would require us to track down and alter every reference made to each of
the dialogs used in the application. Thankfully, all GUI code was written in Lua,
which allowed us to adopt a better approach.

The loading time could be reduced if the `require` calls that created dialogs
were removed from our initialization methods. But, that would leave us with
a lot of missing values in our hands. As mentioned in Section 7, the `index`
metamethod can be used to provide missing values on the fly. Therefore, our
dialogs could be created when needed by loading their defining modules in an
`index` metamethod set in the global environment.

By using this solution we avoided going through all the code of the application. It required, however, knowing the values defined by each module in
the application. A simple table containing module names that are retrieved
from variable names, like the one defined in Listing 2, is all that was necessary.
Granted, creating this table can still require a lot of work. Fortunately, the table
in Listing 2 was generated automatically by using the `newindex` metamethod.

We have implemented the solution in the form of a library we've dubbed
"Origins". The library works in a two-phase approach:

1. During *setup*, the application is executed with the appropriate environment, and the library detects all functions and variables that are loaded,
   tracing each (by name) to its original module;

2. During *run time*, the application is executed and, as it tries to access the
   functions and variables from each module, the library detects the attempt
   and loads the required module.

Each phase depends mainly in a different meta-method. We will examine each
one below.

```
function origins:startWatching()
  origins.original_require = require
  require = origins.new_require
  setmetatable( getfenv(0), origins_metatable )
end

function origins:stopWatching()
  setmetatable( getfenv(0), nil )
  require = origins.original_require
end
```

Listing 3. Watching for definitions.

```
function origins.new_require( name, ... )
  print( "[origins] processing "..name )
  -- preserve previous filename (so we know where variables come from)
  local previousFilename = origins.currentFilename
  -- set current context
  origins.currentFilename = name
  -- call the original function
  origins.original_require( name, unpack( arg ))
  -- restore context
  origins.currentFilename = previousFilename
end
```

Listing 4. Hooking the `require` function.

Setup

During the setup phase we use the `newindex` metamethod to establish which module is providing each global function and variable. This is done by the function `startWatching` presented in Listing 3. First, we hook the loading functions we're interested in (`require` in this case; `dofile` or any other functions that should be processed as well) by replacing their global reference with our own versions. These work as illustrated in Listing 4, keeping track of the lua file (and therefore library module) being currently processed. Our metatable is set on the global environment (acquired via `getfenv(0)`). The `newindex` metamethod, shown in Listing 5, notes each global variable that is set and keeps track of the lua file that was being processed at the time of its definition.

After these proceedings, we can load our application normally. As each new global is set, our variable catalog is built, and by the time the application is up and running — having loaded every variable we're interested in — we can save the stored catalog in a data file that will be used in run time. This is illustrated in Listing 6, and a sample data file is represented in Listing 2. Notice that the data file is simply a Lua code file and that the table data keeps an entry for each variable with the path to its original loading module.

```
local origins_metatable = {
  __newindex = function( table, key, value )
--print( "[origins] newindex: ", key )
    origins.data[key] = origins.currentFilename
    rawset( table, key, value )
  end,
  __index = function( table, key )
--print( "[origins]    index: ", key )
    local source = origins.data[key]
    if source then
      origins.original_require( source )
    end
    return rawget( table, key )
  end,
}
```

Listing 5. The `newindex` and `index` metamethods.

```
function origins:saveData( filename )
  self:stopWatching()
  filename = filename or self.defaultFileName
  local fout = io.open( filename, 'wt' )
  fout:write( "-- generated in "..os.date().." by origins\n" )
  fout:write( "origins.data = {\n" )
  for i,v in pairs( self.data ) do
    fout:write( string.format( "\t[%q] = %q,\n", i, v ))
  end
  fout:write( "}\n" )
  fout:close()
end
```

Listing 6. Saving the catalog data.

Quick setup

It is true that one can execute the setup phase by running the application as normal after calling `startWatching`. However, Listing 7 shows an alternative — artificially loading each module used by the application in a single stretch. This will be enough to refresh all necessary data in most cases, and a proper data file can be generated. This has the additional benefit that we can easily call the setup script in an automated build system, automatically updating the data file as we change the modules.

Runtime

At run time, the application doesn't load its libraries at startup as usual. Instead, it loads the "origins" data file through the `loadData` function, which is

```
-- prepare the application library list
require "origins"
origins:startWatching()

-- these should be in the order they'll be required
require "libUtil"
require "libBeta"
require "libGamma"
require "libAlpha"

-- now save the data
origins:saveData()
```

Listing 7. Loading modules at setup time.

```
function origins:loadData( filename )
  filename = filename or self.defaultFileName
  print( "[origins] loading "..filename )
  dofile( filename )
  origins:startWatching()
end
```

Listing 8. Loading the catalog data.

depicted in Listing 8. This loads the reference catalog (through a trivial `dofile`) and sets the runtime `index` metamethod, shown in Listing 5, which looks for a reference in the catalog in order to load the required module.

After the loading is done, the value that was being sought should be available. The application is not even aware that a module was being loaded on the fly, since it was waiting for the variable referencing to occur while the metamethod was running.

Limitations

The library uses variable and function names as keys; therefore, conditional file loading might cause problems if they define functions by the same name. Consider the code in Listing 9. The execution path taken during setup time would be the one "Origins" considers as the source of `out_write`.

There is a way to pause processing, however (the `stopWatching` method). This enables developers to circumvent said limitation. The use of a quick setup script as described previously would also resolve the situation by not including either module and only loading them at the original point in run time, as intended by the code.

Even if conditional loading is not an issue, what should happen if a global variable is set in more than one module? Such a naming conflict does not

```
if mode == "latex" then
  dofile( "out_latex.lua" )
else
  dofile( "out_html.lua" )
end
-- out_write() is defined in both the files above
out_write( mydata )
```

Listing 9. Conditional `dofiles` could cause problems.

have a resolution we can deem as correct, since even in Lua, the name clash would cause one of the values to be overwritten. We chose not to address this issue in this implementation, but some alternatives would include loading all the modules that defined the conflicting variable (perhaps in the order they originally appeared), printing out warning messages, or even firing an `error` during setup.

Further development

The system introduced here could be the basis for further development. Consider a scheme where standard Lua libraries installed at predetermined path locations were loaded at run time as code in execution needed them, without preloading them through `require`. We could delay library module loading until code is necessary by implementing "Origins" on a system-wide range. One could get rid of `requires` by stipulating that all libraries should be installed through a program responsible for managing a library function catalog, much in the manner of a package manager. After that, any running applications that tried to execute cataloged functions would have the appropriate module loaded and ready at the first call attempt. Module dependencies, of course, would be handled automatically.

Some work would have to be done to keep different versions working correctly together when required. Packaging schemes with property files that describe required module versions come to mind. But scripting, in particular, would greatly benefit from such a scheme — specially if an automated download and installation procedure was available at run time.

Other uses for metatables

Metatables can be used in many ways to significantly change system behavior with little source code alteration. We present some examples below.

Mutexes for concurrent access. If we change an application from a single-threaded approach to a multi-threaded one, access to shared values becomes an issue. Fields in a table (or even global variables) could be watched by a basic monitor paradigm or any kind of mutex solution. This would be easy to implement with metamethods on the lookout for change and access.

Remote procedure calls. Suppose we want to move a component of a modular system to an out-of-process location (and maybe to a remote location accessible by the network). We could use the `call` metamethod to automatically serialize parameters and return values and handle socket communication transparently to the executing process. Of course, this has the disadvantage of hiding important issues like timeouts and communication failures — but on the other hand, programming remains simple and the whole system can be changed in one fell swoop without any perilous search-and-replacing.

Transparent interprocess communication. Not only procedure calls can be sent to other processes; one could implement a shared memory system using sockets or any kind of shared memory access and employ metatables to keep access transparent to the local developer.

Dynamic library loading. Instead of preloading all modules required by the system, we could wait to load each of them as they become needed. This can be done by watching the global environment for access, as shown in the main section of this gem.

It's important to note that these changes are easily made and undone. Since no code is changed in the original application, just setting or not setting the appropriate metatables will activate or deactivate the corresponding functionality. This makes the approach perfect for experimentation, since alternative methods can be kept along with working code in the same development branch.

Another way metatables can help us is on debugging or measuring a system's correctness or performance profile. This can be done in ways such as:

Tracing field access. One could use the `index` and `newindex` metamethods, paired with other debugging information (such as those provided by the `debug` library) to trace which execution paths are altering and accessing a variable or field.

Asserting variable values. Instead of relying on getter and setter functions, one could use appropriate metamethods to check that certain variables always have valid values.

Profiling function calls. The same procedure described for tracing field access, above, could be used to trace function calls. Although a hook could be used to trace every function call in the system and then check for the function names we're interested in, it is probably faster to set a limited number of metamethods. With appropriate timing information or even if we're just tracking the number and/or origin of calls made, one can obtain quite a lot of interesting information with such a system in place.

Conclusion

We have presented in this gem a simple use of what we consider as one of the most versatile and powerful features of Lua. It is easy to see how a simple change implemented this way could alter the execution of a large system as a whole, making a significant and perceptible difference on application performance and usage. In our case it represented the difference between a bit of development work and rewriting the entire GUI system in order to spare processing and memory. By implementing the dynamic loading mechanism presented here we prevented much unnecessary expenditures with little development cost. The most important lesson to keep, however, is that metatables offer a way to effect system-wide change with little use of search-and-replacing and other potentially traumatic methods.

Part II

Design Techniques

8

MVC Web Development with Kepler

André Carregal and Yuri Takhteyev

Kepler is a Lua-based web development platform that is modular and flexible. Kepler 1.1 adds support for the developing web applications using the increasingly more popular Model-View-Controller (MVC) style. This article discusses several approaches to MVC web development and shows how they can be implemented in Kepler.

Introduction

Kepler[1] is an open source web development platform based on Lua that brings many of Lua's advantages to the development of web applications.[2] Like Lua, Kepler is small, portable, and flexible. Kepler 1.1 provides support for web application development that follows the Model-View-Controller (MVC) paradigm, bringing to Lua some of the benefits provided by popular web frameworks written for other programming languages.

MVC refers to the division of application code into three sections and was originally brought to desktop GUI programming by Smalltalk. When applied to

---

[1] http://www.keplerproject.org/

[2] Since this article addresses readers already familiar with Lua, we do not discuss here the exact advantages that Lua offers in general or specifically for web development. Such advantages are discussed, however, on the Kepler site.

Web development, this metaphor has to be adjusted due to the different nature of the interaction: the *model* handles data manipulation and storage, the *view* handles client-side interaction, and the *controller* responds to requests using the model for data manipulation and generating views that are used by the client.

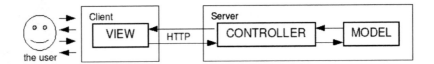

Having the *model* clearly separated is an important part of MVC and the success of such frameworks as Rails had much to do with their handling of the model. The implementation of a model, however, is not specific to web development and we will thus assume here a pre-existing model. We will similarly avoid the discussion of the *view* contents in much detail, since the structure of the view is no way specific to Lua. Instead, we will focus on two problems that must be resolved by the *controller*: dispatching incoming requests (originating from a view) and generating a response that contains a view for the next request.

Request dispatching

Overview

The general problem of HTTP request dispatching is to map an incoming request to an action within the system. The action must at the minimum generate a response that will be sent to the client, but may also have side effects, such as altering the data stored in the model. Here is a general model of the way the MVC controller handles an HTTP request:

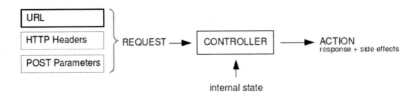

For the purpose of this article we will consider a simplified version of this model, which assumes that the controller relies only on the URL and uses neither other parts of the request nor the internal state: We do not discuss the use of HTTP headers and POST parameters, though those parts of the request are already provided by Kepler in an simple way and their use presents no conceptual challenges.

For the purpose of the this article we will use the term "URL" to refer only to the local part of a URL (/<PATH>?<QUERY>), since the host domain and port number should not concern the web application. As the server dispatches the request, it consumes some part of PATH. The remaining part of PATH is passed to the application and we will refer to it as PATH_INFO.

A common approach to dynamic web development is to structure the application as a collection of functions (in the broad sense of the word) and interpret each request as an identifier of a function and a set of parameters to this function. The traditional use of CGI scripts follows this model: each CGI script acts as a function that accepts a set of parameters (encoded in the QUERY part of the URL). An application is then structured as a collection of scripts, each responsible for a different type of request. Under this approach, a request for wiki/show.cgi?p=HomePage is interpreted as a call to a specific function (/wiki/show.cgi) which is called with one parameter (p=HomePage). If the user clicks on a link to edit the page, they will generate a request for a different function, such as /wiki/edit.cgi?p=HomePage.

Kepler supports this style of web development through "Lua Scripts" or "Lua Pages". This style, however, has been increasingly criticized in the recent years for the insufficient separation between view generation and the application logic. In this article we will show how to use Kepler to implement some of the different alternative approaches that are currently used in some of the popular web frameworks. In doing so, we want to show a range of options available to the developer.

One way of making the dispatching more flexible is to change the way functions and parameters are stored and represented. For instance, we can trivially map /wiki/show onto a Lua function called show, passing to this function the table representing the QUERY parameters. (This would be very similar to the approach used, for example, by CherryPy.) Additionally, we may want to avoid passing parameters via QUERY, as many people find QUERY-free URLs more "clean".

We can do this by implementing a dispatcher similar to Rails' "routes", which will let us map a URL prefix and a sequence of parameters onto a function that would accept a table of parameters:

```
URLs = {
   {"/show/$page_name/$version", show_page}
}
```

This would map a request for /wiki/show/Home_Page/23 onto a call to

```
show_page{page_name="Home_Page, version="23"}
```

which would return version 23 of the page. See *Example 1* in this section for the implementation of this approach.

A yet more flexible and very popular method (used, for example, by Django and web.py) is to determine the function by matching the URL against a list of patterns, each associated with a different function. E.g.:

```
URLs = {
  {"/show/([%w_-]*)/(%d*)", show_page},
  {"/save/([%w_-]*)", save_page}
}
```

The implementation of this approach is discussed in *Example 2*.

In some cases, however, we may want to think of URLs not as selecting functions and passing parameters to them, but as selecting *objects* and sending messages to those objects. This approach is particularly useful if we want to make it easy to override the handling of the action on a per object basis, or if we want to allow custom actions for the objects. For example, we may want some pages of the wiki to be displayed in a special way or to respond to altogether different requests: a page called "History" could have the ability to return the RSS feed for the recent wiki edits. This type of dispatching is presented in *Example 3*.

A complete solution to URL dispatching should also provide for a way to generate URLs that would fit with the dispatching syntax. The ease of doing so would depend on the specific dispatching mechanism. We show how to do this for *Examples 1* and *2*.

Kepler setup

If you do not yet have Kepler installed, please follow the instructions on the Kepler site. Kepler 1.1 default request handler is CGILua, which defaults to CGI-like dispatching with URLs like /index.lp, but also allows the use of more sophisticated dispatchers. The example code available on the Lua Gems site include a gem directory that should be copied to your CGILUA_APPS directory. After that, access /app.lua/gem in your browser to get the examples home page. From that page you can run all the examples.[3]

The following examples will show three different approaches to implementing URL dispatching for a wiki, each using a different URL dispatching model.[4]

Example 1: mapping a sequence to a function and parameters

In this first example we'll use simple patterns that are similar to Rails' "routes", which will allow us to simultaneously identify a function and collect named parameters. The patterns contains $name for each part of PATH_INFO that is to be used as a named parameter. All parameters are considered optional and it is up to the function to determine how to handle unspecified parameters. All code shown in this example is provided in example1.lua.

In the case of the wiki example, we may want to map the requests as follows:

---

[3]The URLs used in this article assume that Kepler is run with Xavante (a lightweight HTTP server written in Lua and included with Kepler). For other servers, please see the Kepler documentation.

[4]Due to space limitations the examples in the text don't show the full HTML used in the sources.

```
URLs = {
  {"/show/$page_name/$version", show_page, "show"},
  {"/history/$page_name/$year/$month/$date", show_history, "history"},
  {"/diff/$page_name/$version1/$version2", show_diff, "diff"},
}
```

Here each mapping consists of three values: a path pattern, a function, and the name of the mapping (used later for generating URLs). So a request for /example1/diff/Home_Page/24/25 would call

```
show_diff{page_name="Home_Page", version1="24", version2="25"}
```

In order to actually dispatch the request we will need a pattern matching function and a function to iterate over the table looking for matches:

```
-- Checks if a URL matches a pattern
function match(url, pattern)
    local params = {}
    -- convert the pattern into a Lua-style pattern
    local lua_pattern = string.gsub(pattern, "(/$[%w_-]+)", "/?([^/]*)")
    -- extract param values from the URL
    local param_values = {string.match(url, lua_pattern)}
    -- save them in table fields
    local i = 1
    for name in string.gmatch(pattern, "/$([%w_-]+)") do
        params[name] = param_values[i]
        i = i + 1
    end
    -- return params or nil
    return next(params) and params
end


-- Maps the correct function for a URL
function map(url)
    for i, v in ipairs(URLs) do
        local pattern, f, name = unpack(v)
        local params = match(url, pattern)
        if params then
            return f, params
        end
    end
end
```

We can now use the map() function to dispatch a request:

```
f, params = map(cgilua.script_vpath)
if f then
    return f(params)
end
```

For this example to work we need to also implement functions show_page, show_history and show_diff. We discuss their implementation later in "Content generation". For now, however, we will only mention that most of such functions will need to generate URLs pointing back to the wiki. We can do this by reusing our URLs table:

```
function makeurl(action_name, params)
   for i, v in ipairs(URLs) do
      local pattern, f, name = unpack(v)
         if name == action_name then
            local url = string.gsub(pattern, "$([%w_-]+)", params)
            url = cgilua.urlpath.."/"..cgilua.app_name..url
            return url
         end
      end
   end
end
```

So we could then write:

```
local template = " <LI><A HREF=%s>v. %s (%s)</A></LI>"
string.format(template, makeurl("show", p), p.version, p.time_stamp))
```

to generate a link for a diff between versions 24 and 25 of Home_Page.

This form of dispatching is so commonly used that CGILua offers a built-in dispatcher for it. Using this dispatcher our example would have simply to return the routing of the URL table:

```
URLs = {
  {"/show/$page_name/$version", show_page, "show"},
  {"/history/$page_name/$year/$month/$date", show_history, "history"},
  {"/diff/$page_name/$version1/$version2", show_diff, "diff"},
}
return cgilua.dispatcher.route(URLs)
```

Note that cgilua.dispatcher.route implements the functions map() and match() shown above. We have shown their implementation here to highlight the similarities and differences between the examples.

Example 2: mapping through Lua pattern matching

In our previous example we presented an approach to request routing that is simple and elegant, but may not give you enough control. Some of the popular web frameworks opt for a more generic approach, mapping regular expressions onto functions. We can do the same with Lua patterns:

```
URLs = {
  {"/show/([^%/]*)/?(%d*)", show_page},
```

```
{"/history", show_history},
{"/history/([^%/]*)", show_history},
{"/history/([^%/]*)/(%d*)/?", show_history},
{"/history/([^%/]*)/(%d*)/(%d*)/?", show_history},
{"/history/([^%/]*)/(%d*)/(%d*)/(%d*)/?", show_history},
{"/diff/(%d*)/(%d*)", show_diff},
}
```

Note that this mapping is more verbose, but allows for more precise selection of URLs. To implement this we use replace the match function of *Example 1* with a simple wrapper around `string.match`:

```
-- Matches a pattern to an URL
function match(url, pattern)
   local match = {string.match(url, pattern.."$")}
   return next(match) and match
end
```

We also make a small change to `map()` since our URLs table now has only two values per row. We then use `map()` in just the same way as we did in `example1.lua`. All code shown in this example is provided in `example2.lua`.

This approach does not allow for such simple generation of URLs as was the case in *Example 1* so this would have to be done manually. (A more complicated version of this method would make URL-generation possible, but will not be discussed here.)

Example 3: delegating action selection to objects

In this last example, adapted from the way request dispatching is done in Sputnik,[5] we will use PATH_INFO to identify the resource object (a wiki page in our case) and the name of the action that the object would be asked to perform. We leave the choice of response to the object however, allowing different objects to respond differently to the same request. To avoid mixing parts of the controller into the model, the model will store references to functions defined elsewhere. In the case of our wiki, the URLs will look like /example3/Page_Name.action_name, optionally followed by additional parameters in the QUERY part of URL. For example,

    /example3/Home_Page.diff?version=24&version2=25

If no .action_name is specified, we shall assume that the action to be show. By default, each action corresponds to a function defined by the controller, but some pages can behave differently. For instance, we might want /History to show recent changes to all pages instead of its own content, /History.rss to return such changes as an RSS feed, /Calendar to show a list of events, and /Calendar.ical to return this list in the iCalendar format. In other words, for

---

[5]http://sputnik.freewisdom.org/

both History and Calendar pages we want to redefine how show is handled as well as define additional actions (rss and ical) that might make little sense for other pages.

We implement our dispatching as follows:

```
local mask = "/([%w_-]+)%.?([^%./]-)$"
local page_name, action_name = string.match(cgilua.script_vpath, mask)
if action_name == nil or action_name == "" then
   action_name = "show"
end

local page = model.get_page(page_name, cgilua.QUERY.version)
local action_function = load_action_function(page.actions[action_name])
local content, content_type =
                    action_function(page, page_name, cgilua.QUERY)
```

Note that the function that is called in the end is determined by the object. The set of functions is thus not limited *a priori* — each object can support different functions, and we can remap them easily. In fact, in the case of Sputnik the functions can be remapped by the visitor to the site. Note that page.actions contains *names* of functions and we rely on load_action_function() to get the actual callable functions:

```
function load_action_function(action_name)
   -- if action contains a dot, assume it's defined in an external
   -- module. if it doesn't, assume it refers to a global function
   if string.find(action_name, "%.") then
      local mask = "([%w_]*)%.([%w_]*)"
      module_name, function_name = string.match(action_name, mask)
      local m = require(module_name)
      return m[function_name]
   else
      return _M[action_name]
   end
end
```

If Home_Page is a standard wiki page, page.actions["show"] should give us a function that simply converts the content of the page to HTML. For the History page, however, we would want "show" to display recent changes to *all* pages. To do this we create a new module and define there additional functions that can return wiki history as HTML or RSS (see the file /gem/lua/example3_history.lua). We then add a new field to the object representing the History page, overriding its action for show and adding a new one for rss (see the file /gem/lua/fake_wiki_model.lua for the whole data structure):

```
Home_Page = {
   title = "Home Page",
   actions = {
      show = "show_page",
      diff = "show_diff",
      history = "show_history",
   }
}

History = {
   title = "Site History",
      actions = {
      show = "example3_history.show_history",
      diff = "show_diff",
      history = "show_history",
      rss = "example3_history.show_wiki_history_as_rss",
   }
}
```

Since we are using standard QUERY parameters, generating URLs can take advantage of the functionality provided by cgilua:

```
function makeurl(page_name, action_name, params)
   local url = "/"..page_name
   if action_name and action_name ~= "show" then
      url = url.."."..action_name
   end
   if next(params) then
      url = url.."?"..cgilua.urlcode.encodetable(params)
   end
   return cgilua.urlpath.."/"..cgilua.app_name..url
end
```

Content generation

Overview

After dispatching, the controller must generate the necessary parts of an HTTP response: the HTTP status, the HTTP headers, and the content part. This section focuses on the approaches to generating content. One approach is to generate the content programmatically, pushing one string after another into a buffer. Another approach is to define template strings that are filled with content when they are processed. We call the first method "scripting" and the second method "templating".

Scripting

The most basic way to do scripting in Kepler is to use cgilua.put to push bits of content. *Example 1* uses this approach:

```
function show_history(params)
    local page = model.get_page(params.page_name)
    local history =
            page:get_history(params.year, params.month, params.date)
    cgilua.htmlheader()
    cgilua.put("<H1>"..page.title.." History</H1>")
    cgilua.put("<UL>")
    for i, p in ipairs(history) do
        p.page_name = params.page_name
        cgilua.put(string.format(" <LI><A HREF=%s>v. %s (%s)</A></LI>",
                makeurl("show", p), p.version, p.time_stamp))
    end
    cgilua.put("</UL>")
end
```

which would give us something like:

```
<H1>Home Page History</H1>
<UL>
 <LI><A HREF=/example1/show/Home_Page/3>v. 3 (2007-05-29 20:02:01)</A></LI>
 <LI><A HREF=/example1/show/Home_Page/2>v. 2 (2007-05-29 10:03:31)</A></LI>
 <LI><A HREF=/example1/show/Home_Page/1>v. 1 (2007-05-29 08:20:00)</A></LI>
</UL>
```

Alternatively, we can use a module like HTK[6] to generate the same HTML (see example4.lua):

```
require"htk"
function show_history(params)
    local page = model.get_page(params.page_name)
    local history =
            page:get_history(params.year, params.month, params.date)
    cgilua.htmlheader()
    cgilua.put(htk.H1{page.title.."History"})
    items = {}
    for i, p in ipairs(history) do
        p.page_name = params.page_name
        local url = makeurl("show", p)
        table.insert(items, htk.LI{htk.A{href=url, "v. ", p.version,
                "(", p.time_stamp, ")"}})
    end
    cgilua.put(htk.UL(items))
end
```

---

[6]HTK, by Tomás Guisassola, is available at http://www.tecgraf.puc-rio.br/~tomas/htk/.

Templating

Another content generation approach uses a template string with placeholders for dynamic content. Such templates allow inclusion of arbitrary code, which blurs the separation between code and presentation; they have both advantages and disadvantages. Alternatively, one can use "safe templates" that can only call the functions that are explicitly given to them. We present here two simple libraries for those two cases, each implemented in under 150 lines of Lua code.

Kepler's solution to arbitrary code templates is "Lua Pages", which are text files with syntax for two types of placeholders. The first allows arbitrary Lua code, using <% cgilua.put(title) %>. The second is a placeholder for a single Lua expression, using <%= title %>

The Lua Pages pre-processor makes global substitutions on the template, searching for matching pairs of markup and generating the corresponding Lua code, which can then be executed.

To use Lua Pages with the dispatching methods discussed in the previous section, we can call them explicitly from inside a Lua script. In example5.lua we implement show_history as follows:

```
function show_history(params)
   local page = model.get_page(params.page_name)
   local history =
           page:get_history(params.year, params.month, params.date)
   local env = {
      page = page, history = history, page_name = params.page_name,
      cgilua = cgilua, ipairs = ipairs, makeurl = makeurl,
   }
   cgilua.handlelp ("example5.lp", env)
end
```

This function delegates most of the content generation to example5.lp, which looks like this:

```
<H1><%= page.title %> History</H1>
<UL>
 <% for i, p in ipairs(history) do
       p.page_name = page_name %>
          <LI>
          <A HREF="<%=makeurl("show", p)%>"> v.<%=p.version%>
          (<%=p.time_stamp%>)</A>
          </LI>
 <% end %>
</UL>
```

Kepler also provides a solution for safe templates through Cosmo, a library that allows two types of template placeholders: $var_name and $fn_name[[template]]. When a template is filled (using cosmo.fill function), a table must be provided in addition to the template string. If cosmo.fill encounters a $var_name pattern it will simply look up the value in the table and substitute it. If it finds something like $fn_name[[...]], it will look up the fn_name field in the table but will assume the corresponding value to be a *function*. Cosmo will then call this function in a coroutine, expecting it to yield one or more tables (using cosmo.yield). Each table that is yielded will be used to fill the template inside [[...]], and all the resulting text will be concatenated and inserted into the output. For example:

```
show_history_template = [==[
<H1>$title History</H1>
<UL>
 $list_versions[[<LI><A HREF="$url"> v. $version ($time_stamp)</A></LI>]]
</UL>]==]

function show_history(params)
   local page = model.get_page(params.page_name)
   local history =
           page:get_history(params.year, params.month, params.date)
   cgilua.htmlheader()
   cgilua.put(cosmo.fill(show_history_template,
                         { title = page.title,
                           list_versions = function()
                               for i, p in ipairs(history) do
                                   p.page_name = params.page_name
                                   p.url = makeurl("show", p)
                                   cosmo.yield(p)
                               end
                           end }))
end
```

Conclusion

Kepler allows for MVC-style web development using many of the currently popular approaches. Instead of locking the user into a specific solutions to such problems as request dispatching and content generation, Kepler focuses on making web applications portable across operating systems and servers, letting the application developers choose higher-level solutions appropriate to their specific case. Your choice between the above mentioned approaches to request dispatching may depend on how "clean" you want your URLs to be, how much control you need over them, and whether the system needs to support resource-specific actions. Similarly, the choice of method for content generation may depend on the degree to which you want to separate design work from programming. Lua Pages may offer a simpler solution in cases where design and coding is done by the same person, while a safe template solution like Cosmo may make your life easier if the design work is to be delegated to a designer or even to anonymous end users.

9

Filters, Sources, Sinks & Pumps
or Functional programming for the rest of us

Diego Nehab

Certain data processing operations can be implemented in the form of filters. A filter is a function that can process data received in consecutive invocations, returning partial results each time it is called. Examples of operations that can be implemented as filters include the end-of-line normalization for text, Base64 and Quoted-Printable transfer content encodings, the breaking of text into lines, SMTP dot-stuffing, and many others. Filters become even more powerful when we allow them to be chained together to create composite filters. In this context, filters can be seen as the internal links in a chain of data transformations. Sources and sinks are the corresponding end points in these chains. A source is a function that produces data, chunk by chunk, and a sink is a function that takes data, chunk by chunk. Finally, pumps are procedures that actively drive data from a source to a sink, and indirectly through all intervening filters. In this article, we describe the design of an elegant interface for filters, sources, sinks, chains, and pumps, and we illustrate each step with concrete examples.

Introduction

Within the realm of networking applications, we are often required to apply transformations to streams of data. Examples include the end-of-line normalization for text, Base64 and Quoted-Printable transfer content encodings, breaking text into lines with a maximum number of columns, SMTP dot-stuffing, gzip compression, HTTP chunked transfer coding, and the list goes on.

Many complex tasks require a combination of two or more such transformations, and therefore a general mechanism for promoting reuse is desirable. In the process of designing LuaSocket 2.0, we repeatedly faced this problem. The solution we reached proved to be very general and convenient. It is based on the concepts of filters, sources, sinks, and pumps, which we introduce below.

Filters are functions that can be repeatedly invoked with chunks of input, successively returning processed chunks of output. Naturally, the result of concatenating all the output chunks must be the same as the result of applying the filter to the concatenation of all input chunks. In fancier language, filters *commute* with the concatenation operator. More importantly, filters must handle input data correctly no matter how the stream has been split into chunks.

A *chain* is a function that transparently combines the effect of one or more filters. The interface of a chain is indistinguishable from the interface of its component filters. This allows a chained filter to be used wherever an atomic filter is accepted. In particular, chains can be themselves chained to create arbitrarily complex operations.

Filters can be seen as internal nodes in a network through which data will flow, potentially being transformed many times along the way. Chains connect these nodes together. The initial and final nodes of the network are *sources* and *sinks*, respectively. Less abstractly, a source is a function that produces new chunks of data every time it is invoked. Conversely, sinks are functions that give a final destination to the chunks of data they receive in successive calls. Naturally, sources and sinks can also be chained with filters to produce filtered sources and sinks.

Finally, filters, chains, sources, and sinks are all passive entities: they must be repeatedly invoked in order for anything to happen. *Pumps* provide the driving force that pushes data through the network, from a source to a sink, and indirectly through all intervening filters.

In the following sections, we start with a simplified interface, which we later refine. The evolution we present is not contrived: it recreates the steps we ourselves followed as we consolidated our understanding of these concepts within our application domain.

A simple example

The end-of-line normalization of text is a good example to motivate our initial filter interface. Assume we are given text in an unknown end-of-line convention (including possibly mixed conventions) out of the commonly found Unix (LF), Mac OS (CR), and DOS (CR LF) conventions. We would like to be able to use the following code to normalize the end-of-line markers:

```
local CRLF = "\013\010"
local input = source.chain(source.file(io.stdin), normalize(CRLF))
local output = sink.file(io.stdout)
pump.all(input, output)
```

This program should read data from the standard input stream and normalize the end-of-line markers to the canonic CR LF marker, as defined by the MIME standard. Finally, the normalized text should be sent to the standard output stream. We use a *file source* that produces data from standard input, and chain it with a filter that normalizes the data. The pump then repeatedly obtains data from the source, and passes it to the *file sink*, which sends it to the standard output.

In the code above, the normalize *factory* is a function that creates our normalization filter, which replaces any end-of-line marker with the canonic marker. The initial filter interface is trivial: a filter function receives a chunk of input data, and returns a chunk of processed data. When there are no more input data left, the caller notifies the filter by invoking it with a nil chunk. The filter responds by returning the final chunk of processed data (which could of course be the empty string).

Although the interface is extremely simple, the implementation is not so obvious. A normalization filter respecting this interface needs to keep some kind of context between calls. This is because a chunk boundary may lie between the CR and LF characters marking the end of a single line. This need for contextual storage motivates the use of factories: each time the factory is invoked, it returns a filter with its own context so that we can have several independent filters being used at the same time. For efficiency reasons, we must avoid the obvious solution of concatenating all the input into the context before producing any output chunks.

To that end, we break the implementation into two parts: a low-level filter, and a factory of high-level filters. The low-level filter is implemented in C and does not maintain any context between function calls. The high-level filter factory, implemented in Lua, creates and returns a high-level filter that maintains whatever context the low-level filter needs, but isolates the user from its internal details. That way, we take advantage of C's efficiency to perform the hard work, and take advantage of Lua's simplicity for the bookkeeping.

The Lua part of the filter

Below is the complete implementation of the factory of high-level end-of-line normalization filters:

```
function filter.cycle(lowlevel, context, extra)
  return function(chunk)
    local ret
    ret, context = lowlevel(context, chunk, extra)
    return ret
  end
end

function normalize(marker)
  return filter.cycle(eol, 0, marker)
end
```

The normalize factory simply calls a more generic factory, the cycle factory, passing the low-level filter eol. The cycle factory receives a low-level filter, an initial context, and an extra parameter, and returns a new high-level filter. Each time the high-level filer is passed a new chunk, it invokes the low-level filter with the previous context, the new chunk, and the extra argument. It is the low-level filter that does all the work, producing the chunk of processed data and a new context. The high-level filter then replaces its internal context, and returns the processed chunk of data to the user. Notice that we take advantage of Lua's lexical scoping to store the context in a closure between function calls.

The C part of the filter

As for the low-level filter, we must first accept that there is no perfect solution to the end-of-line marker normalization problem. The difficulty comes from an inherent ambiguity in the definition of empty lines within mixed input. However, the following solution works well for any consistent input, as well as for non-empty lines in mixed input. It also does a reasonable job with empty lines and serves as a good example of how to implement a low-level filter.

The idea is to consider both CR and LF as end-of-line *candidates*. We issue a single break if any candidate is seen alone, or if it is followed by a different candidate. In other words, CR CR and LF LF each issue two end-of-line markers, whereas CR LF and LF CR issue only one marker each. It is easy to see that this method correctly handles the most common end-of-line conventions.

With this in mind, we divide the low-level filter into two simple functions. The inner function pushchar performs the normalization itself. It takes each input character in turn, deciding what to output and how to modify the context. The context tells if the last processed character was an end-of-line candidate, and if so, which candidate it was. For efficiency, we use Lua's auxiliary library's buffer interface:

```
#define candidate(c) (c == CR || c == LF)
static int pushchar(int c, int last, const char *marker,
    luaL_Buffer *buffer) {
  if (candidate(c)) {
    if (candidate(last)) {
      if (c == last)
        luaL_addstring(buffer, marker);
      return 0;
    } else {
      luaL_addstring(buffer, marker);
      return c;
    }
  } else {
    luaL_pushchar(buffer, c);
    return 0;
  }
}
```

The outer function eol simply interfaces with Lua. It receives the context and input chunk (as well as an optional custom end-of-line marker), and returns the transformed output chunk and the new context. Notice that if the input chunk is nil, the operation is considered to be finished. In that case, the loop will not execute a single time and the context is reset to the initial state. This allows the filter to be reused many times:

```
static int eol(lua_State *L) {
  int context = luaL_checkint(L, 1);
  size_t isize = 0;
  const char *input = luaL_optlstring(L, 2, NULL, &isize);
  const char *last = input + isize;
  const char *marker = luaL_optstring(L, 3, CRLF);
  luaL_Buffer buffer;
  luaL_buffinit(L, &buffer);
  if (!input) {
    lua_pushnil(L);
    lua_pushnumber(L, 0);
    return 2;
  }
  while (input < last)
    context = pushchar(*input++, context, marker, &buffer);
  luaL_pushresult(&buffer);
  lua_pushnumber(L, context);
  return 2;
}
```

When designing filters, the challenging part is usually deciding what to store in the context. For line breaking, for instance, it could be the number of bytes that still fit in the current line. For Base64 encoding, it could be a string with the bytes that remain after the division of the input into 3-byte atoms. The MIME module in the LuaSocket distribution contains many other examples.

Filter chains

Chains greatly increase the power of filters. For example, according to the standard for Quoted-Printable encoding, text should be normalized to a canonic end-of-line marker prior to encoding. After encoding, the resulting text must be broken into lines of no more than 76 characters, with the use of soft line breaks (a line terminated by the = sign). To help specifying complex transformations like this, we define a chain factory that creates a composite filter from one or more filters. A chained filter passes data through all its components, and can be used wherever a primitive filter is accepted.

The chaining factory is very simple. The auxiliary function chainpair chains two filters together, taking special care if the chunk is the last. This is because the final nil chunk notification has to be pushed through both filters in turn:

```
local function chainpair(f1, f2)
  return function(chunk)
    local ret = f2(f1(chunk))
    if chunk then return ret
    else return ret .. f2() end
  end
end

function filter.chain(...)
  local f = arg[1]
  for i = 2, #arg do
    f = chainpair(f, arg[i])
  end
  return f
end
```

Thanks to the chain factory, we can define the Quoted-Printable conversion as such (the encode and wrap factories are also part of LuaSocket's MIME module):

```
local qp = filter.chain(normalize(CRLF), encode("quoted-printable"),
  wrap("quoted-printable"))
local input = source.chain(source.file(io.stdin), qp)
local output = sink.file(io.stdout)
pump.all(input, output)
```

Sources, sinks, and pumps

The filters we introduced so far act as the internal nodes in a network of transformations. Information flows from node to node (or rather from one filter to the next) and is transformed along the way. Chaining filters together is our way to connect nodes in this network. As the starting point for the network, we need a source node that produces the data. In the end of the network, we need a sink node that gives a final destination to the data.

Sources

A source returns the next chunk of data each time it is invoked. When there are no more data, it simply returns nil. In the event of an error, the source can inform the caller by returning nil followed by the error message.

Below are two simple source factories. The empty source returns no data, possibly returning an associated error message. The file source yields the contents of a file in a chunk by chunk fashion:

```
function source.empty(err)
  return function()
    return nil, err
  end
end
```

```
function source.file(handle, io_err)
  if handle then
    return function()
      local chunk = handle:read(2048)
      if not chunk then handle:close() end
      return chunk
    end
  else return source.empty(io_err or "unable to open file") end
end
```

Filtered sources

A filtered source passes its data through the associated filter before returning it
to the caller. Filtered sources are useful when working with functions that get
their input data from a source (such as the pumps in our examples). By chaining
a source with one or more filters, such functions can be transparently provided
with filtered data, with no need to change their interfaces. Here is a factory that
does the job:

```
function source.chain(src, f)
  return function()
    if not src then
      return nil
    end
    local chunk, err = src()
    if not chunk then
      src = nil
      return f(nil)
    else
      return f(chunk)
    end
  end
end
```

Sinks

Just as we defined an interface for a source of data, we can also define an
interface for a data destination. We call any function respecting this interface a
sink. In our first example, we used a file sink connected to the standard output.

   Sinks receive consecutive chunks of data, until the end of data is signaled
by a nil input chunk. A sink can be notified of an error with an optional extra
argument that contains the error message, following a nil chunk. If a sink
detects an error itself, and wishes not to be called again, it can return nil,
followed by an error message. A return value that is not nil means the sink
will accept more data.

   Below are two useful sink factories. The table factory creates a sink that
stores individual chunks into an array. The data can later be efficiently concate-

nated into a single string with Lua's `table.concat` library function. The `null` sink simply discards the chunks it receives:

```lua
function sink.table(t)
  t = t or {}
  local f = function(chunk, err)
    if chunk then table.insert(t, chunk) end
    return 1
  end
  return f, t
end

local function null()
  return 1
end
function sink.null()
  return null
end
```

Naturally, filtered sinks are just as useful as filtered sources. A filtered sink passes each chunk it receives through the associated filter before handing it down to the original sink. In the following example, we use a source that reads from the standard input. The input chunks are sent to a table sink, which has been coupled with a normalization filter. The filtered chunks are then concatenated from the output array, and finally sent to standard out:

```lua
local input = source.file(io.stdin)
local output, t = sink.table()
output = sink.chain(normalize(CRLF), output)
pump.all(input, output)
io.write(table.concat(t))
```

Pumps

Although not on purpose, our interface for sources is compatible with Lua iterators. That is, a source can be neatly used in conjunction with `for` loops. Using our file source as an iterator, we can write the following code:

```lua
for chunk in source.file(io.stdin) do
  io.write(chunk)
end
```

Loops like this will always be present because everything we designed so far is passive. Sources, sinks, filters: none of them can do anything on their own. The operation of pumping all data a source can provide into a sink is so common that it deserves its own function:

```
function pump.step(src, snk)
  local chunk, src_err = src()
  local ret, snk_err = snk(chunk, src_err)
  if chunk and ret then return 1
  else return nil, src_err or snk_err end
end

function pump.all(src, snk, step)
    step = step or pump.step
    while true do
        local ret, err = step(src, snk)
        if not ret then
            if err then return nil, err
            else return 1 end
        end
    end
end
```

The pump.step function moves one chunk of data from the source to the sink. The pump.all function takes an optional step function and uses it to pump all the data from the source to the sink. Here is an example that uses the Base64 and the line wrapping filters from the LuaSocket distribution. The program reads a binary file from disk and stores it in another file, after encoding it to the Base64 transfer content encoding:

```
local input = source.chain(
  source.file(io.open("input.bin", "rb")),
  encode("base64"))
local output = sink.chain(
  wrap(76),
  sink.file(io.open("output.b64", "w")))
pump.all(input, output)
```

The way we split the filters here is not intuitive, on purpose. Alternatively, we could have chained the Base64 encode filter and the line-wrap filter together, and then chain the resulting filter with either the file source or the file sink. It doesn't really matter.

Exploding filters

Our current filter interface has one serious shortcoming. Consider for example a gzip decompression filter. During decompression, a small input chunk can be exploded into a huge amount of data. To address this problem, we decided to change the filter interface and allow exploding filters to return large quantities of output data in a chunk by chunk manner.

More specifically, after passing each chunk of input to a filter, and collecting the first chunk of output, the user must now loop to receive other chunks from the filter until no filtered data are left. Within these secondary calls, the caller passes an empty string to the filter. The filter responds with an empty string when it is ready for the next input chunk. In the end, after the user passes a `nil` chunk notifying the filter that there are no more input data, the filter might still have to produce too much output data to return in a single chunk. The user has to loop again, now passing `nil` to the filter each time, until the filter itself returns `nil` to notify the user it is finally done.

Fortunately, it is very easy to modify a filter to respect the new interface. In fact, the end-of-line translation filter we presented earlier already conforms to it. The complexity is encapsulated within the chaining functions, which must now include a loop. Since these functions only have to be written once, the user is rarely affected. Interestingly, the modifications do not have a measurable negative impact in the performance of filters that do not need the added flexibility. On the other hand, for a small price in complexity, the changes make exploding filters practical.

A complex example

The LTN12 module in the LuaSocket distribution implements all the ideas we have described. The MIME and SMTP modules are tightly integrated with LTN12, and can be used to showcase the expressive power of filters, sources, sinks, and pumps. Below is an example of how a user would proceed to define and send a multipart message, with attachments, using LuaSocket:

```lua
local smtp = require"socket.smtp"
local mime = require"mime"
local ltn12 = require"ltn12"
local message = smtp.message{
  headers = {
    from = "Sicrano <sicrano@example.com>",
    to = "Fulano <fulano@example.com>",
    subject = "A message with an attachment"},
  body = {
    preamble = "Hope you can see the attachment" .. CRLF,
    [1] = {
      body = "Here is our logo" .. CRLF},
    [2] = {
      headers = {
        ["content-type"] = 'image/png; name="luasocket.png"',
        ["content-disposition"] =
          'attachment; filename="luasocket.png"',
        ["content-description"] = 'LuaSocket logo',
        ["content-transfer-encoding"] = "BASE64"},
      body = ltn12.source.chain(
        ltn12.source.file(io.open("luasocket.png", "rb")),
        ltn12.filter.chain(
          mime.encode("base64"),
          mime.wrap()))}}}
```

```
assert(smtp.send{
  rcpt = "<fulano@example.com>",
  from = "<sicrano@example.com>",
  source = message})
```

The `smtp.message` function receives a table describing the message, and returns a source. The `smtp.send` function takes this source, chains it with the SMTP dot-stuffing filter, connects a socket sink with the server, and simply pumps the data. The message is never assembled in memory. Everything is produced on demand, transformed piece by piece, and sent to the server in chunks, including the file attachment which is loaded from disk and encoded on the fly.

Conclusion

In this article, we introduced the concepts of filters, sources, sinks, and pumps to the Lua language. These are useful tools for stream processing in general. Sources provide a simple abstraction for data acquisition. Sinks provide an abstraction for final data destinations. Filters define an interface for data transformations. The chaining of filters, sources and sinks provides an elegant way to create arbitrarily complex data transformations from simpler components. Pumps simply push the data through.

Acknowledgments

The concepts described in this text are the result of long discussions with David Burgess. A version of this text has been released on-line as the Lua Technical Note 012, hence the name of the corresponding LuaSocket module, LTN12. Wim Couwenberg contributed to the implementation of the module, and Adrian Sietsma was the first to notice the correspondence between sources and Lua iterators.

10

Lua as a Protocol Language

Patrick Rapin

This article describes the use of Lua as a communication vector between a client and a server programs. In addition to some implementation choices, we discuss the advantages and drawbacks of this approach, with a special point made on security.

Background

Our company is using a custom source control system program called Code-Administrator, a tool I wrote several years ago in C++ using Microsoft Foundation Classes (MFC). The program has run to satisfaction until now; however it has some limitations: it can only run on Windows and it cannot be used over a regular Internet connection, only through a virtual private network.

We tried to find a way to keep the compatibility of the source database and version numbers, while adding support for Unix-based systems and Internet functionality. An idea for a solution arose: rewrite the core of the program using Lua, into a new tool called Lua CodeAdministrator or LCA. At first at least, there is no need to port all features, notably the administrative tasks, since it is aimed to be a user add-on to the original tool rather than a full replacement. Although the goal of this article is to discuss the ideas beyond the protocol used, it will refer to this particular program when needed for the explanation.

Choice of language

What are the advantages of using Lua to implement a version checking utility? Compared to compiled languages, using a scripting language simplifies the implementation a lot because:

- It is easy to ensure the portability of the program.
- The code is typically shorter compared to C functions.
- It is easy to customize functions, for example by overriding global variables.
- Configuration files can be written in the same language as the main program.
- The protocol itself can use the same language, which is the main subject of this article.

Other scripting languages would certainly also fit the requirements for this tool. The reasons we prefer Lua are the following:

- It is fast, compared to most other scripting languages.
- It is small, thus there is no practical problem embedding it into programs.
- It is easy to compile on all platforms.
- We have a very good experience with the language since we are using it for our printers.

Protocol

Like for example CVS, LCA can be run in four different modes:

Standalone. The user directory and the repository can both be accessed directly, either on a local hard drive or over a mapped network drive. There is no need to worry too much about security in this case: we can assume that the file system management already checks for read and write authorizations.

Client. The user directory can be accessed directly by the program, and any read or write action to the repository must be performed through a request over the network to the server. Security is not a problem on this side; we assume that the user has authorized access to his computer. But the client must be able to provide security checks to the server.

Server. Unlike the other two modes, which are run once for each operation requested, the server must run permanently, as a daemon. It has full direct access to the repository, but each time it needs reading or writing to the user directory, it issues requests back to the client. Security is an important issue for any program accepting requests from the Internet. The user must first log in, and data can be encrypted to ensure confidentiality. Other tricks are used, as discussed later.

CGI Server. It has direct access to the repository, but no knowledge of a user directory. It is not permanent like the previous mode, but is run when needed by the Web server through the CGI interface. It is able to browse the database and produce regular HTML output.

While the repository database format is already strictly defined and cannot be changed without breaking compatibility, we have complete freedom over the protocol used to exchange data. In order to simplify the coding and to unify all concepts, we are using Lua code as the native format.

Any transferred data has the form of some Lua script, normally just a call to a global function with parameters. Parameters values can be arbitrary complex: they may contain big table constructors or embedded files encoded with the string.format("%q") feature. This function is very helpful to embed binary data into valid literal Lua strings. The result is a quoted string, with problematic characters escaped and the other ones copied verbatim.

We also need a command terminator, to synchronize the client and the server through the socket. It is customary in Internet protocols to use a line feed optionally preceded by a carriage return. As this pattern may be present in valid Lua code, we prefer to use the single null character '\0'. This character can only appear inside long strings (those of the form [[···]]), a construction never used in the implementation. A second pattern, consisting of a semicolon immediately followed by a line feed, can only be found at the end of a Lua statement. If the whole request is too big, it is possible to execute it piece by piece by cutting it along this pattern.

A typical transaction looks like the following. The client initiates a socket and sends a request to the server as a Lua chunk followed by a null byte. The server listens to the socket until it finds the termination character. After some basic security checks, it will compile the code and run it. During the execution, results and additional requested information are formatted into another Lua chunk, and sent back to the client followed by the null terminator. The client will then compile and run the response code. An advantage here is that the protocol is fully symmetrical: the client always initiates the connection, but work can be requested by both ends. Also, we can deal with complex situations with hierarchical data and callbacks, without having to define a complicated protocol.

The following code shows the skeleton for the server function (without logging and security checks). Please note the use of setfenv, forcing the chunk to run in a protected environment, where the only global functions are the ones we need to export. The "*z" parameter is a little extension made to LuaSocket library allowing us to read all data up to a null byte (excluded from the result string). At the end, a complete garbage collection is performed. The main server function consists simply in calling ExecuteJob in protected mode and collecting garbage. In case of any error occurring in the job function, the server recovers automatically, because all resources, including sockets, are local variables that will be freed or closed with the collection.

```
local function ExecuteJob()
  local penv = CreateProtectedEnv()
  local sock = assert(socket.bind(config.Host, config.Port))
  local connection = assert(sock:accept())
  repeat
    local line, errmsg, rest = connection:receive("*z")
    line = line or rest
    local funct = assert(loadstring(line))
    setfenv(funct, penv)
    funct()
    collectgarbage()
  until errmsg
end

function Server()
  while true do
    pcall(ExecuteJob)
    collectgarbage()
  end
end
```

The forced garbage collection performed in both functions is not strictly necessary, especially in Lua 5.1, which collects garbage incrementally. But it helps to minimize the memory usage and to close resources in case of errors. It is probably a good idea to free all temporary data after a command execution, so that no useless memory remains allocated during the server idle time.

As a very simple example, here is the checkout of one single file, hello.lua:

```
ExtractFiles("1.0.1", { "hello.lua", }, "~/")\0
```

```
WriteFile("~/hello.lua", "print(\"Hello World!\")", 1023454677)\0
```

The first line is the client request, sending the desired file version, the list of files to retrieve, and the destination directory. The second line is the server response, asking the client to save the given data into a file specifying its full file name and modification time.

Compression

The original database format uses BZIP2 compression library to drastically decrease its size. By the way, we were surprised to observe that CA databases for typical C projects have an overall compression ratio of about 95% (or 20 times)! LCA must of course use this library to open the source code database. The same algorithm is also used to compress the Lua source code stored inside the executable file, and to compress data sent over the Internet socket. The latter is optional, because on a local network the transfer time is probably lower than the compression time, while the inverse yields true over a slow Internet connection. An auxiliary global Load function is used for this task. Its prototype is:

```
Load(flags, string_data)
```

where flags is a combination of Boolean values, indicating whether or not string_data is compressed, and whether or not it is encrypted (see below). The string data is again generated with the string.format("%q") feature.

Encryption

Optionally, data can also be encrypted using an MD5 library in cypher-feedback mode. We chose this algorithm simply because a standard Lua module exists. The security of this algorithm is certainly enough for our application. The same Load function is used for this case. This is no requisite; an idiom like this one would do the same thing, although it is a little more verbose:

```
loadstring(Uncompress(Decrypt(string_data)))()
```

Of course, when combining compression and encryption, we must first apply compression and then encryption; inversely, first decryption and then decompression. This is because an encrypted message compresses very badly, since it just looks like random data.

Secured mode

There are two running modes for the server: secured and unsecured. The unsecured mode is targeted to be used inside a secured local network, while the secured mode could be opened on the whole Internet.

In secured mode, the authorized user must log in with a password before he can make any operation. An MD5 hash of a challenge phrase is used for the authentication procedure. Before login is complete, the only global value in the environment is the authorization function itself. The server will check and refuse any request that do not look like a valid authorization request.

If the login succeeds, most of the other custom functions become available, as in the unsecured mode. Critical functions that could destroy the database may only be executed over a secured local network.

Benchmark

A small benchmark run between the original MFC program and the Lua-based version showed surprising results, which may be of interest to other Lua programmers. For the key feature of extracting a version, the equivalent of cvs checkout -r tag, LCA in standalone mode happens to take roughly the same time as its C++ counterpart. It uses however about twice as much of memory. We can probably explain these measures with the observations in the next paragraph.

All CPU intensive operations (compression, checksum computation, merge) are implemented in C code, using the same libraries. The core work of both implementations is to build the file lists of any version from the incremental database. For these, we mainly use strings, and data structures like arrays and hashes. In Microsoft Foundation Classes these are implemented using CString, CArray and CMap objects respectively. In Lua, we of course use native strings and tables. While Lua is itself interpreted, which is a performance penalty over C++, its native implementation of strings and tables seems to be faster than the equivalent MFC classes. Concerning the memory usage, we can argue that objects are not freed immediately when they are not needed anymore, like in C++, but incrementally collected by the garbage collector. Using default settings, the garbage collector of Lua 5.1 has a step pause of 200%, meaning that it waits until the memory used has doubled compared to last collection before running again. This factor is approximately the one we saw in the benchmark.

In client/server mode, if both programs runs on the same computer, the checkout time using raw transfers is about 20% higher than in standalone mode. The overhead rises to about 60% when using both compressed and encrypted transfers.

Security

Security is a major issue for any system opening sockets over the Internet. As the protocol consists of plain scripting code, this is quite an invitation for hackers to send malicious code to the server!

Library functions

Fortunately, Lua gives us some weapons to fight against hacking. First, in this language we have full control of which functions are exported into the global environment. None of the standard Lua functions is present in the environment used to evaluate external command scripts. These functions are in reality present in Lua state memory, but only as local variables, so there is no way to access them even with a malicious code.

Of the standard libraries, the coroutine, math, table and string libraries are normally harmless. They are not exported nevertheless because we do not need them, and do not want to give these facilities to the outside world.

On the other hand, the io, os, and debug libraries are very dangerous. If a hacker has direct access to io.open or os.execute function, he can delete or create files on the server system nearly as he wants (just limited by the operating system permissions). The base function dofile and the package library may be used to run external Lua code present somewhere on the server hard disk, providing the hacker has the knowledge of the place to find these.

The debug library opens a more subtle security backdoor. Using debug.getlocal, you can access local variables, and with debug.getupvalue, non-local variables. These are normally completely inaccessible to an outside program, but if a malicious code can use debug.getupvalue to gain access to the os table stored as a non-local variable, we have lost the game.

Buffer overrun

The most common security issues using networking programs are the so-called buffer overrun bugs. They typically occur when reading data coming from the outside world without checking for the maximum size. A simple example in C is this one:

```
int InputNumber(void)
{
  char buffer[100];
  gets(buffer);
  return atoi(buffer);
}
```

Instead of the expected number, a hacker can send more than 100 non-null characters and patch the function return address normally found in memory just after the buffer. This forces the program to jump to an arbitrary address, typically the function buffer itself, where the hacker just placed some executable code!

Here is the very good news: this type of bugs is impossible in Lua language (and in most other scripting languages), provided that there is no remaining bugs in the implementation that could be exploited by malicious people. Because Lua has been used and tested much more than our application, we can reasonably assume that there is no security issue related to buffer overruns.

Denial of service

A hacker may also attack a server trying to overflow the computer performance. There are plenty of possibilities there: opening hundreds of simultaneous connections without closing them, overwhelming the bandwidth by requesting huge amount of data, asking the server for too complex requests, etc. This type of attack is not as harmful as the previous ones, because no private data can be stolen this way from the server, and there should not be any data loss. Restarting the server program (or the whole computer) is enough to recover from such a problem. Nevertheless, it harms regular users, who won't be able to access the server for some period of time. Some critical services cannot afford such a risk of interruption and must take important measures against denial of service attacks. For others, it may be enough to guarantee that no data loss or corruption occurs, and that the server will be up again in a reasonable amount of time.

Using Lua as a protocol language makes it very easy to overwhelm the server. Here are some examples:

1. `while true do end`

2. `function f() return f() end; f()`

3. `a = " "; for i=1,math.huge do a = a..a end`

4. `a = " "; a=a..a; a=a..a; a=a..a; a=a..a; ...`

5. `a = "An infinite string.  An infinite string.  An ...`

The first request uses 100% CPU time, and never finishes. The second example too: as this is a tail call, it does not consume any stack space and there is no limit on the call level. The third line will exponentially eat all the available virtual memory on the computer (physical memory and swap file), until an out-of-memory error occurs. This shows that loops and tail calls are dangerous and should be forbidden. But even without loops we can achieve the same result with a finite but long enough command as shows code 4. If we also forbid concatenation, there is still the possibility to send a huge command like code 5, supposing the hacker has even bandwidth and time for his attack.

It is very difficult to protect against all possible attacks. However, a small number of checks can be done to drastically decrease vulnerability. There are not always necessary; it depends on the application design and the desired security level.

- Limit the number of simultaneous connections.

- Place a maximum size for any request.

- Before login is complete, refuse any request not matching a strict string pattern.

- Place a lower limit for memory allocation than the total available on the computer. For that you just have to provide a custom `lua_Alloc` function to `lua_newstate`, counting allocated memory.

- Run a separate program that will monitor CPU and memory usage of the server, like `top` on Unix or the task manager on Windows. If this usage goes higher than a reasonable limit, the program will kill and rerun the server.

- Forbid some Lua virtual machine opcodes. This can be achieved by first compiling the received chunk, then analyzing the binary code. We just have to avoid 3.5 instructions out of 38:

  - JMP with a negative offset, found at end of `while` loops;

  - FORLOOP, at end of `for` loops;

  - TAILCALL, used for tail calls;

  - CONCAT, used for string concatenation.

The code below implements this check. Notice that it needs private headers and structures. So it is neither portable nor advisable: use it only when necessary.

```
#include "lstate.h"
#include "lopcodes.h"

static int checkfct(const Proto* f)
{
  const Instruction* code=f->code;
  int i,n=f->sizecode;
  for (i=0; i<n; i++)
  {
    Instruction instr=code[i];
    OpCode o=GET_OPCODE(instr);
    if(o == OP_FORLOOP || o == OP_CONCAT || o == OP_TAILCALL)
      return 0;
    if(o == OP_JMP && GETARG_sBx(instr) < 0)
      return 0;
  }
  n = f->sizep;
  for(i=0;i<n;i++)
  if(!checkfct(f->p[i]))
    return 0;
  return 1;
}

static int check_opcode (lua_State *L)
{
  luaL_checktype(L, 1, LUA_TFUNCTION);
  lua_pushboolean(L, checkfct(clvalue(L->base)->l.p));
  return 1;
}
```

Conclusion

This experience shows that it is possible to use Lua as a protocol language over an Internet socket. Such a protocol simplifies the implementation and debugging of the communication tool, if a Lua interpreter is used for other tasks as well. However, it is clearly not a good choice for critical services, because the scripting language opens a number of security issues. This approach is best targeted to quickly developed enterprise tools, run over a secured local area network.

11

Lua Script Packaging

Han Zhao

Why do we need to package script files together?

In real world applications, the logic or data described in Lua will be distributed into many .lua files that may be scattered in different directories. During development this directory structure reflects the organization of modules or resources (if Lua serves as a data description language). But when release time comes, there might be too many files to deliver. After installation, all script source files will be visible to the end user — that may not be acceptable for a commercial product for both maintenance and security reasons. A packaging mechanism is necessary to avoid exposing the internal details of an application.

First try: luac -o

During development, .lua files are usually organized in a directory hierarchy. If you use luac to compile .lua source files into a single pre-compiled file as in

```
luac -o dest-file src-file-list
```

the directory hierarchy will be lost — all source files are compiled and packed together flatly. For simple projects, it's possible to build a utility to map the directory hierarchy to the flat structure of the release package. But there will be a maintenance overhead — the developer will have to keep in mind where a file is located in the release package. We don't want our modularization strategy for development to compromise our deployment requirements. Sometimes we also need to dynamically load a .lua resource file from the package, but luac doesn't offer this facility either.

Mock require and dofile

To load Lua files from a package, we need to modify the default behavior of standard require and dofile.

How does the standard require work?

According to Programming in Lua Chapter 15.1, the require function works in following steps:

> "Its first step is to check in table package.loaded whether the module is already loaded. If so, require returns its corresponding value. Therefore, once a module is loaded, other calls to require simply return the same value, without loading the module again. If the module is not loaded yet, require tries to find a loader for this module [...] Its first attempt is to query the given library name in table package.preload. If it finds a function there, it uses this function as the module loader."

Besides the internal mystery require does, require itself is just a normal Lua function which we can replace with our mocked package-friendly one.

Mock require

We'll leverage the module loading mechanism described above to build a decorator around the standard require to do the extra work: plugging our module loader onto package.preload table to load a .lua file from package and leaving the rest to the standard require.

The mocked require looks like this:

```
-- rename standard require
local lua_require = require
-- mocked require
function require(mod_name)
  -- redirect loading function to our package (.dat) loader
  package.preload[mod_name] = fio_loader
  -- Lua standard loading routine
  lua_require(mod_name)
end
```

The package loader (fio_loader) will convert the given module name to a format needed by the packaging format. Then fio_loader will load the module (.lua file) referenced by module name from the package:

```
function fio_loader(mod_name)
 print('fio require '..mod_name)

 -- replace '/' with '\' for path separator in package (.dat)
 mod_name = string.gsub(mod_name, '/', '\\')
 local ref_name = mod_name..'.lua'

 local ret = FioG.c_load_chunk_from_dat(ref_name, FioG.fio_script_dat)

 if(type(ret) == 'string') then
  -- error while loading chunk
  print(ret)
 elseif(type(ret) == 'function') then
  -- if the loader returns any value, require returns this value and
  -- stores it in table package.loaded to return the same value in
  -- future calls for this same library
  -- passing in the mod name, module(..., package.seeall) will need it
  return ret(mod_name)
 else
  error('unknown chunk type '..type(ret))
 end
end
```

In the code above FioG is a name space. The .dat package format will be described in later section. You can choose a common format or implement a specific one for your project.

FioG.fio_script_dat is a global user data of type DatFileReg. It holds the .dat package and keeps a map from module name to an offset to access a specific module file in the package.

FioG.c_load_chunk_from_dat is an imported C function. It will locate the script in the package, load it using lua_load, and return the result: a Lua function or an error message. Since lua_load just loads the chunk without running it, we need to invoke the returned function with the module name passed in:

```
return ret(mod_name)
```

(For Lua 5.0, the module name (mod_name) can be ignored. If you're using the module function introduced in Lua 5.1: module(..., package.seeall), it is obligate to be passed in.)

The implementation of FioG.c_load_chunk_from_dat in C++ is:

```
static int s_load_chunk_from_dat(lua_State* L){
 const char* ref_name = lua_tostring(L, 1);
 DatFileReg* reg = (DatFileReg*)lua_touserdata(L, 2);
      // locate the script chunk in the packed .dat file
 reg->offset(ref_name);
      // construct a packed file to read
 DatFile file(reg->handle());
      // callback argument:
      // struct ZipWrap{
      //     DatFile* fp_;
      //     int left_bytes_;
      // };
 ZipWrap zip_wrap = {&file, reg->size(ref_name)};
      // load script, {file and file size} is the opaque value
      // passed to the lua_Reader callback function
 int load_rslt = lua_load(L, call_back_lua_Reader, &zip_wrap, ref_name);
 // return result of lua_load
 return 1;
}
```

DatFile is the actual reader of packed script — it implements the gzip algorithm
for .dat file. It's held by a ZipWrap struct which is passed into lua_load as the
opaque data value for the lua_Reader callback function:

```
const char* call_back_lua_Reader(lua_State* L, void* data, size_t* size){
      // unpack zip wrap to get dat file and number of bytes to read
 DatFile* fp = ((ZipWrap*)data)->fp_;
 int& left = ((ZipWrap*)data)->left_bytes_;
      // load script into buffer
 int nread = fp->read(chunk_buf, min(left, NBUF));
 switch(nread){
 case -1:
   // gzip read error
   assert(false && "gzip reading failed");
   return 0;
 case 0:
   // eof
   return 0;
 default:
   // discount bytes to read
   left -= nread;
 }
 *size = nread;
 return chunk_buf;
}
```

call_back_lua_Reader works just as lua_load requested: "Every time it needs another piece of the chunk, lua_load calls the reader, passing along its data parameter. The reader must return a pointer to a block of memory with a new piece of the chunk and set size to the block size. The block must exist until the reader function is called again. To signal the end of the chunk, the reader must return NULL. The reader function may return pieces of any size greater than zero."

chunk_buf is a global buffer of NBUF bytes to hold and return the read script chunk. It can be a static buffer or a dynamically allocated one from heap. You can try different buffer sizes to balance the loading time and space requirement. In my projects, a 100K buffer in heap works well (1K and 10K buffers will consume a little more time).

Since it is hard to get original size of a zipped module file without completely inflating it, we keep the size in DatFileReg and pass it to call_back_lua_Reader in the field ZipWrap->left_bytes_.

Mock dofile

The dofile function "opens the named file and executes its contents as a Lua chunk." Unlike require, each time dofile invoked, a fresh piece of script will be loaded and executed.

dofile is useful when you use Lua for configuration or resource description. For example, in a game project, a map is a .lua file which contains tables of cells, items, and critters. When the player steps into a new level, dofile will dynamically load the map file into memory to construct the level. Like mocked require, mocked dofile also relies on FioG.c_load_chunk_from_dat, as shown in Listing 1. Here we use absolute path (home_dir) for dofile, e.g., to load a game map:

```
dofile(home_dir..'master.dat\\level\\dungeon.lua')
```

Then pattern matching is applied on the path to get the directory where the script is and the reference name (in the example, the directory is 'master.dat' and the reference name is 'level/dungeon.lua'). After adjusting reference name format, we are able to load the file from corresponding packed .dat file (here, FioG.fio_master_dat) just like what we've done for mock require.

Sometimes it's not necessary to pack all resource files into packages. In the code above, when directory is 'savegame', we use standard dofile (renamed to lua_dofile) to load the saved game record which is just a .lua file saved in 'savegame' directory. Thus we have the flexibility to load file from both package and normal file system; this is a powerful mechanism for loading Lua-described resources.

From separate Lua files to packed .dat — How to organize?

In development, we use separate files (in hierarchical directory) to modularize and use require to model dependencies between modules. It's important that

```lua
function FioG.mock_dofile()
 -- save standard dofile
 local lua_dofile = dofile
 function dofile(filename)
   -- find script directory and reference name
   local b, e, dir, ref = string.find(filename,
                           home_dir..'([%a%.]+)\\([%a%p%d]+)')

   if(b) then
     -- adjust for reference name in .dat
     ref = string.gsub(ref, '/', '\\')
     local ret = nil

     if(dir == 'master.dat') then
       ret = FioG.c_load_chunk_from_dat(ref, FioG.fio_master_dat)
     elseif(dir == 'critter.dat') then
       ret = FioG.c_load_chunk_from_dat(ref, FioG.fio_critter_dat)
     elseif(dir == 'savegame') then
       -- saved game is not packed in .dat, using lua's dofile
       lua_dofile(filename)
       return
     else
       error('load file unknown dir type '.. dir)
     end
     if(type(ret) == 'string') then
       error(ret)
     end
     -- execute loaded chunk
     ret()
   else
     error('load file invalid format, '..filename)
   end
 end
end
```

Listing 1.

the packaging (or deploying) strategy doesn't interfere with the development file organization structure. A smooth transfer from separate development files to packed ones for release is necessary. Otherwise, we will have to manually maintain the mapping between development structure and release package structure.

As we've seen, there's a code snippet to adjust reference name in both mocked require and dofile. This snippet automatically maps the development structure to release package structure. And the mapping reserves the directory structure (e.g., 'utility/utf8') in the reference name.

For require, during development we put all the files under a directory named 'script', creating subdirectories for submodules if necessary. The standard require will find and load these files based on package.path or LUA_PATH and reference name (e.g., require'utility/utf8').

In the release build, we pack all the files in 'script' directory into a .dat file with the reference names and file sizes built in. The packed .dat file will be loaded during startup (in a DatFileReg object named FioG.fio_script_dat in Lua) and the standard require is also mocked here. Later when we require a module, the mocked one will be invoked. It'll find the script in the .dat and load it as described in previous section.

dofile works in a similar but more flexible way: you can choose to pack resources into more than one packed file for a better organization.

When to mock?

It depends on your project. The following loading steps work well in several projects:

1. Two config.lua files: one for development and one for release. It should contains a field 'packed' which is false for development and true for release. The config.lua file works like a compiler switch for mocking.

2. Mock functions (mock require, mock dofile) in a separate .lua file. The two mock functions are defined and loaded here.

3. Your first Lua entry file. This is the bootstrap file which requires other .lua files. After reading the config.packed field from C++ , we can decide which loader to invoke: if the project is in development phase, using the standard lua_load; or in release, using a function like FioG.c_load_chunk_from_dat to load. The file should contain following initialization code at the top:

```
if(config.packed) then
  mock_require()
  mock_dofile()
end
```

For released project, all later require and dofile are mocked hereafter.

Choose a packaging algorithm/utility

The mocked `require` and `dofile` hides the file loading mechanism from Lua. We can choose any packaging algorithm that best suits our needs. Though the zlib-alike .dat format we've used for illustration is good enough for general purpose packaging, you can build your own home-brew format or even no packaging at all, just a dumb wrapper around the standard `require` and `dofile`.

.dat format

Here is a brief description of the .dat format.

.dat is a format used in Black Isle Studio's Fallout role-playing game series for game resource packaging. Its simple structure makes it a good candidate. A .dat file contains a sequence of gzip compressed files with a record at the tail describing each file's reference name, file size, and offset.[1] In our implementation, `DatFileReg` holds the .dat file, maintains a map from reference name to offset; `DatFile` is responsible for reading a single zip file (located by a reference name) in which a resource file is packed. The format has been well studied and supported by the Fallout modding community—there are many .dat packers/unpackers available (both command line and GUI ones).[2] It's convenient to choose this format instead of inventing a new one and building the tool set from scratch.

Compiled vs plain .lua files

Simple packaging of plain .lua files has one drawback: anyone can view the source code with a text editor. To protect the source code, you can pack compiled .lua files instead of plain source files. Since the Lua file loader treats both formats in the same way, here's a trick to make our mocked `require` and `dofile` still work for compiled files: when compiling, you just need to name the output file the same as the original .lua file:

```
luac -o output\foo.lua foo.lua
```

Or use the following command if you're working in batch mode on Windows:

```
for %%f in (*.lua) do luac -o output\%%f %%f
```

Please note that the compiled file is still easy to be hacked—there are some decent decompilers for Lua out there. You can use the technique described here as a starting point to build more advanced features like accessing verification or encryption into your packaging algorithm to protect the source code.

---

[1] .dat file format description: http://wiki.fifengine.de/index.php?title=DAT_architecture#DAT2

[2] .dat file tools: http://www.teamx.ru/eng/files/utils/ F2 DAT-files packer/unpacker (DAT2), command line tool; DatMan! Light, GUI tool.

Patching

Another consideration on choosing a packaging algorithm is patching. After the product gets shipped, we'll have to maintain it, fix bugs, or upgrade. The modified script files need to be delivered to the user and installed there.

For small projects, we can just repack all files together and release the new package. But this is not convenient or feasible for large projects. For example, in a game project you might have packed the scripts with other resources (image, video, sound, map files, etc.) into one file (perhaps hundreds of megabytes). It's awkward for a player to download a big patch just to update several kilobytes of script files.

Depending on your project, the patching requirement might be vital. There are two approaches for patching: replacing an existing file in the package, or appending one or more files to the package.

The 'append' approach is easier to implement. If other decisions like encryption get in the way of the 'replace' approach, you can use the 'append' approach instead: the new file will be appended at the tail of the package and you only need to adjust the mapping from reference name to the new file's offset without touching the existing old file which is buried in the package.

Several utilities for .dat format have implemented both the 'replace' and the 'append' functionalities.

Conclusion

We started from Lua's basic facilities (`require`, `dofile`, and the binding API) to build a flexible and powerful packaging mechanism. With Lua script packaging, we can setup a direct mapping from the development structure to the deployment structure that hides internal organizing details from the end user. The application will be easier to develop, deploy, and maintain.

The technique described here has been applied in two game projects and a shareware product.

12

Objects, Lua-style

Reuben Thomas

Object-oriented programming is one of the most thoroughly explored and hotly debated topics in Lua, as in so many languages that lack built-in objects. Considerable effort has been expended to implement objects in many different existing styles. Often the aim is to integrate smoothly with existing OO systems, in C, C++ or Java; sometimes it seems to degenerate into a "me-too" exercise. Rarely is the question approached from the other direction: what is the most Lua-ish way to do objects? In a sense, the answer is already present: the language already has basic support for object orientation, with tables as objects, the `table:function()` syntactic sugar for method dispatch, and the `__index` metamethod for inheritance. However, there is no built-in instantiation or subtyping mechanism.

I present a prototype-based object implementation in 35 lines lines of Lua (most of which is actually just three important functions on tables). Although the framework is based on a consideration of the design of Lua, rather than that of any particular OO system, it has been successfully used with existing code, in particular to wrap non-OO C code into easier-to-use OO Lua. It fits well with the Lua philosophy, and adds little overhead, in space, time or complexity.

Having presented, examined and discussed the model and implementation, I end by re-examining the justification for programming in an OO style in Lua at all, and suggest that it is needed less often than one might think.

The object model

It's so simple that there's little more to do than state the obvious. First, note that there is no *a priori* distinction between objects and classes, though it is common to make "class objects" that are used to create all objects of a class, and for no other purpose. Below, class objects' names are capitalized. Similarly, fields and methods are only distinguished by type: a field which is a function, or a table with a __call metamethod, is usually considered to be a method.

Create an object: `object = prototype{value, ...; field = value, ...}`
> `object` is created by cloning `prototype` (typically, a class object). The table passed to it is used to initialize fields as follows: keyed fields are straight-forwardly initialized, while unkeyed fields (to be precise, non-negative integer fields) are assigned to the fields whose keys are listed in the prototype object's init field, as a convenience (any excess arguments are simply kept as a fields with numeric indices). This is best illustrated:
>
> ```
> Point = Object{_init = {"x", "y"}}
> p = Point{-5, 3; color = "blue"}
> ```
>
> assigns −5 to p's x field, 3 to its y field, and "blue" to its color field. (Note that we use a table rather than a normal argument list so that both named and unnamed fields may be conveniently initialized.)
>
> Strictly speaking, the above is only true when the prototype object's _code field is unmodified. It may usefully be overridden to add initialization code.
>
> An object has no record of its prototype. One can be made explicitly, or a _prototype field could be set by the default _clone method.
>
> By convention, fields have string keys, and private fields have keys starting with an underscore. Since private fields aren't hidden, it's up to the programmer to ensure they don't clash.

Access field: `object.field`
> Since object fields are normal table entries, the standard syntax is used to read and write to them.

Call method: `object:method(...)`
> As for field access, method invocation works using the standard syntax.

Call class method: `Class.method(object, ...)`
> The obvious way to call a class method is used: simply use dot rather than colon notation, to pass the object explicitly.

A judicious justification

By now, some readers are probably verging on apoplexy, either because of the use of prototypes, or because of the object model's extreme simplicity. Such readers may be particularly irritated that the design was foisted on them without motivation or justification. I did this because I thought it better to let the design speak for itself before wading into the inevitable controversy. Nonetheless, the design is a good general-purpose object implementation for Lua:

It is simple. The simple, even minimal, design fits with the Lua philosophy. For every OO devotee bemoaning its naivety there will be a Lua purist who thinks it's superfluous.

Prototypes are natural in Lua. Prototypes sit well with Lua's weakly-typed and dynamic nature.

It works for ad-hoc wrapping... As well as working for pure Lua programs, this object model can be used for ad-hoc wrapping of other object models. I've used it to make OO interfaces to C structures, for example (sadly, it's not code I can share).

... but doesn't claim to be the one true way. If you're trying to make an extensive, easy-to-use, and above all automatic wrapper for another object model, you should be rolling your own Lua implementation, because it's easy and will work better than compromising with an existing model: this is a case in which having multiple OO implementations is a good thing.

A delightful detour

Our object implementation needs some basic functions which should be in any Lua programmer's toolbox: clone, merge and rearrange. The following implementations are taken from the stdlib project (http://luaforge.net/projects/stdlib). The code verges on the trivially simple; precisely for this reason I reproduce it here for the reader's enjoyment. Of crucial importance is that all three routines are *functional*: they do not have any side effects. Though Lua is an imperative language, it is well-suited to a functional style, which in my opinion should be used whenever applicable, as it encourages clear, robust and re-usable code.

clone makes a shallow copy of a table, including any metatable:

```
function clone(t)
  local u = setmetatable({}, getmetatable(t))
  for i, v in pairs(t) do
    u[i] = v
  end
  return u
end
```

merge merges two tables. The merge, like assignment, goes right to left: fields of the second argument override those of the first, but the result's metatable, if any, is that of the first argument. The left-hand argument, though, is not overwritten.

```
function merge(t, u)
  local r = clone(t)
  for i, v in pairs(u) do
    r[i] = v
  end
  return r
end
```

rearrange rearranges the keys of a table. Its first argument is a map from old keys to new keys, and its second argument is a table. Only the keys mentioned in the map are rearranged.

```
function rearrange(p, t)
  local r = clone(t)
  for i, v in pairs(p) do
    r[v] = t[i]
    r[i] = nil
  end
  return r
end
```

(Note that both here and later I omit distracting details important in a production implementation, such as packaging the code as a requirable module. This is done in stdlib.)

Implementation

Given the functions above, the actual object implementation is brief.

```
Object = {
  _init = {},
  _clone = function(self, values)
             local object = merge(self, rearrange(self._init, values))
             return setmetatable(object, object)
           end,
  __call = function(...)
             return (...)._clone(...)
           end,
}
setmetatable(Object, Object)
```

The careful reader will want to check that the innocuous-looking first line of _clone really does what it should, and note that the odd-looking implementation of __call really is correct: the first (...) adjusts the list to one element, the object, while the second passes the entire argument list to _clone, which is really a method, so its first argument is indeed the object itself.

Weaknesses

The default _clone could be made to discard excess numbered initializers, but that feels un-Lua-ish, as it imposes behavior that is not required for correct functioning.

There are also some obvious major omissions. First, since our objects can be indexed just like ordinary Lua tables, there's nothing to stop the programmer treating them as such. In other words, we lack information hiding, one of the main planks of object orientation. I don't think this is a problem, however. Lua is not designed for opacity, and is not a good choice when strong type discipline is required. (This is not to ignore Lua's excellence as a language for safe, sandboxed scripting, which rests on its namespace control.)

Secondly, there is no multiple inheritance. With prototypes, multiple inheritance is often replaced by aggregation: a number of classes objects are cloned and merged together. For example:

```
o = merge(c1._clone(), merge(c2._clone(), c3._clone()))
```

This could be abbreviated

```
o = subclass(c1, c2, c3)
```

where subclass is defined:

```
function subclass(...)
  local r = {}
  for c in {...} do
    r = merge(r, c)
  end
  return r
end
```

I didn't include this in the package because I haven't yet needed it.

Inconclusion

In conclusion, we can pertinently wonder whether having a general-purpose object system in Lua is useful at all. The principle advantages of an OO style in Lua are encapsulation of readable syntax for well-structured data types supporting a limited range of operations. However, it's often possible to write shorter, clearer code without objects. For example, when processing poorly structured, unstructured or arbitrarily structured data, such as text, tag soup or XML, a table-oriented approach is often clearer, and a functional style briefer. One example of this is the utility functions used to implement objects, which perform general table operations. The use of general-purpose functions, helps ensure that the object model has no undefined behavior and is robust, as well as avoiding the need to write special-purpose code.

The real conclusion is that Lua is flexible, and lends itself to a variety of approaches. Each should be used when appropriate, but none taken too far.

13

Exceptions in Lua

John Belmonte

Despite the well known advantages of using exceptions for program errors, the mechanism is underutilized in Lua — both in quantity and quality. One aspect of this relates to the Lua core and standard library, which tend to raise exceptions only in the most serious situations such as parse errors, type errors, and invalid arguments. When exceptions are thrown, they are exclusively string values which are not enumerated as part of the API. Tables, the primary data structure, yield nil for a nonexistent key rather than raise an error. All of this leads to an unspoken bias in Lua that exceptions are something to be thrown but rarely caught — that they are serious errors which normally go unhandled. In the few situations where we do catch them, no distinction is made with respect to the cause of the error.

The core and standard libraries arguably work well as they are, and their use of errors may not warrant meddling. But why are exceptions also under-utilized within Lua programs and third party modules? One problem is the unfriendliness of Lua's protected call interface to programmers expecting a native try–catch construct. This in turn discourages library authors from using exceptions for fear of alienating users. The inability to use coroutines within a protected call also works to limit uptake by libraries.

Lua possesses the necessary building blocks for exceptions; however, rough edges appear when one tries to assemble them. This perpetuates disuse of exceptions and strengthens anti-exception patterns such as signaling errors by way of return values. To break the cycle, we first need to promote idioms and know-how for richer use of exceptions. As more Lua developers encounter the same rough spots, the necessary motivation will exist for some incremental improvements in the core and language itself.

This gem intends to start the process by presenting some exception tools and know-how for Lua. First we spell out a criteria as to when a function should raise an exception versus simply return an error status. For handling the exceptions, we present a simple try–catch idiom that works with today's stock Lua. We then cover why custom error objects are important and address gaps in Lua regarding their use. Finally, we set out to find the right pattern for exception safety in Lua.

What is an error?

What failure situations should be considered a first-class error, warranting the use of exceptions? Calling a function with invalid arguments is an obvious error. In contrast, a negative result from a string matching function is normally not considered an error. In between these is an expanse of various error-like situations. What about an attempt to append to a read-only file; a failed hash table lookup; a database conflict; or an HTTP connection failure? We need a guideline for evaluating these.

On this subject, "Programming in Lua" suggests that if an error cannot be easily avoided, it should be signaled with a return code rather than exception. This logic is geared towards letting you handle error situations without the need for a try–catch — a decidedly conservative view on the use of exceptions. What effect does it have on a program?

Let's consider a Lua program which outputs the length of a file given its name on the command line:

```
local f = io.open(arg[1])
local length = f:seek('end')
print(length)
```

The program lacks error handling — it may be the work of a novice programmer or a lazy expert programmer. How does it behave when things go wrong? Let's try an input file, "abc", which doesn't exist:

```
$ lua file-length.lua abc
lua: file-length.lua:2: attempt to index local 'f' (a nil value)
```

The good news is that an unhandled exception occurred, causing the program to return a non-zero exit code. This is the bare minimum behavior we need from a command-line program on error. The error message, however, is not very helpful. In this simple program we can look at the source code and quickly deduce that io.open returned nil instead of a file object, causing an error on call of the seek method. In a complex program, debugging could be much more difficult. The file object could be passed to a different place in the program, and perhaps not used until long after the io.open call.

Wrapping the io.open call in assert would address this error situation, producing an exception with an accurate location and message.[1] However, the novice programmer didn't consider that, and the expert programmer either didn't think his program would be used so foolishly, or didn't care. In large programs such negligence can go unnoticed until a certain obscure code path is encountered. Arguably, it's better not to present the opportunity for an oversight.

A more liberal guideline for errors is this: if a failure situation is most often handled by the immediate caller of your function, signal it by return value. Otherwise, consider the failure to be a first-class error and throw an exception. The effect is to use exceptions when errors are communicated two levels up the call stack or higher (including possible program termination). This is intended to extract the best value from exceptions. When an error is likely to traverse several levels, we relieve intermediate code from having to propagate the error — a task which is error prone and clutters both code and API. On the other hand, when a failure is usually consumed by the caller, we spare the extravagance and expense of a throw and catch.

What is the outcome when this guideline is applied to io.open? It's subjective, but programs usually have a strong dependency on the files they open. When a problem occurs — whether it be a full storage device, permission error, or missing file — it tends to require handling at a high level in the program, if it is handled at all. It's a good guess that the error will be traveling up past the immediate caller of the I/O function.

A simple try–catch construct

Now that we've planted the seed for more exceptions, we can focus on how to catch them. As mentioned, Lua lacks the common try–catch construct for dealing with exceptions, which may put off some programmers. By creating something in pure Lua close to that familiar construct, perhaps we can lower the barrier to more extensive use of exceptions.

Lua supports catching of exceptions through a functional interface, namely pcall. It expects that the code to be attempted is itself defined as a function. Those constraints leave us with few options — our try–catch will have to be functional also, with the "try" and "catch" blocks of code passed in as functions. Nonetheless, with the help of in-line anonymous functions and some creative formatting, we can approach the feel of a native try–catch construct. Here is a template for use of our utility function, simply called "try":

---

[1] Wrapping a call with assert assumes it follows the convention of returning a nil and error message tuple on failure. The convention can't be used, however, if nil or false happen to be valid outputs. It can also interfere with code readability when a function has multiple outputs and the caller elects not to wrap with assert (e.g., a function returns coordinates x and y, but on error y doubles as a message).

```
try(function()
    -- Try block
end, function(e)
    -- Catch block.  E.g.:
    --    Use e for conditional catch
    --    Re-raise with error(e)
end)
```

The catch function, should it be invoked, receives the error object as an argument. After inspecting the error, it can elect to either suppress the exception by taking no action, re-raise the existing error, or throw a different error.

A notable limitation of using functions to define our code blocks is that flow control statements, such as return and break, cannot cross outside the try–catch. For example, the following code would not work as expected:

```
function foo()
    try(function()
        if some_task() then
            return 10 -- does not cause foo() to return 10
        end
    end, function(e)
        -- ...
    end)
    return 20
end
```

Lua's pcall operates by calling the function given to it. Any exception will be trapped, returning nil and the error object. Based on that, the definition of our try function is trivial:

```
function try(f, catch_f)
    local status, exception = pcall(f)
    if not status then
        catch_f(exception)
    end
end
```

Unfortunately coroutines do not mix well with pcall, so this will preclude their use within our try block. The problem is well known and has various workarounds, ranging from a pcall replacement implemented in pure Lua to an extensive Lua core patch.

Custom error objects

Putting our new try–catch construct to use, let's say we have a transactional database application. If a database conflict error occurs — perhaps because two programs tried to increment the same balance field of some record — we'd like to retry the transaction. Coding our simplistic example:

```
try(function()
    do_transaction()
end, function(e)
    log('Retrying database transaction')
    do_transaction()
end)
```

The issue here is that we end up retrying the transaction not only when there is a database problem, but also for any other error. This could mask bugs such as calling a function with the wrong arguments, producing strange program behavior. Clearly we want to be more selective by handling only the errors we understand and letting the rest pass through. Given the common practice of throwing strings, however, this becomes tricky. We are faced with fragile parsing of exception messages which may change in the future, especially if they originate from a third party's module.

To address this problem, we take advantage of the often-overlooked ability of error to throw values other than strings. A table is the natural choice, leaving room for expanded functionality by way of methods and internal state. The database module might simply contain the following definition:

```
ConflictError = {}
```

This approach serves not only to allow positive identification of an exception, but also to enumerate the errors which can be raised by a module— it should be considered part of the API. Now the database module can signal a conflict with error(ConflictError) and our catch function can be refined as follows:

```
function(e)
    if e == db.ConflictError then
        log('Retrying database transaction')
        do_transaction()
    else
        error(e)  -- re-raise
    end
end
```

A new problem is lurking however. What if the database conflict should go unhandled? Let's simulate the situation in Lua's interactive interpreter:

```
> error({})
(error object is not a string)
```

Unfortunately, the uncaught exception handler which lives inside Lua's standard interpreter refuses to do anything with a non-string error value. We're missing the human-readable message and call stack which are essential for locating the source of the error. The required improvement to the interpreter is minor however: just pass the error value through tostring before invoking debug.traceback. This change is planned for the next version of Lua. With this change in the interpreter, and by enhancing our error object with an appropriate __tostring metamethod, the behavior becomes:

```
> MyError = setmetatable({},
>>   {__tostring = function() return 'My error occurred' end})
> error(MyError)
My error occurred
stack traceback:
        [C]: in function 'error'
        stdin:1: in main chunk
        [C]: ?
```

While this is a significant improvement, there is sill one detail missing from
the trace: the file name and line number of the exception. Normally, with
a string value, the error function adds this information at the point of the
exception by prefixing it to the string. For other value types the location is
omitted. While the association between an error and its location might best be
maintained by the Lua core, such a change would be substantial. A compromise
is to alter the error function to store the location in a field (assuming the value
is a table) and have it picked up by the interpreter's handler. This location fix
and the aforementioned tostring fix are available together as a "custom errors"
patch to Lua. (See http://lua-users.org/wiki/LuaPowerPatches.)

Continuing with our database application, suppose we wish to catch any
exception specific to the database module. Or perhaps the module author decides
to distinguish between read and write conflicts using separate error types, while
our handler remains interested in both cases. It would be unfortunate to have
to spell out each error to be caught when all we mean is "any database module
error" and "any conflict error", respectively. This suggests the need for an error
hierarchy, where we can test if a certain instance belongs to a given class of
errors.

In other languages, an error hierarchy tends to be defined by class inheritance. In Lua we are free to do the same, but without a standard class system
the error values from various modules and our own code will lack a common root
and API. As a compromise, the database module author might make a utility
available for testing inheritance among the module's own objects. The implementation should be robust, yielding a negative result for foreign values. Our
catch function then becomes:

```
function(e)
    if db.instance_of(e, db.ConflictError) then
        log('Retrying database transaction')
        do_transaction()
    else
        error(e)
    end
end
```

Note that such an inheritance test becomes mandatory should we choose to
make error objects something more than a simple table constant. For an error

having internal state, a new instance must be created for each exception thrown. In that case equality cannot be used to identify the exception.

The argument for custom errors is that a human-readable error message, while essential, should be only one component of a richer error object. Errors should be enumerated as part of an API, providing the ability to positively identify exceptions and perhaps locate their place within a hierarchy of errors. Custom error objects can also serve to store arbitrary state at the time of an exception, which may be useful for debugging and error reporting. All of this is light work for Lua tables, although the need for hierarchy testing does present an interoperability issue between modules.

Exception safety

With exceptions comes the issue of exception safety — proper cleanup of acquired resources and program state when an exception does occur. Acquired resources might include memory allocated from special pools, device handles, and mutex objects. Consider the following simplistic function to paint a logo onto the screen:

```
function display_logo(display_buffer, x, y)
    local canvas = allocate_canvas(50, 50)
    render_logo(canvas)
    display_buffer:lock()
    display_buffer:copy(canvas, x, y)
    display_buffer:unlock()
    canvas:free()
end
```

During the course of this function we acquire a graphic canvas (perhaps off-screen video memory) and a lock on the display buffer. If the render_logo function happens to throw an exception then the canvas may not be freed in a timely manner — it may happen automatically when the canvas value is garbage collected, but we don't know when that will be. More seriously, if the display_buffer:copy call throws an exception because the input coordinates are out of range, the display is never unlocked. Clearly, if resources like this are going to be exposed to the scripting environment, we need a way to free them even if an exception occurs.

Even if we decide not to expose management of critical resources to scripting, there are common cases where we must ensure that some program state is restored despite an error. Say we'd like the text output of a certain third party function directed to a file, but the module has been hard-coded to use standard output. We could work around the limitation by changing Lua's default output temporarily:

```
local out = io.output()
io.output(log_file)
somelib.do_task()
io.output(out)
```

The problem here is that if do_task throws an exception, the default output will never be restored. One may argue that restoring this state doesn't matter because the process will be terminated anyway. This overlooks the possibility that the exception may be handled at a higher level in the execution stack, allowing the program to continue. That a certain error is too dire to be intercepted usually turns out to be a myopic view since, at the highest level of the program, there are always options such as reattempting an operation or switching to a failover routine. This makes proper exception safety especially important when implementing a library, where the author cannot imagine all usage scenarios.

Now that we've identified the need for exception safety, how is it accomplished? The solutions are all variations on one theme: install cleanup code to be run on exit of the current scope, whether that be normally or by exception. Traditionally, programming languages have two mechanisms available for this. One is the try-finally construct, where the scope is defined by a "try" block, and the cleanup code placed in a "finally" block which always runs afterward. As a language construct, however, try-finally has fallen out of fashion. To consider why, let's pretend that Lua supported try..finally..end and apply it to our display_logo function:

```
function display_logo(display_buffer, x, y)
    local canvas = allocate_canvas(50, 50)
    try  -- no such thing in Lua
        render_logo(canvas)
        display_buffer:lock()
        try
            display_buffer:copy(canvas, x, y)
        finally
            display_buffer:unlock()
        end
    finally
        canvas:free()
    end
end
```

The issue is one of code readability and maintenance. A nested try-finally is needed for each consecutive resource acquired, making the flow of the original program difficult to follow. Moreover, although having "try" come before "finally" is most intuitive and the common layout, it tends to maximize the distance between acquisition and cleanup code. This problem becomes more pronounced as the size of the function grows—to the point where the programmer cannot see them on the screen together, and could modify one without considering the other.

The other traditional mechanism for exception safety is the use of a custom object which is referenced solely by the local scope. The cleanup code exists in the destructor of the object so that it will be invoked as the value goes out of scope. Rather than defining an ad hoc type for each cleanup situation—which becomes verbose and a burden to maintain—the use of a generic "scope manager" object is becoming common (e.g., the C++ scope guard pattern, or the D "scope" statement). A scope manager allows the registration of arbitrary code which will be called at scope exit. Since registration can take place multiple times and throughout the scope, it enables natural placement of cleanup code. In some languages it's possible for the manager to know if the scope exited normally or by exception, further enhancing the utility of this pattern.

Unfortunately, Lua provides no way to hook into scope exit.[2] As object destruction is subject to the whim of the garbage collection system, the trick of using an object referenced only by the local scope does not provide deterministic cleanup. As in our try–catch implementation, however, it's possible to approximate such a hook by way of an explicit function scope and pcall. We'll use that to create a simple scope manager in Lua for our cleanup needs.

A simple scope manager

We define a utility function "scope", which takes a single function argument and calls it. Within the environment of the given function, an on_exit function is made available for registering cleanup functions. Here is how the scope utility looks when applied to our display_logo example:

```
function display_logo(display_buffer, x, y)
    scope(function()
        local canvas = allocate_canvas(50, 50)
        on_exit(function() canvas:free() end)
        render_logo(canvas)
        display_buffer:lock()
        on_exit(function() display_buffer:unlock() end)
        display_buffer:copy(canvas, x, y)
    end)
end
```

Notice that no nesting is needed for consecutively acquired resources as in the try-finally solution. Also, each piece of cleanup code is positioned logically so that, as the code is read from top to bottom, one can see exactly when it becomes active within the scope.

To round out our cleanup utility, we'll make two more registration functions available within the scope: on_failure and on_success. The on_failure hook might be used to roll back a pending database transaction or other tentative state change. Although a try–catch could be used here instead, on_failure is more readable and avoids having the user take responsibility for re-raising the caught error. The on_success hook will likely be least used of the three, but

---

[2]The ability to hook into scope exit is the only fundamental building block I've noticed as missing from Lua 5.1. I hope that this can be resolved in a future version of the language — perhaps by creating a new class of variable which notifies its value when it goes out of scope, or by adding a construct along the lines of Python's "with" statement.

again it offers more flexibility on placement of cleanup code. Here is the scope function implementation:

```lua
function scope(f)
    local function run(list)
        for _, f in ipairs(list) do f() end
    end
    local function append(list, item)
        list[#list+1] = item
    end
    local success_funcs, failure_funcs, exit_funcs = {}, {}, {}
    local manager = {
        on_success = function(f) append(success_funcs, f) end,
        on_failure = function(f) append(failure_funcs, f) end,
        on_exit = function(f) append(exit_funcs, f) end,
    }
    local old_fenv = getfenv(f)
    setmetatable(manager, {__index = old_fenv})
    setfenv(f, manager)
    local status, err = pcall(f)
    setfenv(f, old_fenv)
    -- NOTE: behavior undefined if a hook function raises an error
    run(status and success_funcs or failure_funcs)
    run(exit_funcs)
    if not status then error(err, 2) end
end
```

Like the try–catch implementation, this scope hook suffers from an incompatibility with coroutine yield, and the inability to use flow control statements across the scope's boundary (i.e., return, break, etc.). A more fundamental limitation exists however: cleanup code itself must not raise an exception. Allowing this would create at least two ambiguities: 1) if an exception happens in one piece of cleanup code, should the entire cleanup contract be invalidated? 2) if there are multiple, logically parallel exceptions, which is to be propagated? The situation is best avoided and, in the implementation presented, its behavior is left undefined.

A slightly different design for the scope utility would be to pass the manager object to the user's function as an argument. Besides eliminating the complexity of making on_exit and the other registration methods appear implicitly within the function, this would allow the manager to be passed to utility functions. For example, the allocate_canvas function could take a scope manager as an optional argument, and in that case register the canvas cleanup code for us. On the other hand, the explicit manager variable makes the user's code more verbose in the simple case, and opens the door for confusion should someone try to operate on the manager of an already expired scope.

This pattern to assist with exception safety is the final component in our bag of exception tools. Combined with custom error objects, which allow discerning between errors, and a try–catch construct implemented in pure Lua, programmers can explore richer use of exceptions in their programs and libraries. Limitations and rough spots exist for sure, but hopefully this situation is temporary — the authors of Lua have a good track record of improving the flexibility of the language and its implementation over time.

Part III

Algorithms
and
Data Structures

14

Word Ladders

Gavin Wraith

Word Ladders or *Doublets* is a word game whose invention has been attributed to Lewis Carroll. The idea is to transform one word into another by changing only a single letter at each step.

Here is a simple example:

BEST → PEST → POST → POSE → ROSE → RISE → RISK

We present a small Lua program which, given a lexicon of words as a command line argument, takes a word from the standard input and prints the words in the lexicon that can be obtained from it by such transformations. This program is really just an excuse for presenting a more abstract application: a module for calculating the strata of the connected component of a vertex in an undirected graph.

Undirected graphs

From the earliest days of programming this game has been a vehicle for demonstrating algorithms about undirected graphs. An undirected graph may be defined as a set of *vertices* together with a Boolean-valued function on the set of unordered pairs of distinct vertices, which tells which vertices are joined by an *edge*. In what follows the term *graph* should be read as *undirected graph*.

If two vertices can be joined by a sequence of edges then we say that they belong to the same *component* of the graph. Given a lexicon of words we can construct a graph whose vertices are words, where two vertices are joined by an edge if the corresponding words differ by only one letter. The Word Ladder game is about finding a path from a given word to another.

The mathematical notion of graph is an abstraction. The Word Ladder game has various features which are thrown away by this abstraction — the significance of the words, for example, or the fact that we can enumerate words in lexicographic order. If a program is to be reusable it should be as faithful as possible to the mathematical abstraction, and avoid building in specific features of this or that example. However, there is a problem. Mathematicians tend to use the notion of *set* in contrast to the notion of *enumerated set*. Programming languages, on the other hand, having developed in an era of serial processors, are usually better adapted to handle enumerated sets. Of course, every finite set can be enumerated in some way or other (and if you believe the axiom of choice, every set can be totally ordered), but if a problem does not mandate a particular enumeration it seems rather ugly to have to choose one in order to program a solution.

The fundamental datatype in Lua is the table. Any value except **nil** can be a key in a table. We can use tables to represent both enumerated sets, using integers starting from 1 as keys, and non-enumerated sets by taking as the elements keys with value **true**. Lua has two iterator functions for tables: ipairs iterates over integer keys in order starting from 1 and so is appropriate for enumerated sets, and pairs iterates over all keys but in no predictable order, and so is appropriate for non-enumerated sets. This unpredictability is the serial processor's apology, so to speak, to the parallel world of mathematical sets (logicians may be thinking of *permutation models* at this point).

Although a component of a graph may have no natural enumeration, once we have chosen a particular vertex in it we get a natural stratification of it. The first stratum consists just of the chosen vertex. The n-th stratum consists of those vertices having a shortest path of $n - 1$ edges to the chosen vertex. Each stratum has no particular enumeration itself, and so should be represented by a Lua table whose values we may take to be **true**. The collection of all the strata does have an enumeration, and so is represented as an array of tables.

Listing 1 shows a module, graph, that calculates the array of strata, given a graph and a vertex of it. A graph is a table with keys vertex and edge. The value for vertex is a **true**-valued table. The value for edge is a Boolean valued function on pairs of distinct keys of the vertex table. It should be *symmetric*, that is to say if g is a graph then g.edge(x,y) and g.edge(y,x) should have the same value for any keys x, y of g.vertex.

The function graph.component makes a copy of the table mygraph.vertex and points the local variable vertex at it. It initializes the strata array to a single stratum containing just the start node, and then removes the start node from vertex. It defines a local function, more, which searches the nodes of vertex to see if they are joined by an edge to the current stratum. If they are, they are removed from vertex (which is why we had to make a copy of mygraph.vertex) and put into the next stratum. This avoids redundancy. The more function is called repeatedly until no more strata can be found.

```
-- graph
--[[component of start node in graph as a list of sets of nodes]]

local insert = table.insert
local pairs = pairs

module "graph"

component = function(mygraph,start)
  local vertex,edge = {},mygraph.edge
  for node,val in pairs(mygraph.vertex) do
    vertex[node] = val
  end -- for
  local strata  = {{ [start] = true }}
  vertex[start] = nil
  local more = function()
      local new,change = {},nil
      for x,_ in pairs(strata[#strata]) do
       for y,_ in pairs(vertex) do
        if edge(x,y) then -- x cannot equal y
          change = true
          new[y] = true
         end -- if
        end -- for
      end -- for
      if change then
       insert(strata,new)
       for x,_ in pairs(new) do vertex[x] = nil end -- for
      end -- if
      return change
     end -- function
  repeat until not more() -- add new vertices while possible
  return strata
 end -- function
```

Listing 1. The graph module

The number of calls to the function mygraph.edge is given by

$$nm + n^2 + \sum_i \frac{x_i^2}{2}$$

where n is the number of vertices in the component, m is the number of vertices not in the component and x_i is the number of vertices in the i-th stratum. This number cannot be made smaller.

Word Ladder game

The Word Ladder game itself can be coded as in Listing 2. The program uses a lexicon of words in a file whose pathname is passed in as a command line argument, and a starting word which is input by the user. It outputs the words in the strata in order.

The program asks for the start word to be input, and transforms it to lower case. The lexicon is a file consisting of lower case words separated by white space and newlines. The table called lexicon is set to have as keys the words found in the lexicon file to be of the same length as the start word, as this version of the game does not allow the length of words to change. A function string.vary is added to the string library which creates a pattern matched by any word that differs in only one letter from its first argument, whose position is the second argument. The reason for adding it to the string library is a trivial aesthetic one: it makes the pretty colon notation available. The function differby1 is a Boolean-valued function that tells when words differ by only one letter. The graph wordgraph is defined by the lexicon table and the differby1 function. A function printout is defined to print out the contents of the strata; it converts all words to upper case and first prints the stratum level. The graph library is loaded and finally the result is output.

Summary

The graph module and the ladder program that uses it are tiny and straightforward, and in themselves unremarkable. They are simply pegs on which to hang some observations. Readers are, of course, free to quarrel with my personal preferences.

- I like to use comments, but not too many. It is pointless to overcomment if meaningful variable names tell the story.
- I like to indent to make chunks easily identifiable.
- I like to comment the **end** keyword whenever feasible.
- I like to reduce the use of global variables as much as possible.

```
-- ladder
-- arg[1] holds pathname of lexicon
do
 local read,lines = io.read,io.lines
 print "Enter a word from the lexicon"
 local startword = (read()):lower()
 local n = #startword
 local pat = ("%a"):rep(n) -- pattern for words of same size
 local lexicon = {}
 for line in lines(arg[1]) do
  line:gsub(pat,function(word) lexicon[word] = true end)
 end -- for
 -- add vary to string library
 string.vary = function(s,i)   -- pattern - vary i-th char
             return s:sub(1,i-1).."."..s:sub(i+1,-1)
            end -- function
 local differby1 = function(x,y)
        local n = #x
        for i = 1,n do
           if y:match(x:vary(i)) then return true end -- if
        end -- for
        return false
        end -- function
 local wordgraph = { vertex = lexicon; edge = differby1; }
 local printout = function(strata)
           for i,stratum in ipairs(strata) do
            for word,_ in pairs(stratum) do
             print(i,": ",word:upper())
            end -- for
           end -- for
           end -- function
 require "graph"
 printout(graph.component(wordgraph,startword))
end -- do
```

Listing 2. The main program

- I am proud that in Lua functions are first-class values. For that reason I make it clear that function definitions are assignments, and I do not use the syntactic sugar provided to conceal this fact, lest it be misinterpreted as apologetic. If you have got it, flaunt it!

The choice of data structures and the division of labour between main program and required modules should follow from analysis of the abstractions thrown up by the problem. In this case the analysis is the trivial fact that a vertex in a graph stratifies the component in which it lives. It tells us loud and clear that we need a function that returns a list of tables and not just their union, as a superficial reading of the task might suggest.

15

Building Data Structures and Iterators in Lua

Luis Carvalho

Besides being lightweight and fast, Lua is also highly regarded for being an elegant and expressive language. The main purpose of this gem is to reinforce this impression by showing how powerful and straightforward the concerted application of tables, metamethods, and coroutines is in the implementation of complex data structures and their iterators.

Here we implement a graph object module where graphs are modeled using a vertex set, a weighted edge/arc set and adjacency lists (set objects are as described in "Programming in Lua" (PiL)). Graph vertex sets can be iterated by depth first search (DFS), breadth first search (BFS), and topological sorting, which illustrate well the application of closures and coroutines. Moreover, classical routines for shortest paths from a vertex and minimum spanning tree (MST) are also provided. These routines require additional data structures in order to achieve optimal time complexity: queues (similar to the ones implemented in PiL) are used in the BFS iterator, while heaps and partition sets (both as trees with special properties) are used in the MST routine. Each data structure, on its own, comprises an individual pure Lua module whose methods satisfy the usual colon calling convention for objects. A few examples and direct applications of the routines are also presented.

Introduction

The study and development of algorithms and data structures are tightly coupled together: appropriate data structures are the core of well designed, optimal algorithms. Besides designing suitable data structures, it is also important to use a programming language that allows easy specification and implementation of a data structure and that is rich and expressive enough to favor the realization of abstract concepts and possible future extensions. This gem aims to show that Lua is such a language: with its many appealing resources — including a powerful unique data structure building block, the table, metamethods, and coroutines — we can implement many data structures effortlessly.

The main data structure portrayed in the text is a graph, but we also present others in order to solve some classical graph problems efficiently. A complete listing of all routines, which are encapsulated in modules, one per data structure, can be found in the gem repository.

Although we provide an explanation for each method in the text, we try to be as terse as possible to keep the text short. Familiarity with data structures and design of algorithms is highly desirable — this way you can concentrate in enjoying the Lua code! — but not necessary; however, the reader should refer to many excellent books that cover these topics for more details[1]. We should mention the excellent *"Programming in Lua"* (PiL)[2], by Roberto Ierusalimschy, one of Lua's creators: we make many references to it, and try to draw inspiration from it whenever possible.

Queues

Our first data structure is a *queue*, a list in which elements are always inserted to the *front* and retrieved at the *rear*, that is, in a first-in, first-out fashion. Although simple, our queue implementation will be useful later on this chapter when we talk about graph traversal and can serve as good warm-up exercise. The implementation comprises a module Queue, very similar to the one in PiL: a queue object is a table with two pointers, first and last, indicating the current positions of the queue's front and rear. A queue is then initialized by

```
local modenv = getfenv() -- module environment
function new ()
  return setmetatable({first = 1, last = 0}, {__index = modenv})
end
```

where we use __index to enable colon call notation in our objects. Note that getfenv takes 1 as default argument and returns the current, module, environ-

---

[1]We particularly recommend the classical *"Design and analysis of computer algorithms"*, by Aho, Hopcroft and Ullman, and the more modern *"Introduction to algorithms"*, by Cormen, Leiserson, Rivest, and Stein.

[2]PiL's first edition is available online at http://www.lua.org/pil.

ment. The methods in the environment are the typical `insert` and `retrieve`, as presented in PiL[3],

```
function insert (Q, v)
  assert(v ~= nil, "cannot insert nil")
  local last = Q.last + 1
  Q[last] = v
  Q.last = last
end
```

```
function retrieve (Q)
  local first = Q.first
  assert(Q.last >= first, "cannot retrieve from empty queue")
  local v = Q[first]
  Q[first] = nil -- allow GC
  Q.first = first + 1
  return v
end
```

and the useful check:

```
function isempty (Q) return Q.last < Q.first end
```

Thanks to the `__index` metamethod we are able, for example, to simply issue `Q:retrieve()` instead of `Queue.retrieve(Q)`. We will be following this practice of defining `__index` as the module environment for all objects in this chapter, and so the queue module gives the reader a good opportunity to get familiarized with this prototype-based convention[4].

Heaps

We now implement a *heap* data structure, which is a binary tree stored in an array. For each node in the tree we associate a `record` *numeric* field such that the tree satisfies the (min) heap property: for every node v, $\text{record}(v) \leq \min\{\text{record}(l), \text{record}(r)\}$, where l and r are the left and right children of v. If a tree is a heap, its root contains the smallest `record` over all nodes in the tree.

Heaps have many applications, but in this gem we focus on heaps as *priority queues*, that is, as a data structure for keeping a set of objects ordered by their `record` field. Priority queues will be at the core of our solutions to the minimum spanning tree and shortest path problems in a latter section about graphs. Since records in a heap represent some object feature — such as the time of occurrence of events in a simulation engine — it is then desirable to have a correspondence between nodes in the heap and objects. We use two additional fields for this

---

[3]They are called *push* and *pop* in PiL.

[4]For a more thorough presentation, check PiL's chapter on object-oriented programming, more specifically on the section about classes.

intent: key stores object labels and ref stores references from keys back to heap nodes. Of course, key[ref[k]] = k and ref[key[n]] = n for all keys k and nodes n. Since this correspondence between objects and the heap will be useful for us later on, our heap methods are implemented with it in mind.

Heaps are similar to queues since we can insert elements, retrieve them, and check the heap for emptiness. Insertions are performed at the leaves, filling each level of the tree before going to the next, while retrieval is performed at the root. Heaps differ from queues in that they also have an *update* operation that rearranges the heap after some record is decreased. Still, our main concern should be for the tree to keep the heap property after each of these operations.

We create heap objects with

```
function new ()
  return setmetatable({record={}, key={}, ref={}}, {__index = modenv})
end
```

where our tree is represented by integer-keyed tables record, key and ref in the following way: if i is a position representing a node in the tree, then $2i$ is the left child of i, $2i + 1$ is the right child of i, and thus $\lfloor i/2 \rfloor$ is the parent of i. Since we are going to need parents of nodes a lot, it is convenient to provide:

```
local function parent (n) return (n - n % 2) / 2 -- floor(n / 2) end
```

The update method is listed below; we maintain the heap property by percolating the node i with key k and new record value v < record[ref[k]] up the tree until the property is again satisfied:

```
function update (H, k, v)
  local record, key, ref = H.record, H.key, H.ref
  local i = ref[k]
  local p = parent(i)
  while i > 1 and record[p] > v do -- climb tree?
    -- exchange nodes
    record[i], key[i], ref[key[p]] = record[p], key[p], i
    i, p = p, parent(p)
  end
  record[i], key[i], ref[k] = v, k, i -- update
end
```

Note how we actually update three trees, one for each field in the heap, as we exchange parent and child nodes, but use record exclusively for comparisons. Insertions are now straightforward; we simply insert a new leaf and call update to maintain the heap property:

```
function insert (H, v, k)
  local ref = H.ref
  assert(ref[k] == nil, "key already in heap")
  ref[k] = #H.record + 1 -- insert reference
  update(H, k, v) -- insert record
end
```

Updates and insertions are simple because there is a unique path from any node to the root and so we just need to follow that path up looking for a suitable position to place our new or updated object. Retrieval is a bit more complicated since it comprises extracting the root and swapping the rightmost leaf (the last position in the array) by the root: both left and right subtrees from the root are still heaps, but now the root might be violating the heap property. The task of fixing the tree in case this happens is handled recursively by heapify:

```
local function heapify (record, root, key, ref, n)
  local left, right = 2 * root, 2 * root + 1 -- children
  local p, l, r = record[root], record[left], record[right]
  -- find min := argmin_{root, left, right}(record)
  local min, m = root, p
  if left <= n and l < m then min, m = left, l end
  if right <= n and r < m then min, m = right, r end
  if min ~= root then -- recurse to fix subtree?
    record[root], record[min] = m, p -- exchange records...
    key[root], key[min] = key[min], key[root] -- and keys
    if ref ~= nil then -- fix refs?
      ref[key[root]], ref[key[min]] = root, min
    end
    return heapify(record, min, key, ref, n)
  end
end
```

Complementary to update, heapify percolates down any offending node root at a subtree root until the whole tree becomes a heap. Note that heapify is *tail* recursive, and so we should profit from Lua's implementation of proper tail recursion to allow an arbitrary number of calls. The use of a ref field is optional in heapify, but we need to specify the size of the heap as a last argument; this interface is more general, and will be justified when we talk about heapsort.

Finally, we can now extract the minimum record from the heap with

```
function retrieve (H)
  local record, key, ref = H.record, H.key, H.ref
  assert(record[1] ~= nil, "cannot retrieve from empty heap")
  local n = #record -- heap size
  local minr, mink = record[1], key[1]
  record[1], key[1], ref[key[n]] = record[n], key[n], 1 -- leaf to root
  record[n], key[n], ref[mink] = nil, nil, nil -- remove leaf
  heapify(record, 1, key, ref, n - 1) -- fix heap
  return minr, mink
end
```

while the check for emptiness is implemented by

```
function isempty (H) return H.record[1] == nil end
```

Heapsort

We could not talk about heaps and not mention one of their main applications: to sort an array. The concept is an ingenious derivation from retrieve: we can sort an array in-place by iteratively replacing the root by the rightmost leaf—the first position by the last position in the array—and not actually removing the root, but simply reducing the heap size. By performing the whole sorting in-place, we do not need to insert elements either[5]. However, since we have a min heap, we sort *decreasingly*; to sort increasingly we would need a max heap, which can be trivially obtained by swapping record comparisons in heapify and insert. Our heapsort routine does not use a ref field and needs to explicitly set the size of the heap in heapify since no elements are removed from the heap:

```
function heapsort (t)
  local n = #t -- heap size
  local k = {} -- key: position in t
  for i = 1, n do k[i] = i end
  for i = parent(n), 1, -1 do -- build heap
    heapify(t, i, k, nil, n)
  end
  for i = n, 2, -1 do -- sort in-place
    k[1], k[i] = k[i], k[1] -- exchange keys...
    t[1], t[i] = t[i], t[1] -- ...and records
    heapify(t, 1, k, nil, i - 1)
  end
  return k
end
```

The motivation behind using the key field to store the original position of the entries in the array to be sorted is to illustrate an interesting use of key: we can recreate the original state of a sorted table, as in

```
function permute (t, o)
  local p = {}
  for i = 1, #t do p[o[i]] = t[i] end
  return p
end

local k = heapsort(t) -- sort
-- do something with t
t = permute(t, k) -- restore
```

---

[5]You might ask: why not implement heapsort using insertions and retrievals? This is possible, of course, but less efficient: the "build heap" loop in heapsort has complexity $O(n)$, n being the heap size, as opposed to $O(n \log n)$ if the heap is built using insert.

Partition sets

Consider now a set S and a *partition* $\{S_i\}$ over S, that is, the sets S_i are disjoint, $\cap_i S_i = \emptyset$, and their union is S, $\cup_i S_i = S$. We want an efficient way to implement two operations for partition sets: *merge* two sets into their union and, given an element $e \in S$, *find* the set to which e belongs.

A good representation for partition sets is a forest where every set is represented by a tree and is identified by the element at the root of its tree. This way, merging two sets S_1 and S_2 requires a simple attachment of the tree representing S_1 as a subtree in S_2. In addition, finding the set that contains a random element involves a tree climbing routine from the element up to the root of the tree representing the containing set. As we will see shortly, to guarantee efficiency we also need to perform these operations according to some rules, but for now let's just assume that we need to keep track of the number of elements in each set.

Our partition sets are represented by a table with two fields: card, a table storing the cardinality of each set, and parent, a table storing the parent of an element in its containing set. An element e is the root of a set S if and only if card[e] contains the number of elements in S — e represents S — and parent[e] == nil. New partition objects are created with

```
function new ()
   return setmetatable({card = {}, parent = {}}, {__index = modenv})
end
```

while set takes a new element and creates a new set in the partition containing only the argument,

```
function set (P, e)
   assert(e ~= nil, "set cannot contain nil")
   assert(P.card[e] == nil and P.parent[e] == nil,
       "element already in partition")
   P.card[e] = 1 -- e is root of new set
end
```

and sameset checks if two elements belong to the same set in the partition:

```
function sameset (P, e1, e2)
   return find(P, e1) == find(P, e2)
end
```

Now we need to provide find. As stated before, to find to which set an element e belongs, we just need to climb the tree from e up to the root. It is clear that the shorter the tree the more efficient this task is; to favor this feature in our sets, we then implement a compacting rule where all the internal nodes in the path from e up to the root are collapsed into one level with the internal nodes becoming children of the root:

```
function find (P, e)
  local parent = P.parent
  assert(P.card[e] ~= nil or parent[e] ~= nil,
      "element not in partition")
  -- climb tree up to root r
  local r = e
  while parent[r] do r = parent[r] end
  -- compacting rule for tree paths
  local u = e
  while u ~= r do -- collapse nodes from e to r
    u, parent[u] = parent[u], r
  end
  return r -- root identifies set
end
```

For merge we also try to keep the tree shorter by applying a weighting rule: when merging two sets, attach the smaller set to the larger set. This rule requires the use of card to keep track of set sizes. The best way to connect the two sets is then to redefine the root of the smaller set as a child of the root of the larger set.

```
function merge (P, e1, e2) -- merge sets containing e1 and e2
  local s1, s2 = find(P, e1), find(P, e2)
  if s1 ~= s2 then -- merge needed?
    local card = P.card
    -- weighting rule: merge with largest set
    if card[s1] > card[s2] then s1, s2 = s2, s1 end
    P.parent[s1] = s2
    card[s1], card[s2] = nil, card[s1] + card[s2]
  end
end
```

You might be asking: how much do we actually gain by incorporating the path compression and weighting rules? After all, the path compression rule is responsible for roughly half of find's running time, while we need to allocate extra space for card to implement the weighting rule. A rigorous analysis is beyond the scope of this text, but the gains can be summarized, for $O(n)$ merge and find operations, as follows: with no rules it costs $O(n^2)$ time units, with only the weighting rule it becomes $O(n \log n)$, and with both rules the complexity becomes almost linear[6]. More details can be found in "Design and analysis of computer algorithms", by Aho, Hopcroft and Ullman.

---

[6]It is actually $O(nG(n))$, where G is a very slowly increasing function related to a functional inverse of the Ackermann's function.

Graphs

There are many ways to represent a graph data structure, each being better suited to a particular application. For our graph object we adopt a representation using *adjacency lists* — or better, tables — where the keys are vertices and the values hold adjacency relations.

Vertices can be of any type but `nil`, and are stored in the graph's vertex set, `vset`; similarly, we store the edges or arcs of a graph, if it is undirected or directed respectively, in its edge (or arc) set `eset`. To avoid redundancy, `vset` is actually the adjacency list: `vset[v]` is a table where each key is a neighbor `u` of `v` and the corresponding value is the edge {u,v}, also a table. The edge set `eset` can be a regular set as presented in PiL — keys are edges and values are `true` — or values can hold edge *weights*.

Graphs are created with our (now canonical) `new` method:

```
function new()
  return setmetatable({vset = {}, eset = {}}, {__index = modenv})
end
```

As basic graph operations we offer the addition of vertices,

```
function addvertex (G, v)
  assert(v ~= nil, "cannot add nil as vertex")
  local vs = G.vset
  assert(vs[v] == nil, "vertex already in graph")
  vs[v] = {} -- new adjacency list
end
```

and edges to a graph,

```
function addedge (G, v1, v2, w)
  assert(v1 ~= nil and v2 ~= nil, "cannot add nil as vertex")
  local vs = G.vset
  -- add v1 and v2 if not in G
  if not vs[v1] then vs[v1] = {} end
  if not vs[v2] then vs[v2] = {} end
  -- update v1 and v2 adjacency lists
  local e = {v1, v2} -- new edge
  vs[v1][v2] = e -- v1 -> v2
  vs[v2][v1] = e -- v1 <- v2
  -- update edge set
  G.eset[e] = w or true
end
```

Addition of arcs can be handled by a very similar method where the adjacency lists are updated only according to the arc direction.

It is useful to have some iterators for traversing the vertex and edge sets, and the *neighborhood* of a vertex `v` — the set of vertices adjacent to `v`. We can derive such iterators by mimicking the stateless `pairs` iterator:

```lua
function vertices (G) return next, G.vset, nil end

function edges (G) return next, G.eset, nil end

function neighborhood (G, v)
  local adjv = G.vset[v]
  assert(adjv ~= nil, "vertex not in graph")
  return next, adjv, nil
end
```

It should be noted that, even though `pairs` can be used instead of each iterator, we explicitly define them to keep our following graph methods abstract, that is, independent of our particular underlying graph implementation: if we later decide to change the graph representation to solve some problem more efficiently our higher level algorithms should require minimum modifications, or even none at all.

In the next sections we treat a few classical graph problems that arise from many applications. All problems have a theme in common, graph connectivity, that allow us to exploit our chosen adjacency list representation.

Graph search

Many graph related problems involve a search through the graph's vertex set in order to, say, verify some property or compute some desired quantity. It is often the case when the vertices should be visited in some specific order as required by the task at hand. The most common orderings are provided by two graph search procedures: *depth-first search* (DFS) and *breadth-first search* (BFS).

Both procedures take a vertex in the graph as a starting point. As the names suggest, depth-first search follows some edge leaving the current vertex in the search as deep as possible, backtracking to explore more vertices when the options are exhausted, while breadth-first search explores the neighborhood of the current vertex before attempting to branch the search further.

Let's address DFS first; check Listing 1. Our DFS method is actually an iterator wrapped around an auxiliary routine, `search`. Thanks to Lua's coroutines, implementing such an iterator is simple even when it involves a recursive routine since we can yield from it. In `dfs`, `visited` is a control variable that keeps a set of already visited vertices. As an iterator, `dfs` is not as efficient as `neighborhood` since a new closure is created for each search; however, even though `dfs` is algorithmically more complex, it is, at the same time, semantically as simple as `neighborhood` thanks to Lua's generic `for`.

A *subgraph* S of a graph G is a graph such that $V(S) \subseteq V(G)$ and $E(S) \subseteq E(G)$, where $V(G)$ and $E(G)$ are the vertex and edge sets of G respectively. A *component* C of a graph G is a maximal connected subgraph of G: any two vertices in C have a path connecting them, that is, C is connected, and any vertex not in C has no edges to a vertex in C, that is, if we add any other vertex, C is not connected anymore. An important application of graph searches is to

```
local function search (G, v, visited)
  visited[v] = true -- mark v as visited
  coroutine.yield(v)
  for u in G:neighborhood(v) do -- branch search
    if not visited[u] then -- search deeper?
      search(G, u, visited)
    end
  end
end

function dfs (G, s)
  assert(G.vset[s] ~= nil, "vertex not in graph")
  local visited = {} -- control variable (set)
  return coroutine.wrap(function()
    return search(G, s, visited)
  end)
end
```

Listing 1. Depth-first search for G, starting at s.

identify the components of a graph; the following method is our first application of dfs and returns a table containing vertex sets for each component of a graph:

```
function components (G)
  local comp = {} -- holds components
  local S = {} -- unvisited vertices
  for v in G:vertices() do S[v] = true end
  for v in pairs(S) do
    local C = {} -- component set
    for u in G:dfs(v) do -- or bfs
      C[u] = true -- add to C
      S[u] = nil -- remove from S
    end
    comp[#comp + 1] = C
  end
  return comp
end
```

We can also have *true* iterators, as discussed in PiL, by implementing a factory that returns a DFS iterator starting at a provided vertex as a closure on the graph, the control variable, and the auxiliary search routine; see Listing 2. The iterator takes two functions as optional arguments, visit and finish, that perform some action as the vertex is visited and finished, respectively. By a finished vertex we mean a vertex that had all its neighbors traversed by DFS. Using dfs from the listing above, we can, for example, print the order in which the vertices are discovered by DFS from a vertex s by just creating an iterator dfser = dfs(G, s) and then calling dfser(print). This last dfs has a strong

```lua
function dfs (G, s)
  assert(G.vset[s] ~= nil, "vertex not in graph")
  local dfsaux, visited
  dfsaux = function (v, visit, finish)
    visited[v] = true
    if visit ~= nil then visit(v) end
    for u in G:neighborhood(v) do
      if not visited[u] then
        dfsaux(u, visit, finish)
      end
    end
    if finish ~= nil then finish(v) end
  end
  return function(visit, finish) -- true iterator
    visited = {}
    dfsaux(s, visit, finish)
  end
end
```

Listing 2. DFS iterator factory.

functional flavor—it is a higher order function (HOF) that returns another HOF!—that corroborates to its powerful semantics but increased complexity when compared to previous iterators.

A more elaborate application is to sort a directed acyclic graph (DAG) *topologically*, that is, to order its vertices such that there are no arcs from u to v if u is after v in the ordering. For example, if in a graph G the vertices represent subtasks and the arcs precedence rules, a topological sort of G gives a valid way of executing a procedure.

Listing 3 provides a simple routine for topologically ordering a graph G: we just need to execute a depth-first search on G that computes the *finishing times* of its vertices and then sort the vertices decreasingly by the finishing times. We need to keep a notfinished set because dfs iterates only over one component at a time, and we need an ordering over all vertices.

While depth-first search required a recursion to perform the search, breadth-first search can be implemented iteratively using a queue, as presented in Listing 4; note that bfs requires our Queue module.

The BFS iterator can still be viewed as a wrapper around an auxiliary routine, an iterative one, nevertheless. Observe the similarities between dfs and bfs: while the former performs the search as soon as it finds an unvisited vertex, the latter stores the unvisited neighbors in a queue for later traversal. As a matter of fact, we can construct an iterative version of DFS by using an explicit *stack* to traverse the graph, and so the only difference between BFS and DFS is how the neighborhood of a vertex is visited: if in first-in-first-out order, as in BFS, or in last-in-first-out order, as in DFS.

```
function toporder (G, s)
  local s = s or next(G.vset) -- optional start
  local n = 0 -- number of vertices
  local i = 0 -- finishing time
  local f = {} -- vertices in decreasing time
  local notfinished = {} -- set
  for v in G:vertices() do
    n = n + 1
    notfinished[v] = true
  end
  local function finish (v)
    if notfinished[v] then
      notfinished[v] = nil -- finish v
      i = i + 1 -- advance time
      f[n - i + 1] = v -- store reverse order
    end
  end
  while s do -- any unfinished vertex left?
    dfs(G, s)(nil, finish)
    s = next(notfinished) -- start at other component
  end
  -- return iterator
  i = 0
  return function ()
    i = i + 1
    return f[i]
  end
end
```

Listing 3. Topological sort of graph G, optionally starting at s.

Minimum spanning trees

Given a *weighted* undirected graph G, the *minimum (weight) spanning tree* (MST) problem asks us to find a spanning tree T of G — an acyclic connected subgraph of G that covers all its vertices — such that the sum of the weights of the edges in T is minimum over all possible spanning trees of G[7].

The MST problem can be solved efficiently by Kruskal's algorithm: initially put each vertex of G in a component and tentatively add an edge to the tree if the edge is not incident to vertices in the same component; when an edge is added to the solution we merge the components the edge connects proceeding iteratively until all edges have been visited. Of course, for the resulting spanning tree to have minimum total weight we need to visit the edges in some fashion, and that turns out to be in increasing weight order.

---

[7]In general, if G is not connected, we want the minimum spanning *forest* of G.

```
function bfs (G, v)
  assert(G.vset[v] ~= nil, "vertex not in graph")
  local visited = {} -- control set
  local Q = Queue.new()
  return coroutine.wrap(function()
    Q:insert(v)
    while not Q:isempty() do -- any vertex left?
      local u = Q:retrieve()
      if not visited[u] then
        visited[u] = true
        coroutine.yield(u)
      end
      for w in G:neighborhood(u) do
        if not visited[w] then Q:insert(w) end
      end
    end
  end)
end
```

Listing 4. Breadth-first search for G, starting at s.

Listing 5 presents an implementation of Kruskal's algorithm where we use Heap to keep the edges sorted by weight, and Partition to handle the components. By using our optimized heap and partition operations, mst(G) achieves the optimal complexity of $O(m \log m)$, where m is the number of elements in G.eset[8].

Shortest paths

Consider now two distinct vertices u and v in a connected graph G: there may be many paths in G connecting them. However, if we attribute to each edge in G a positive *cost*, we are usually more interested in a *shortest path* between u and v, that is, a path of minimum total cost. The cost of a path between u and v is called the *distance* between u and v, and comprises the sum of the costs over all edges in the path.

Dijkstra's algorithm finds the shortest paths between a source v and all other vertices in G[9]. His algorithm iteratively marks a vertex once its shortest path to the source is known, and visits the unmarked vertices in order of increasing distance to the source. Since the costs are positive, shortest paths leading to unmarked vertices can only pass through already marked vertices. Thus, we can compute the distance from an unmarked vertex to the source by only considering the known distance from one of its marked neighbors to the source.

---

[8] You cannot sort a list of n elements with complexity less than $O(n \log n)$.

[9] Even if we are only interested in the shortest path between two specific vertices, an algorithm for that problem would not be more efficient in the worst case than the best single-source algorithm.

```
function mst (G)
  local T = Graph.new() -- min spanning tree
  local VS = Partition.new() -- component sets
  local H = Heap.new() -- keep edges ordered by weight
  -- fill heap with all edges
  for e, w in G:edges() do H:insert(w, e) end
  -- each vertex in a component
  for v in G:vertices() do VS:set(v) end
  while not H:isempty() do -- any edge left?
    local w, e = H:retrieve() -- min weight edge
    local v1, v2 = unpack(e)
    if not VS:sameset(v1, v2) then
      -- v1 and v2 in different components?
      VS:merge(v1, v2) -- merge components
      T:addedge(v1, v2, w) -- grow tree
    end
  end
  return T
end
```

Listing 5. Kruskal's algorithm: minimum spanning tree of a graph G.

We present shortestpath in Listing 6. A heap H is used to keep track of the vertices to be visited in order of increasing distance; as we retrieve from H we mark the vertex that minimizes the distance to the source. The previous table stores information about the predecessor of a vertex as it is marked; using previous we can construct the shortest paths from the source to all other destinations. The method returns dist, a table with vertices as keys and shortest distances to the source as values, and previous.

Although previous contains all the information needed to construct the shortest paths, it is desirable to have this information in a more convenient format. As a matter of fact, it is not immediate which vertex was used as source to derive previous. Alternatively, it would be nice to have, similarly to dist, a function that takes a destination and returns the shortest path, as a table, from the source to the argument. Here is one way to do it: we can define a factory,

```
function backtracker (previous)
  return function (dest)
    return function(p, v) return p[v] end, previous, dest
  end
end
```

that creates stateless iterators that backtrack from the destination to the source along the shortest path, and use one such iterator to implement a path builder:

```lua
function shortestpath (G, v)
  -- initialize
  local cost = G.eset -- alias
  local dist, previous = {}, {}
  local H = Heap.new() -- keep unmarked vertices ordered by dist
  for u in G:vertices() do dist[u] = math.huge end
  dist[v] = 0
  for u, d in pairs(dist) do H:insert(d, u) end -- build heap
  -- iterate
  while not H:isempty() do -- any vertex left?
    local du, u = H:retrieve() -- du = min_v dist[v], u marked
    -- update distances
    for w, e in G:neighborhood(u) do
      -- dist[w] = min{dist[w], dist[u] + cost(w, u)}
      local dw = dist[w]
      local d = du + cost[e]
      if dw > d then -- update w?
        dist[w] = d
        previous[w] = u
        H:update(w, d)
      end
    end
  end
  return dist, previous
end
```

Listing 6. Dijkstra's algorithm: single-source shortest paths in graph G from v.

```lua
function buildpath (btrack, dest)
  local p = {dest} -- path
  for v in btrack(dest) do -- dest -> source
    p[#p + 1] = v
  end
  local c = #p
  for i = 1, #p / 2 do -- reverse path
    p[i], p[c] = p[c], p[i]
    c = c - 1
  end
  return p
end
```

Of course, buildpath could have previous as direct argument, but backtracker gives you the functionality to traverse shortest paths for purposes other than building paths. Moreover, backtracker abstracts from previous and it is more meaningful.

Conclusions

This gem highlights Lua's simplicity and expressiveness through the implementation of data structures and iterators. Data structures are easily realized by using tables and their `__index` metamethod for object-like notation, while iterators can be build using Lua's generic `for` loop, closures and coroutines. The resulting code is simple, high-level and abstract, mostly composed of table accesses and object method calls.

One of the main motivations of this text is to show many possible ways of achieving a goal in Lua. For instance, there are many ways to construct an iterator in Lua according to PiL; we cover them all here. Another motivation is to be true to one of Lua's maxims in PiL — "Lua gives you the power, you build the mechanisms" — by providing iterators instead of tables, for example, or ways of generating a desired table instead of the table itself, as in the `backtracker` factory.

16

A Primer of
Scientific Computing in Lua

Luis Carvalho

Lua is a fast, resourceful, easily embeddable and extensible programming language; this set of features makes Lua very suitable for scientific computing applications. This gem implements a simple interface to two cornerstones of scientific computing: numerical linear algebra and discrete Fourier transforms (DFTs). More specifically, one module for (two-dimensional) matrices is implemented using some of Lua's unique resources, namely: weak tables, coroutines, metamethods, and environments.

The matrix module defines a matrix object and its methods. A matrix object is a userdatum containing a lua_Number pointer as the data core and other descriptive parameters: number of rows and columns and stride. Data cores are allocated as new matrices are created and are then stored in weak-keyed table as values, whereas the corresponding keys are matrices that reference them. Matrix rows are objects where the data core is a pointer to the "parent" matrix's data core, and are lazily interned on the parent's userdatum environment table when a call to __index is made. Most routines, like addition and scalar multiplication, are thin wrappings around simple (level 1) routines in the ubiquitous BLAS library. A routine to perform the discrete cosine transform of a vector is also provided based on a routine from the — equally ubiquitous — FFTW library. The C side of the matrix module is kept to the minimal necessary extent for wrapping and performance sensitive routines, and it is further extended by Lua code. Other examples with applications of the matrix module are presented.

Introduction

Lua tables are fast enough for many numerical applications. However, for more specific applications performance is usually critical. One way to achieve a high performance environment in Lua is to extend the language with suitable objects and methods from efficient numerical libraries. Of course, these extensions should profit from Lua's expressiveness and resourcefulness.

In this gem we explore two common numerical extensions: matrices and discrete Fourier transforms. These together allow us to implement many standard scientific computing algorithms including numerical linear algebra, interpolations, and quadratures. Moreover, with Lua we are able to devise very efficient implementations that can beat even well-known scientific computing software!

We assume the reader is fairly familiar with Lua's C API and feels comfortable managing the Lua–C virtual stack. Due to the numerical nature of the text, a background in engineering or numerical analysis is desirable, but not needed; the last section, however, deals with more mathematically sophisticated applications and relies on some knowledge of elementary calculus and linear algebra.

Matrices

In order to keep our interface simple our matrices are real two-dimensional arrays stored in column-major order. Column-major order is essential because we will be using Fortran libraries, and that is Fortran's storage mode for arrays.

The first issue we need to address when representing matrices in Lua is indexing. For a one-dimensional array (a vector) that is simple enough: just create a userdatum with fields size and data and return data[i] for index i. For matrices this is a bit more complicated since we have to go through two dimensions to access an entry. One solution to accessing index (i, j) is to return the i-th row as a matrix which in turn behaves like a vector and returns the j-th entry.

Since matrices are stored in column-major order, rows in a matrix have an offset from one entry to the next, that is, between consecutive columns. This row offset is the number of rows from the matrix referenced by the row. We call this offset *stride*, and we keep track of it in our data structure.

It is not uncommon to use a matrix without referencing its entries, that is, by only using matrix operations. That is actually the most efficient way to use our library: operate in the higher level, say, adding, multiplying or transforming matrices, and leave the heavy-duty operations to the optimized, architecture-dependent libraries under the hood; seasoned users of numerical software usually refer to this strategy as "vectorizing your code". This practice suggests that we should adopt a *lazy interning* strategy and only create the rows

of a matrix when needed, that is, when some entry is requested. To intern the
rows of a matrix we can use the environment table of the matrix's userdatum.
The straightforward association is then to store the i-th row at entry i in the
environment table.

The next issue is memory allocation and deallocation. Suppose that we
decide to allocate a memory block to store both structure (number of rows,
columns, and stride) and data of a matrix; what would happen if we attribute one
row of this matrix to a variable and then garbage-collect the matrix? The data
would be collected along, and the variable would be left dangling. To avoid this,
we separate the structure and data of a matrix and allocate them individually. A
data memory block can only be collected once all the matrices referencing it have
been collected. To this end, we use a *weak-keyed table* where the keys are matrix
userdata holding both the structure and a pointer to a data memory block, and
the values are the referenced data memory blocks. To avoid extra table lookups
we do not create a dedicated table to hold the matrix to data associations, but
instead use the matrix userdatum metatable as a holder.

After all these considerations our matrix should have the following structure:

```
typedef struct {
    int rows;
    int cols;
    int stride;
    lua_Number *data;
} lua_Matrix;
```

To create a new matrix, we then use

```
static int matrix_new (lua_State *L) {
    int r = luaL_checkinteger(L, 1);
    int c = luaL_optinteger(L, 2, 1); /* vector as default */
    int i, n;
    lua_Number *data;
    if (r < 1 || c < 1) luaL_error(L, "invalid size to matrix");
    lua_settop(L, 2);
    n = r * c; /* data size */
    data = lua_newuserdata(L, n * sizeof(lua_Number)); /* data block */
    for (i = 0; i < n; i++) data[i] = 0; /* initialize to zeros */
    pushmatrix(L, r, c, 1, data, 3);
    return 1;
}
```

where `pushmatrix` handles matrix userdatum allocation and matrix-to-data associations in Listing 1. Note that we need to control the size of the stack
(`lua_settop`) in `matrix_new`, since the last parameter to `pushmatrix` is assumed
to be an absolute stack position.

The purpose of `pushmatrix` will be clearer shortly, but it should be intuitive
that we might want to create references to a data block that is already in the

```
static lua_Matrix *pushmatrix (lua_State *L, int rows, int cols,
    int stride, lua_Number *data, int dataidx) {
  lua_Matrix *m = lua_newuserdata(L, sizeof(lua_Matrix));
  lua_pushvalue(L, -1);
  lua_pushvalue(L, dataidx); /* data block */
  lua_rawset(L, LUA_ENVIRONINDEX); /* env[matrix] = data */
  m->data = data;
  m->rows = rows;
  m->cols = cols;
  m->stride = stride;
  lua_pushvalue(L, LUA_ENVIRONINDEX); /* metatable */
  lua_setmetatable(L, -2);
  if (rows > 1 && cols > 1) { /* not a vector? */
    lua_newtable(L); /* new matrix environment */
    lua_setfenv(L, -2);
  }
  return m;
}
```

Listing 1. Auxiliar routine to `matrix_new`.

stack and that needed not to be previously allocated. It is important to observe that all functions that call `pushmatrix` should have the `matrix`'s metatable as environment. Also note that if a matrix is not a vector it receives a new table as its environment to store rows.

One advantage of using a userdatum metatable as environment to its methods is that it is easy and efficient to check a userdatum in the stack: we just need to verify the existence of a metatable and equality of this metatable to the calling function's environment first, as in `checkmatrix` below:

```
static lua_Matrix *checkmatrix (lua_State *L, int pos) {
  lua_Matrix *m = NULL;
  if (lua_isnoneornil(L, pos)
      || !lua_getmetatable(L, pos)) /* no MT? */
    return NULL;
  if (lua_rawequal(L, -1, LUA_ENVIRONINDEX)) /* MT == env? */
    m = (lua_Matrix *) lua_touserdata(L, pos);
  lua_pop(L, 1); /* lua_Matrix MT */
  return m;
}
```

and then check for a null pointer:

```
lua_Matrix *m = checkmatrix(L, pos);
if (m == NULL) luaL_argerror(L, pos, "matrix expected");
```

This routine should be performed whenever we expect a matrix as argument. It assumes that the calling function has the appropriate environment, as pushmatrix does. As a first example, `matrix_size` returns the dimensions of a matrix userdatum:

```
static int matrix_size (lua_State *L) {
  lua_Matrix *m = checkmatrix(L, 1);
  if (m == NULL) luaL_argerror(L, 1, "matrix expected");
  lua_pushinteger(L, m->rows);
  lua_pushinteger(L, m->cols);
  return 2;
}
```

From now on, to make the code conciser, we implicitly perform all matrix checks and assume the arguments given to all functions are consistent: for example, if we are adding two matrices, they should have the same number of rows and columns[1].

Metamethods

To access entries in our matrix we need to implement two metamethods: `__index` and `__newindex`. Let's start with `__index`. Since we want to enable colon call notation for matrix methods — like `m:method(...)` — our `__index` should first check if the key is a number, in which case an entry is requested, or otherwise delegate to a metatable lookup. Next, if the key is numeric, we should check if it is valid, that is, if it is positive and less than or equal to the size of the matrix. Now, according to our previous discussion, we decided for lazily interned rows when indexing a matrix and for a direct entry if the matrix is a vector; if the row is interned, we should just get it from the userdatum's environment, otherwise intern it before returning. This discussion leads to `matrix__index` in Listing 2.

The first part of `__index`, when the key is a valid numeric index, is expected: it returns an entry if the matrix `m` is one-dimensional or a row if not, taking care to store the row if it is not interned yet. The row interning procedure comprises three steps: getting the data block `data` associated with `m` from the function environment; pushing a new row `r` such that `r->rows = 1`, `r->cols = m->cols`, `r->stride = m->rows`, and `r->data = data[k - 1]` using `pushmatrix`, since the `r`'s data block is only referenced, not allocated; and finally interning `r` as the k-th entry in `m`'s environment.

If the key is not a number we resort to a metatable lookup. The *class table* containing all matrix methods is the first upvalue in the `__index` closure; more details on how this is set up will appear when we talk about `luaopen_lmatrix` in the "Library setup" section.

Matrix entry attribution is accomplished through `__newindex` only on one-dimensional matrices. The procedure is very similar, but simpler; it is listed in Listing 3 for the sake of completeness.

We can also implement a `__len` metamethod,

---

[1]Don't worry: the complete code in the repository contains all the consistency checks.

```
static int matrix__index (lua_State *L) {
  lua_Matrix *m = (lua_Matrix *) lua_touserdata(L, 1);
  if (lua_isnumber(L, 2)) {
    int k = lua_tointeger(L, 2);
    if (k < 1 || (m->rows == 1 && k > m->cols)
        || (m->cols == 1 && k > m->rows))
      luaL_error(L, "matrix index out of range");
    if (m->rows == 1 || m->cols == 1) /* vector? */
      lua_pushnumber(L, m->data[(k - 1) * m->stride]);
    else {
      lua_getfenv(L, 1); /* matrix env */
      lua_rawgeti(L, -1, k);
      if (lua_isnil(L, -1)) { /* isn't row k interned? */
        lua_Number *data;
        lua_pop(L, 1); /* nil */
        lua_pushvalue(L, 1); /* matrix */
        lua_rawget(L, LUA_ENVIRONINDEX); /* push data */
        data = (lua_Number *) lua_touserdata(L, -1);
        /* new row: */
        pushmatrix(L, 1, m->cols, m->rows, data + k - 1, 4);
        lua_pushvalue(L, -1);
        lua_rawseti(L, -4, k); /* matrix env[k] = new row */
      }
    }
  }
  else { /* meta lookup? */
    lua_pushvalue(L, lua_upvalueindex(1)); /* class */
    lua_pushvalue(L, 2);
    lua_rawget(L, -2);
  }
  return 1;
}
```

Listing 2. __index metamethod for matrices.

```
static int matrix__newindex (lua_State *L) {
  lua_Matrix *m = (lua_Matrix *) lua_touserdata(L, 1);
  int k;
  lua_Number v;
  if (m->rows > 1 && m->cols > 1)
    luaL_error(L, "can't assign to matrix row");
  if (!lua_isnumber(L, 2) || !lua_isnumber(L, 3))
    luaL_error(L, "wrong type to matrix assignment");
  k = lua_tointeger(L, 2);
  v = lua_tonumber(L, 3);
  if (k < 1 || (m->rows == 1 && k > m->cols)
      || (m->cols == 1 && k > m->rows))
    luaL_error(L, "matrix index out of range");
  m->data[(k - 1) * m->stride] = v;
  return 0;
}
```

Listing 3. __newindex metamethod for matrices.

```
static int matrix__len (lua_State *L) {
  lua_Matrix *a = lua_touserdata(L, 1);
  lua_pushinteger(L, a->rows);
  return 1;
}
```

which is really useful only for column vectors since it only returns the number of rows — we have matrix_size to retrieve both dimensions if needed — and a __tostring metamethod for pretty printing:

```
static int matrix__tostring (lua_State *L) {
  lua_pushfstring(L, "matrix: %p", lua_touserdata(L, 1));
  return 1;
}
```

Since we are dealing with matrices, it is only natural to expect arithmetic metamethods; these will be addressed in pure Lua in the "Lua side" section, after we talk about library bindings.

Core methods

Now, true to our intention of pushing the heavy-duty work to the C side of our library, we need to provide some basic methods that operate over all entries of a matrix.

Our first routine, matrix_fill, sets all entries of a matrix to a number given as argument:

```
static int matrix_fill (lua_State *L) {
  lua_Matrix *m = checkmatrix(L, 1);
  lua_Number s = luaL_checknumber(L, 2);
  int i, n = m->rows * m->cols * m->stride;
  lua_settop(L, 2);
  for (i = 0; i < n; i += m->stride) m->data[i] = s;
  lua_pop(L, 1); /* number */
  return 1; /* matrix */
}
```

This routine is a good example of two important practices in our matrix methods:
the stride should always be used when traversing a matrix, as in the for loop;
and the input matrix should always be returned for notational convenience[2] as
it allows consecutive colon calls in Lua, as in r,c = m:fill(1):size(). Note
that, since we are returning the first argument, we set the stack top and pop the
second argument.

   A useful routine is scalar summation, where a matrix m is added to a number
s yielding a matrix m + s. Although this routine produces a new matrix by
definition, we can use an *in-place* version of it, which we call matrix_shift, by
simply changing the for loop at line 6 in matrix_fill to

```
for (i = 0; i < n; i += m->stride) m->data[i] += s;
```

   In-place routines, where the entries of a matrix are updated, should always
be preferred. This guideline is justified, at this lower level of our implementation, as a way to avoid unnecessary memory allocations; if we really need to copy
a matrix, we should explicitly do so. To perform scalar summation on m and s, for
example, we would copy m to another matrix c and then apply c:shift(s). Scalar
summation will be treated shortly, when we discuss the __add metamethod. An
efficient implementation of a matrix copying routine is presented in the "External libraries" section.

   We also need some operations, that is, routines that take two matrices with
same number of columns and rows and return another matrix consistent with
the arguments. An important operation is the element-wise multiplication[3] of
two matrices:

```
static int matrix_ewmul (lua_State *L) {
  lua_Matrix *a = checkmatrix(L, 1);
  lua_Matrix *b = checkmatrix(L, 2);
  int i, n;
  lua_settop(L, 2);
  n = a->rows * a->cols;
  for (i = 0; i < n; i++) a->data[i * a->stride] *= b->data[i * b->stride];
  lua_pop(L, 1); /* b */
  return 1; /* a */
}
```

---

[2]Some might disagree and point out that such feature actually reduces code readability.
[3]Also known as Hadamard product, but .* should be more familiar.

Note that operation is in-place for the first argument, and that the strides of both arguments are used in the update.

Functional facilities

In the previous section we managed to avoid loops that update entries in a matrix by providing specialized routines. After all, we do not want to incur in metatable overheads for calling __index and __newindex on loops like

```
for i = 1, #v do
  v[i] = foo(v[i])
end
```

if foo is simple enough to be coded as a library core method. However, instead of providing specific methods for every foo function, we should do so only if foo is common enough to warrant a method on its own and such that the resulting method is more efficient than a general method that takes a function like foo as argument. This was the case for the methods in the previous section; now we address the general case.

The best way to avoid the loop in the last listing is to provide a higher level function that takes a matrix m, a function f, and *maps* each entry e in m to f(e) if f(e) is a number:

```
static int matrix_map (lua_State *L) {
  lua_Matrix *m = checkmatrix(L, 1);
  int n, i;
  luaL_checktype(L, 2, LUA_TFUNCTION);
  lua_settop(L, 2);
  n = m->rows * m->cols * m->stride;
  for (i = 0; i < n; i += m->stride) {
    lua_pushvalue(L, -1); /* function */
    lua_pushnumber(L, m->data[i]); /* entry */
    lua_call(L, 1, 1);
    if (lua_isnumber(L, -1)) m->data[i] = lua_tonumber(L, -1);
    lua_pop(L, 1);
  }
  lua_pop(L, 1); /* function */
  return 1; /* matrix */
}
```

Our mapping method is a well-known functional facility. Another useful one is a method that takes the same arguments as matrix_map, an optional initial value for an *accumulator* a, traverses m in increasing column-major order updating a to f(a, e), and returns the final value of a[4]:

---

[4]Exactly, a *left* fold.

```
static int matrix_fold (lua_State *L) {
  lua_Matrix *m = checkmatrix(L, 1);
  int n, i;
  luaL_checktype(L, 2, LUA_TFUNCTION);
  lua_settop(L, 3);
  n = m->rows * m->cols * m->stride;
  for (i = 0; i < n; i += m->stride) {
    lua_pushvalue(L, -2); /* function */
    lua_insert(L, -2); /* accumulator */
    lua_pushnumber(L, m->data[i]); /* entry */
    lua_call(L, 2, 1);
  }
  return 1;
}
```

Besides the obvious difference of returning an accumulation instead of a mapped matrix, note that matrix_fold's function f accepts two arguments instead of one in matrix_map's f. Also note the order in which the arguments to f are pushed in both methods, and how we need to pop the result from lua_call in matrix_map but not in matrix_fold.

A practical application of fold is to compute the sum of the entries of a matrix

```
function sum (m)
  return matrix.fold(m, function(x, y) return x + y end, 0)
end
```

where zero should be given as initial value[5]. Functions of the form

```
function(x, y) return alpha * x + y end
```

are actually very common, and we refer to folds arising from their application as *linear folds*. Since linear folds can be parameterized by alpha, we can define a simpler version of matrix_fold:

```
static int matrix_linfold (lua_State *L) {
  lua_Matrix *m = checkmatrix(L, 1);
  lua_Number alpha = luaL_optnumber(L, 2, 1);
  lua_Number x = luaL_optnumber(L, 3, 0);
  int n, i;
  lua_settop(L, 2);
  n = m->rows * m->cols * m->stride;
  for (i = 0; i < n; i += m->stride) x = x * alpha + m->data[i];
  lua_pushnumber(L, x);
  return 1;
}
```

---

[5]Not necessarily true: we can always test the first argument of the function against nil to provide a suitable initial value, but this is more efficient (not to mention traditional).

Now we can simply define `sum` = `matrix.linfold`. Another neat application of `linfold` is to implement polynomial evaluation using Horner's scheme: if c is a vector where `c[i]` is the coefficient of x^{n+1-i} in a polynomial P of degree n (== `#c - 1`) on x, then

```
function poly (c)
  return function(x) return c:linfold(x) end
end
```

returns an evaluator for P.[6]

External libraries

So far we have been able to provide efficient routines for simple methods in our matrix library. For many other specialized and more complex matrix routines — like computing the norm of a matrix, or solving a linear system, or inverting a matrix — we can resort to optimized code from external libraries.

For our basic needs here we are going to use the high-quality ubiquitous BLAS (Basic Linear Algebra Subprograms) library, or better, an optimized version of it[7].

Our first routine using BLAS is a method to copy matrices:

```
static int matrix_copy (lua_State *L) {
  lua_Matrix *m = checkmatrix(L, 1); /* source */
  lua_Matrix *d = checkmatrix(L, 2); /* dest [optional] */
  int n;
  lua_settop(L, 2);
  n = m->rows * m->cols;
  if (d == NULL) { /* no destination? create new matrix */
    lua_Number *data = lua_newuserdata(L, n * sizeof(lua_Number));
    int inc = 1;
    dcopy_(&n, m->data, &m->stride, data, &inc);
    pushmatrix(L, m->rows, m->cols, 1, data, 3);
  }
  else dcopy_(&n, m->data, &m->stride, d->data, &d->stride);
  return 1;
}
```

The actual copying is done by the BLAS routine at lines 10 and 13, which have signature

```
dcopy_(int *n, double *x, int *incx, double *y, int *incy);
```

---

[6]An easy polynomial object from c:
`getmetatable(c).__call = function(v, x) return v:linfold(x) end`

[7]BLAS is in public domain and can be found at `http://www.netlib.org/blas`. There are many optimized versions of BLAS, depending on the platform, but the most common open source version is ATLAS: `http://math-atlas.sourceforge.net`.

where x is to be copied to y, n is the size of x and y and incx and incy are
the strides of x and y respectively. Note that all arguments are pointers; since
BLAS's natural implementation is in Fortran[8] and Fortran passes arguments
by reference, we should provide variables by their memory addresses. Of course,
we are assuming that lua_Number is defined as double, as in vanilla Lua. We
should also always provide strides for our matrix arguments, similar to what we
did in the previous sections. As a matter of fact, all BLAS routines that we use
here have a common signature pattern: the size of the argument(s) comes first,
followed in some routines by a number meant for scalar multiplication, and then
the matrix argument(s) as a data block address and a stride.

We can provide an optional destination to matrix_copy as a second argument.
If no destination is specified, a data block is allocated and a fresh matrix is
pushed; otherwise, we just copy to the provided destination matrix — of course,
as in our previous routines, we are assuming the matrices are consistent and do
not set any checks in our prototype. The main reason for using a copy destination
is when a procedure performs a copy operation often and we can then use a
buffer to avoid new matrices being created at each operation. Also, note that we
return the copy destination matrix, as expected.

To *scale* a matrix m by a number s, that is, to multiply each element in m by a
scalar s, we use

```
static int matrix_scale (lua_State *L) {
  lua_Matrix *m = checkmatrix(L, 1);
  lua_Number s = luaL_checknumber(L, 2);
  int n = m->rows * m->cols;
  lua_settop(L, 2);
  dscal_(&n, &s, m->data, &m->stride);
  lua_pop(L, 1); /* scale */
  return 1; /* matrix */
}
```

where dscal performs the hard work. The signature pattern should be already
familiar. As usual, we provide references as arguments to dscal and return the
scaled matrix.

Continuing with in-place linear operations, we have a routine that incre-
ments a matrix y by a * x, where a is a (not necessarily positive) optional number and x is consistent with y:

```
static int matrix_add (lua_State *L) {
  lua_Matrix *y = checkmatrix(L, 1);
  lua_Matrix *x = checkmatrix(L, 2);
  lua_Number a = luaL_optnumber(L, 3, 1.0); /* defaults to 1.0 */
  int n;
  lua_settop(L, 3);
  n = y->rows * y->cols;
```

---

[8]This also explains the ugly underscore after a Fortran routine's name when calling from C.

```
    daxpy_(&n, &a, x->data, &x->stride, y->data, &y->stride);
    lua_pop(L, 2); /* x, a */
    return 1; /* y */
}
```

Finally we can compute the dot product of two consistent column vectors with

```
static int matrix_dot (lua_State *L) {
    lua_Matrix *x = checkmatrix(L, 1);
    lua_Matrix *y = checkmatrix(L, 2);
    int n = x->rows * y->rows;
    lua_pushnumber(L,
        ddot_(&n, x->data, &x->stride, y->data, &y->stride));
    return 1;
}
```

where `ddot_` returns a `double`.

Library setup

Now that we have all methods, we can register them in our library. For this purpose we create two `luaL_regs`, one for class methods and other for metamethods,

```
static const luaL_reg lmatrix_func[] = {
    {"new", matrix_new},
    /* ... list other methods here ... */
    {"dot", matrix_dot},
    {NULL, NULL}
};

static const luaL_reg lmatrix_mt[] = {
    {"__newindex", matrix__newindex},
    {"__len", matrix__len},
    {"__tostring", matrix__tostring},
    {NULL, NULL}
};
```

where `__index` is not included in `lmatrix_mt` because it requires the class table as an upvalue.

Our library entry point is in Listing 4. Recall that we need to complete three tasks: set the environment for all our methods as the matrix class metatable for `pushmatrix` and `checkmatrix` to run correctly; define the environment, which holds matrix to data block associations, as a weak-keyed table; and set the class table as an upvalue to `matrix__index`. We also need to fill the class table and metatable, as it is usually done in entry point routines.

The comments in `luaopen_lmatrix` should guide the reader through all these steps, and it is a good exercise to keep track of the stack as the code is executed. Note that the resulting C library should be called `lmatrix` and linked against `-lblas`; adjust your files and compiling targets accordingly.

```
int luaopen_lmatrix (lua_State *L) {
  lua_newtable(L); /* class */
  lua_newtable(L); /* new environment */
  lua_pushvalue(L, -1);
  lua_replace(L, LUA_ENVIRONINDEX); /* set as default environment */
  /* fill class */
  lua_pushvalue(L, -2); /* class */
  luaL_register(L, NULL, lmatrix_func);
  /* class as upvalue for __index: */
  lua_pushcclosure(L, matrix__index, 1);
  lua_setfield(L, -2, "__index");
  luaL_register(L, NULL, lmatrix_mt); /* fill env/metatable */
  /* set environment as weak-keyed table: */
  lua_newtable(L); /* env metatable */
  lua_pushstring(L, "k");
  lua_setfield(L, -2, "__mode");
  lua_setmetatable(L, -2);
  /* return class */
  lua_pop(L, 1); /* env/metatable */
  return 1;
}
```

Listing 4. `lmatrix` entry point.

Lua side

Now that everything is set up on the C side, we can turn to Lua to enhance our library, `matrix.lua`. First of all, we need to load all methods from `lmatrix`,

```
matrix = require "lmatrix" -- create global
module(...)
```

Since `matrix` is global and also the name of our library, the class table returned by `require"lmatrix"` becomes the environment after the call to `module`.

As promised before, we now provide arithmetic metamethods for our matrix userdata based on `add`, `shift`, and `scale` in Listing 5. All these metamethods should return a new table, and so we use `copy` to explicitly copy the values and apply any needed transformation in-place. Depending on the second argument to `__add` and `__sub`, we either `shift` or `add` the copy s of the original matrix a. Note that `__unm` uses consecutive calls in colon notation, which could also be used for `__add`, for example,

```
mt.__add = function(a, b)
  return type(b) == "number" and a:copy():shift(b) or a:copy():add(b)
end
```

but at the cost of being less clear.

```
local mt = getmetatable(matrix.new(1))
mt.__unm = function(m)
  return m:copy():scale(-1)
end
mt.__add = function(a, b)
  local s = a:copy()
  if type(b) == "number" then s:shift(b) else s:add(b) end
  return s
end
mt.__sub = function(a, b)
  local s = a:copy()
  if type(b) == "number" then s:shift(-b) else s:add(b, -1) end
  return s
end
```

Listing 5. Remaining arithmetic metamethods for matrices.

Sometimes we need to fill a vector v of size n *linearly* starting from a number a, v[1] = a, and finishing at a number b, v[n] = b. This could be done in-place, but the need for a new vector is far more common, leading us to linspace

```
function linspace (a, b, n)
  assert(type(a) == "number" and type(b) == "number",
    "number expected")
  local n = n or math_abs(b - a) + 1
  assert(type(n) == "number" and n > 0, "unexpected number of steps")
  local s = (b - a) / (n - 1)
  local l = a - s
  return matrix.new(n):map(function() l = l + s; return l end)
end
```

where math_abs is a local for math.abs defined before the module call.

It is also handy — but not necessarily efficient — to have a method similar to pairs for matrix traversal. The idea is simple: we just need to keep two control variables as row and column indexes and update them as we traverse the matrix. Our first try, in Listing 6, uses coroutines; local variables i and j are controls for row and column indexes respectively, while v is used to cache the i-th row and avoid metatable lookup overhead.

Vectors are treated differently because there is actually only one dimension to traverse. We chose to assert this case here to save space, but it should be simple to implement it by adapting from the matrix case[9]. As expected, coroutine_wrap and coroutine_yield are locals to their respective methods, coroutine.wrap and coroutine.yield.

---

[9]Or by drawing inspiration from ipairs. The complete version of entries can be found in the repository.

```lua
function entries (m)
  local r, c = m:size()
  assert(r > 1 and c > 1, "vectors not allowed")
  local i, j, v = 0, c
  return coroutine_wrap(function()
    repeat
      if j == c then  -- next row
        i, j = i + 1, 1
        v = m[i]
      else  -- next column
        j = j + 1
      end
      coroutine_yield(i, j, v[j])
    until i == r and j == c
  end)
end
```

Listing 6. Matrix traversal routine.

Although coroutines provide a flexible and easy way of implementing matrix iterators, we can do better by simply providing a suitable closure on the control variables that returns instead of yielding[10]:

```lua
function entries (m)
  local r, c = m:size()
  assert(r > 1 and c > 1, "vectors not allowed")
  local i, j, v = 0, c
  return function()  -- closure on i and j
    if j == c then  -- next row
      i, j = i + 1, 1
      v = m[i]
    else  -- next column
      j = j + 1
    end
    if i <= r then return i, j, v[j] end
  end
end
```

Applications

Armed with our `matrix` module, we can now work on some applications. Since the methods we implemented are basic, we need to illustrate their power with some simple—but not elementary!— applications. In the next sections we will first exercise our module with some straightforward tasks to gain more

---

[10]A good exercise is to provide a *stateless* iterator for vectors; check the repository for a solution.

familiarity, and then deal with variations on a theme: interpolation. We will talk about the most common interpolation, Lagrangian interpolation, then discuss discrete Fourier transforms, and finally apply another type of interpolation to compute the quadrature of an arbitrary function.

This section, and in particular the latter part, is more mathematically involved, but we try to keep the text as self-contained as possible without going too much into details. The applications are standard in numerical computing, and the interested reader can refer to a number of good books in the subject to quench the curiosity for more details and the desire for more rigor. The last application demands some degree of familiarity with more complex math, but serves well to illustrate how versatile and powerful Lua is; it was largely inspired by some of Prof. Lloyd Trefethen's works[11].

Basic operations

Let's first take our matrix module for a test drive in an interpreter session. We start off by checking some basic operations:

```
$ lua
Lua 5.1.2  Copyright (C) 1994-2007 Lua.org, PUC-Rio
> require "matrix"
> n = 4
> a = matrix.linspace(1, n) -- [1, 2, ..., n]'
> b = matrix.new(n) -- [0, 0, ..., 0]'
> x = matrix.linspace(0, math.pi, n) -- [0, pi/(n-1), ..., pi]'
> x:copy(b):map(math.cos) -- b[i] = cos(x[i])
> s = -(a + 1 + b - 1 - b) -- __add, __sub, __unm
> for i = 1, n do print(a[i], x[i], b[i], s[i]) end
1       0           1         -1
2       1.0471975511966 0.5   -2
3       2.0943951023932 -0.5  -3
4       3.1415926535898 -1    -4
```

Everything works as expected. Now, as a warm up, let's define a function that returns the dot product of two vectors, that is, the sum of their entry-wise product:

```
function dot(a, b)
  local t = a:copy() -- t[i] = a[i]
  t:ewmul(b) -- t[i] = a[i] * b[i]
  return t:linfold() -- sum_i a[i] * b[i]
end
```

Our `dot` is clearly less efficient than `matrix.dot` since it needs a copy of the first argument, but it provides a good exercise nonetheless. For instance, once

---

[11]In particular, "Is Gauss quadrature better than Clenshaw–Curtis?" and "An extension of Matlab to continuous functions and operators".

we are more comfortable with the colon notation, we can drop temporary local variables like t above and just concatenate operations — being careful not to abuse notation at the cost of readability! — as this quick test shows:

```
> print(a:dot(b), dot(a, b), a:copy():ewmul(b):linfold())
-3.5     -3.5      -3.5
```

Next, we can compute the p-norm of a vector,

$$\|v\|_p = \left(\sum_{i=1}^{n} |v_i|^p \right)^{1/p}$$

by implementing norm directly from the definition:

```
function norm (v, p)
  local s = 0
  for i = 1, #v do s = s + math.abs(v[i]) ^ p end
  return s ^ (1 / p)
end
```

A more generic version of norm could be devised using functional facilities if we observe that we actually do not need to index the entries, but only a fold (summation) over a map on the entries (p-th power of the absolute value):

```
function norm (v, p)
  local f = function(a, e) return a + math.abs(e) ^ p end
  return v:fold(f, 0) ^ (1 / p)
end
```

This last version is directly applicable to matrices as well. As a matter of fact, we can define the Frobenius norm of a matrix, that is, the square root of the sum of its squared entries, as

```
function frobenius (m) return norm(m, 2) end
```

As p grows, the norm converges to the inf-norm

$$\|v\|_\infty = \max_{i=1,\dots,n} |v_i|$$

which we can compute similarly by

```
function infnorm (v)
  local f = function(a, e)
    local t = math.abs(e)
    return a > t and a or t  -- a = max(a, |e|)
  end
  return v:fold(f, 0)
end
```

Let's make a quick check on `norm` and `infnorm`:

```
> for p=1,n do print(p, norm(a,p)) end; print("inf", infnorm(a))
1       10
2       5.4772255750517
3       4.6415888336128
4       4.3376131365334
inf     4
```

As another interesting simple application, we can write a pretty-printer for matrices that returns a row per line and tab-separated column entries. To simplify the implementation, we print a vector as a row even if it is a column vector, and so to print a matrix we just need to iterate over its rows:

```
function pretty (m)
  local r, c = m:size()
  if r == 1 or c == 1 then -- vector?
    local t, l = {}, r > c and r or c -- l = max(r, c)
    for i = 1, l do
      t[i] = string.format("%g", m[i])
    end
    print(table.concat(t, "\t"))
  else
    for i = 1, r do pretty(m[i]) end
  end
end
```

Note the common Lua practice of storing strings to be concatenated in a table and then using `table.concat` instead of using the concatenation operator `..` directly.

Finally, to test our pretty printer, let's create a special type of matrix. A *Pascal* matrix P_n is a symmetric matrix of order n where the elements $p_{i,j}$ in the anti-diagonal where $i + j = k + 2$ are the binomial coefficients in the expansion of $(x + y)^k$, namely

$$p_{i,j} = \binom{i+j-2}{i-1} = \begin{cases} 1, & i = 1 \text{ or } j = 1 \\ p_{i,j-1} + p_{i-1,j}, & \text{otherwise} \end{cases}$$

that is, if we look at the anti-diagonals starting at the top-left corner of the matrix we see the rows of Pascal's triangle. The recursive definition above stems from a well-known binomial coefficient identity[12] and it is particularly useful for our implementation:

---

[12] $\binom{k+1}{l} = \binom{k}{l} + \binom{k}{l-1}$, where $k = i + j - 3$ and $l = i - 1$.

```
function pascal (n)
  local p = matrix.new(n, n)
  local c, r = p[1] -- current and previous rows
  c:fill(1) -- first row, i = 1
  for i = 2, n do -- remaining rows
    r, c = c, p[i]
    c[1] = 1 -- first column, j = 1
    for j = 2, n do -- i ~= 1 and j ~= 1: p[i][j] =
      c[j] = c[j - 1] + r[j] -- = p[i][j-1] + p[i-1][j]
    end
  end
  return p
end
```

An important point to observe in pascal is how we have used references r and c
to the previous, p[i-1], and current, p[i], rows respectively to avoid __index
lookup overheads. Before moving on to more elaborated applications, let's check
pascal (and pretty):

```
> pretty(pascal(5))
1        1        1        1        1
1        2        3        4        5
1        3        6        10       15
1        4        10       20       35
1        5        15       35       70
```

Lagrangian interpolation

Given n points in the plane, (x_i, y_i), $i = 1, \ldots, n$, with distinct x_is, the interpolation problem requires us to find an *interpolating* function f — the interpolant —
such that $f(x_i) = y_i$. Interpolants are usually expressed as a linear combination
of a set of *basis functions* $b_1, \ldots, b_n$: $f(x) = \sum_{k=1}^{n} c_k b_k(x)$, where the coefficients
c_k are to be determined in order to satisfy the interpolation criterion

$$f(x_i) = \sum_{k=1}^{n} c_k b_k(x_i) = y_i, \quad i = 1, \ldots, n. \tag{16.1}$$

Since we have n points, it is reasonable to define f as a suitable polynomial
of degree not greater than $n - 1$. The first natural choice is to pick the mono-
mial basis, $b_k(x) = x^{k-1}$, and find c_k by solving the linear system defined by
equation (16.1):

$$\mathbf{B}^T \mathbf{c} = \begin{bmatrix} 1 & x_1 & \cdots & x_1^{n-1} \\ 1 & x_2 & \cdots & x_2^{n-1} \\ \vdots & \vdots & \ddots & \vdots \\ 1 & x_n & \cdots & x_n^{n-1} \end{bmatrix} \begin{bmatrix} c_1 \\ c_2 \\ \vdots \\ c_n \end{bmatrix} = \begin{bmatrix} y_1 \\ y_2 \\ \vdots \\ y_n \end{bmatrix} = \mathbf{y}$$

The matrix B above has a particular structure where the i-th row can be obtained from the $i - 1$-th row by element-wise product with x; B is then said to be a *Vandermonde* matrix with basis x and order n[13]. We can easily generate a Vandermonde matrix with

```
function vandermonde (b, n) -- basis b, order n
  local _, m = b:size() -- row vector
  local v = matrix.new(n, m)
  local r = (n > 1 and v[1] or v):fill(1)
  for i = 2, n do
    r = r:copy(v[i]):ewmul(b) -- v[i] = v[i-1] .* b
  end
  return v
end
```

Observe how we specify the copy destination in the for loop and use the colon notation: r is v[i-1], and what gets multiplied by b is v[i], the copy destination.

For small n this method works fine, but even though B is not singular it might get ill-conditioned as n grows—even singular to machine precision—resulting in very sensitive coefficients. Moreover, we still need to solve the system in equation (16.1) by providing more bindings to our matrix library from other external libraries[14].

Another option is to specify a different, more numerically stable, basis. For instance, if we choose the *Lagrangian* basis

$$b_k(x) = \prod_{j \neq k} \frac{x - x_j}{x_k - x_j}, \quad k = 1, \ldots, n,$$

then $c_k = y_k$ (B is the identity matrix), and we do not need to solve a linear system anymore. Since f has a closed-form expression now,

$$f(x) = \sum_{k=1}^{n} \left(\prod_{j \neq k} \frac{x - x_j}{x_k - x_j} \right) y_k$$

we can even implement it efficiently using tables. On the other hand, a version using matrices should avoid explicit loops to be more efficient. Listing 7 presents both versions in interp1t and interp1 respectively.

In interp1, b computes $b_k(z)$ by folding a closure on x_k that accumulates the product over x. We avoid the singularity when $j == k$ by comparing xk directly to xj and doing nothing, that is, passing t untouched, if they are equal[15]. After evaluating $b_k(z)$ by mapping b to x, we apply a dot product to y to obtain the

---

[13]Some authors actually define the transpose of a Vandermonde matrix as Vandermonde.

[14]BLAS provides methods for solving linear systems only when B is triangular, and so we need to resort to BLAS's big brother, LAPACK (http://www.netlib.org/lapack), to solve general linear systems. Unfortunately, this is out of our scope.

[15]Assure yourself that it is ok here to compare floating point numbers directly.

```lua
function interp1t(x, y)
  local n = #x
  assert(n == #y, "sizes differ")
  return function(z) -- f
    local p = 0 -- f(z)
    for k = 1, n do
      local xk = x[k]
      local t = 1 -- b_k(z)
      for j = 1, n do
        if j ~= k then
          local xj = x[j]
          t = t * (z - xj) / (xk - xj)
        end
      end
      p = p + t * y[k]
    end
    return p
  end
end

function interp1(x, y) -- x, y: column vectors
  local n = #x
  assert(n == #y, "sizes differ")
  local p = matrix.new(n) -- proxy
  return function(z)
    local b = function(xk) -- b_k(z)
      return x:fold(function(t, xj)
        return xk == xj and t or t * (z - xj) / (xk - xj)
      end, 1)
    end
    return matrix.dot(x:copy(p):map(b), y)
  end
end
```

Listing 7. Lagrangian interpolation using tables, `interp1t`, and matrices, `interp1`.

final linear combination. Since we would alter x by mapping b, we need to use a proxy by copying x to p.

Despite using functional facilities, `interp1` is still slower than `interp1t`, approximately two times slower on my machine. However, since we often want to interpolate many numbers at a time, we could provide a version of `interp` that takes a vector z of abscissae, instead of a single one, to be interpolated and returns a vector containing $f(z)$. This version is illustrated in Listing 8.

```
function interp(x, y) -- x, y: column vectors
  local n = #x
  assert(n == #y, "sizes differ")
  return function(z)
    local m = #z -- column vector
    local v, t, p = matrix.new(m), matrix.new(m), matrix.new(m)
    for k = 1, n do
      local xk = x[k]
      t:fill(1) -- b_k(z), a vector
      for j = 1, n do
        if j ~= k then
          local xj = x[j]
          t:ewmul(z:copy(p):shift(-xj)) -- t = t .* (z - x[j])
          t:scale(1 / (xk - xj)) -- t = t / (x[k] - x[j])
        end
      end
      v:add(t, y[k])
    end
    return v
  end
end
```

Listing 8. Vectorized Lagrangian interpolation.

We can think of `interp` as a vectorized version of `interp1t`. However, if we add another loop in `interp1t` to compute interpolations for each entry in z, and hence offer a facility similar to `interp`, we now observe that `interp` is faster than its table version. As a matter of fact, it is close to five times faster on my machine.

Fast Fourier transforms

While modeling cyclic data, it is often more appropriate to use trigonometric functions — sines and cosines — as basis functions instead of polynomials, as we did in the previous section. Also in contrast to common polynomial interpolation, *trigonometric* interpolation presents a recursive structure and can be done efficiently by an algorithm called the *fast Fourier transform* (FFT).

FFTs compute *discrete Fourier transforms* (DFTs): given a complex data vector $\mathbf{x} = [x_0, \ldots, x_{n-1}]^T$, its DFT $\mathbf{y} = [y_0, \ldots, y_{n-1}]^T$, a consistent complex vector, is such that

$$y_m = \sum_{k=0}^{n-1} x_k \omega_n^{mk}, \quad m = 0, \ldots, n-1,$$

where $\omega_n = \exp(-2\pi i/n)$. This is also known as the *forward*, or direct, transform, and a similar expression exists for the *backward*, or inverse, transform that maps y back to x.

Another important transform arises when x is real and even around x_0 and x_{n-1}, that is,

$$\mathbf{x} = [x_0, x_1, \ldots, x_{n-2}, x_{n-1}, x_{n-2}, \ldots, x_1],$$

where the actual size of x is $2(n-1)$. In this case, we can save space by only declaring the first n entries of x. Moreover, the DFT of x is also a real and even vector, and so we can also save space by returning only the first n entries. By considering only the non-redundant first half of x and computing its DFT assuming evenness, we have a *discrete cosine transform* (DCT). DCTs can be computed using an adapted version of FFT that deals with storage for reals only and evenness: a fast cosine transform (FCT).

The most well-known library for FFT computing is FFTW (Fastest Fourier Transform in the West)[16], and that is the library we are going to use to implement a FCT for our matrix library. FFTW works through the concept of *planners*: it does not use a fixed, one-size-fits-all algorithm, but it rather learns the fastest way to compute the transform on the underlying hardware and then executes the learned plan to yield the desired transform.

Our new method, `matrix_fct`, is presented in Listing 9. Since the actual size of x is $2(n-1)$, we need to allocate it physically to perform the transform. We use `buf` for this intent. Besides the (now hopefully familiar) routine of allocating a matrix's data block (`data`) and then pushing its structure with `pushmatrix`, the DCT is computed by: copying the first half of x to `buf` using `dcopy` (no need to initialize `buf` as it is updated in-place); creating a `plan` for a DCT, which is specified as real-to-real one-dimensional (`fftw_plan_r2r_1d`) real-even (`FFTW_REDFT00`) forward transform; executing and destroying the plan; and finally copying back the first half of `buf` to `data`. Since the transforms computed by FFTW are unnormalized, we fix this by scaling `data` by the inverse of x's actual size.

A nice optimization to this method would be the implementation of a buffering system with `lua_Number` units to avoid the creation and collection of `buf` at every run of `matrix_fct`[17]. FCTs are the core of our next, and final, application.

Clenshaw–Curtis quadrature

Suppose now that we want to compute the integral of an arbitrary function f. An approximative approach is to sample f at a number of distinct abscissae x_k,

---

[16]FFTW is free software and can be found at http://www.fftw.org.

[17]In case you are wondering: yes, there is one such implementation in the repository, and it is very educative on its own.

```
static int matrix_fct (lua_State *L) {
  lua_Matrix *x = checkmatrix(L, 1);
  lua_Number s, *data, *buf;
  fftw_plan plan;
  int n, inc = 1;
  lua_settop(L, 1); /* needed for pushmatrix */
  n = (x->rows == 1) ? x->cols : x->rows; /* x is a vector */
  /* fct(x)'s data block: */
  data = lua_newuserdata(L, n * sizeof(lua_Number));
  /* DCT */
  buf = lua_newuserdata(L, 2 * (n - 1) * sizeof(lua_Number));
  dcopy_(&n, x->data, &x->stride, buf, &inc);
  plan = fftw_plan_r2r_1d(n, buf, buf, FFTW_REDFT00, FFTW_FORWARD);
  fftw_execute(plan);
  fftw_destroy_plan(plan);
  dcopy_(&n, buf, &inc, data, &inc);
  lua_pop(L, 1); /* buf */
  /* renormalization */
  s = 1.0 / (2 * (n - 1));
  dscal_(&n, &s, data, &inc);
  pushmatrix(L, n, 1, 1, data, 2);
  return 1;
}
```

Listing 9. A fast cosine transform method for vectors.

obtain an interpolant $\hat{f}$ as an approximation to f, and compute $\hat{f}$'s integral, which should be simpler. The whole process can be summarized by

$$\int_a^b f(x)dx \approx \int_a^b \hat{f}(x)\,dx = \int_a^b \sum_{k=1}^n c_k b_k(x)\,dx = \sum_{k=1}^n c_k \left(\int_a^b b_k(x)\,dx \right) = \sum_{k=1}^n c_k w_k$$

which amounts to computing the c_ks and w_ks. This procedure is known as *interpolatory quadrature*.

It turns out that if we choose the basis functions to be *Chebyshev* polynomials and judiciously choose the sampling abscissae x_k, than c_k and w_k are easy to evaluate. The n-th Chebyshev polynomial is defined on the interval $[-1, 1]$ by $T_n(x) = \cos(n\cos^{-1}(x))$, which hints at the oscillatory nature of T_n[18]. In fact, Chebyshev polynomials have an important property known as equi-oscillation: successive extrema of T_n are equal in magnitude and alternate in sign. Remarkably, if we choose the sampling points $x = \{x_k\}$ to be these extrema, known as *Chebyshev points*,

$$x_k = \cos\left(\frac{k\pi}{n}\right), \quad k = 0, 1, \ldots, n,$$

---

[18]$\cos^{-1}(x)$ is $\arccos(x)$, not $1/\cos(x)$, and T_n is *really* a polynomial.

then c_k can be obtained by a discrete cosine transform on $f(\mathbf{x})$ and w_k are simply:

$$w_k = \int_{-1}^{1} T_k(x)\, dx = \begin{cases} 0, & k \text{ odd} \\ 2(1 - k^2)^{-1}, & k \text{ even} \end{cases}$$

The quadrature we obtain by using Chebyshev polynomials is known as *Clenshaw–Curtis* quadrature. It has many attractive properties besides simplicity: it is also stable, accurate, and progressive. By progressiveness we mean that we do not need to re-evaluate f at every sample point in case we want to enhance the precision by adding more sample points. For our particular choice of x_k, if we have n sample points and want $2n - 1$, then only $n - 1$ new points and function evaluations are needed.

Back to Lua, we can implement this discussion with Listing 10. cheb has only one method, new, that returns an object to compute an approximate definite integral using Clenshaw–Curtis quadrature. Method new takes a function f and a number of points n as arguments, computes x, the Chebyshev points, and w, the integral weights, using linspace, and returns a table storing f and n with a __call metamethod to compute the quadrature.

To allow general, but finite, integration limits — since Chebyshev polynomials are defined only on $[-1, 1]$ — we apply a linear transformation:

$$\int_{a}^{b} f(t)\, dt = \left(\frac{b - a}{2} \right) \int_{-1}^{1} f\left(\frac{b - a}{2} x + \frac{b + a}{2} \right) dx.$$

There is still room for improvement in cheb. For one, we could provide a precision as argument instead of the number of sample points, and control the precision by selecting the appropriate number of points. Another improvement, or better, extension, would be to implement an interpolation routine that computes an approximation to $f(x)$ at arbitrary x based on our Chebyshev interpolant.

By choosing a suitable transformation, we can even approximate improper integrals. Consider the tangent transform,

$$\int_{a}^{b} f(t)\, dt = \frac{\pi}{2} \int_{2\tan^{-1}(a)/\pi}^{2\tan^{-1}(b)/\pi} f\left(\tan \frac{\pi x}{2} \right) \sec^2 \frac{\pi x}{2}\, dx,$$

and its implementation based on cheb in Listing 11.

With ttintegral we can now implement, for example, pnorm, the cumulative function for the standard normal distribution:

```
do
  local f = function(x)
    return 1 / math.sqrt(2 * math.pi) * math.exp(-x * x / 2)
  end
  local g = ttintegral(f, 1000)
  pnorm = function(x) return g(-math.huge, x) end
end
```

```
require "matrix"
local linspace, dot = matrix.linspace, matrix.dot
local pi, cos, setmetatable = math.pi, math.cos, setmetatable

module(...)

function new (f, n)
  local x = linspace(0, pi, n + 1):map(cos) -- Chebyshev points
  local w = linspace(0, n, n + 1):map(function(i) -- weights
    return (i % 2 == 0) and 2 / (1 - i * i) or 0
  end)
  return setmetatable({f=f, n=n}, {
    __call = function(c, a, b) -- integral by linear transform
      local s = (b - a) / 2
      -- compute f(s * x + (b + a) / 2)
      local p = x:copy()
      p:scale(s):shift((b + a) / 2) -- p = s * p + (b + a) / 2
      p:map(f) -- p = f(p)
      -- compute interpolating coeffs
      local c = p:fct():scale(2) -- c = 2 * dct(p)
      c[1], c[n] = c[1] / 2, c[n] / 2
      -- compute integral
      return s * dot(w, c)
    end
  })
end
```

Listing 10. The cheb module.

```
require "cheb"
function ttintegral (func, n) -- tangent transform
  local p2 = math.pi / 2
  local f = function(x)
    local v = x * p2
    local c = 1 / math.cos(v) -- sec(pi * x / 2)
    return func(math.tan(v)) * c * c
  end
  local c = cheb.new(f, n)
  return function(a, b)
    return p2 * c(math.atan(a) / p2, math.atan(b) / p2)
  end
end
```

Listing 11. Improper integral through tangent transform.

We can also implement the gamma function:

```
gamma = function(t, n)
  assert(t >= 1, "argument is lesser than 1: " .. t)
  local n = n or 1000
  local f = function(x) return x ^ (t - 1) * math.exp(-x) end
  return ttintegral(f, n)(0, math.huge)
end
```

Conclusions

In this gem, we have implemented a matrix library and a few applications. Lua's resources, including userdatum environments, metamethods, function closures, first class functions, and proper lexical scoping were invaluable for a simple yet powerful implementation: our matrices have lazily interned rows, efficient functional facilities, and proper arithmetic operators, while our Chebyshev interpolants can compute the integral of any function with arbitrary precision and limits of integration.

Thanks to the C API, it is almost straightforward to extend Lua by either wrapping routines from high performance, specialized, external libraries or providing your own routines. We hope this gem inspires the reader to create new libraries — especially numerical ones! — by following the same approach. One could also extend the current implementation as suggested in the footnotes, or even by enhancing the matrix object to account for multidimensionality and a typing system that would elect the best routine for a specific task if the matrix were, say, triangular or symmetric. For an implementation of these latter improvements and other scientific computing facilities, including random deviates for a number of probability distributions, complex number support, and specialized functions, the reader can refer to the *Numeric Lua* project at http://numlua.luaforge.net.

17

Complex Structured Data Input

Julio M. Fernández-Díaz

Lua is very good at describing (often complex) data structures through tables. However, apart from spotting syntax errors, Lua cannot deal directly with the logical structure of read tables.

This gem explains a small library which, in combination with data templates, enables the user to: introduce complex, controlled structures to any depth; include test functions to check the validity of the input; declare optional values at any level for missing fields, if desired; etc. An example, including the appropriate driver, which runs in a convenient protected mode, is also shown.

The problem

As a developer, you are preparing a program (to be used by other people) which requires (relatively general) data to be processed: control parameters in a chemical plant, objects characteristics in an arcade game, etc.

You may also wish to develop programs that allow some external configuration: sometimes for self use; at other times, the end users wish to adapt the program to their particular needs (which always adds value to the product).

On other occasions, you are preparing a complex program with a graphical user interface: windows, menus, buttons, radio-buttons, etc. A tool to facilitate the implementation would be welcome: a system that describes the menu structure both well and clearly (with the corresponding actions) would be very useful. Then, by adding only a general function for managing the structure, we have nearly all the necessary parts for an operative program.

Let us show an example (for the sake of brevity, this is somewhat simplified compared with a more realistic case). In a program to make book covers, a box is described in the form:

```
box "box 1" "front" "c" 90 10 40 10 20 0.5 0.3 0
```

Our program manages it well, but the user will probably have to go to the 'manual' to understand the meaning of each item. It is evident that a descriptive format (even with comments) is much better:

```
box {
  -- this is a comment
  id = "box 1",
  place = "front",
  adjust = "c",
  angle = 90,                    -- another comment
  position = {x = 10, y = 40},
  width = 10,
  height = 20,
  fill = {color = {r = 0.5, g = 0.3, b = 0}}
}
```

This second fragment, apart from data, is a chunk of Lua code, which has to be processed using a function named box (defined in another place inside the program). Some of the characteristics of the box may even be optional and have default values. These improvements are easy to implement in the latter case, but not in the former.

Lua is very good at describing data with a complex structure through tables (see Section 10.1 in PIL2 for an example). However, the Lua interpreter is not able to deal directly with the logical structure of those tables, to determine whether a field must exist or not, to distinguish correct fields from wrong ones, etc. For example, if the user types plaxe instead of place, the program should throw an error. If the user inputs r = 2 (forbidden because the amount of red must be between 0 and 1), the program must signal it. Therefore, a data description 'shell' should be included.

Besides, the possibility of optional fields (with default values or not) should also exist. Sometimes the program should hinder the use of fields different from a given set, but at other times this restriction is inadmissible (because the data file is also used by other programs with diverse necessities).

Thus, we have a problem which may be stated as follows:

> *To develop a Lua library that allows the input of complex structured data, with complete control and validation of the contents.*

The solution

The initial idea was to include in the program a table with the structure of the desired input data and to compare the value type field by field. However, this

```
require "datatest"
local positive  = datatest.numrange(0, math.huge)
local purecolor = {VALUE = 1, TEST = datatest.numrange(0, 1)}
local rgbcolor = {r = purecolor, g = purecolor, b = purecolor}
local places = datatest.inset({"front", "back", "spine"},string.lower)

template = {} -- to store data templates
template.box = {ALLSTRICT = true,
  CONTAINS = {
    id       = {VALUE = "a box"},
    place    = {VALUE = "front", TEST = places},
    fill     = {OPTIONAL = true,
                 CONTAINS = {color = {CONTAINS = rgbcolor}}},
    adjust   = {VALUE = "l", OPTIONAL = true, DEFAULT = "l",
                 TEST = datatest.inset({"l", "c", "r"}, string.lower)},
    angle    = {VALUE = 0, OPTIONAL = true, DEFAULT = 0},
    position = {CONTAINS = {x = {VALUE = 0}, y = {VALUE = 0}}},
    width    = {VALUE = 10, TEST = positive},
    height   = {VALUE = 20, TEST = positive},
  }
}
```

Listing 1. An example of a template for a `box` in a cover design. Other templates (`template.arc`, `template.isbn`, etc.) could be developed for other elements.

does not allow other validations. For example, we could not distinguish between different numbers (some correct, others not).

The solution found uses data templates as well, but also includes information about the actual fields. Besides, the template structure must be related to the data to be input, with the aim of facilitating their management from Lua.

Using the above example, we shall present and comment on a suitable template for a box. Subsequently, we shall set out the design of a function to manage the data. A version for the example is shown in Listing 1 (in a realistic case, more fields could appear). This listing is almost self-descriptive. The template is a table with sub-tables. The fields placed at an odd depth are control fields, with information about the treatment of the fields placed at the next depth. A level n in the data table corresponds to fields in CONTAINS (or VALUE) at level $2n$ in the template. The possible control fields are described in Table 1.

In the example, only the shown fields are allowed, because in the first level the control ALLSTRICT = true is declared. Some fields are optional, such as fill and angle, although the latter has a default value of 0 if not given, due to its control DEFAULT = 0. For some fields, the unique check is data type (i.e., id must be a string), but other fields have testing functions (such as the color element fill.color.r: the number must be between 0 and 1). The adjust field, which is optional with a default value "l", is solely able to take the values "l", "L", "c", "C", "r" or "R".

VALUE	Indicates a terminal datum; it is any value of the expected type.
CONTAINS	Indicates a non-terminal datum; it is a table with the substructure of the branch.
TEST	A function to check the value in case of terminal data.
STRICT	true if the field cannot contain other fields not provided in CONTAINS.
ALLSTRICT	true if the CONTAINS fields and all embedded ones cannot contain other fields not given in the corresponding CONTAINS.
OPTIONAL	true if the field is optional.
DEFAULT	Default value for an optional field if not provided in data; both terminal and non-terminal data can have default values.

Table 1. Control fields in templates. Table templates can be recursively nested through CONTAINS fields to any depth. VALUE and CONTAINS cannot be used simultaneously at the same level.

The content of a field VALUE is any value of the expected type (even a function or a table), which is used for type checking. The contents of the field CONTAINS ('non-terminal data') must be a table with a sub-template.

Although the description of possible contents in a box is somewhat verbose, the versatility is apparent. It should be borne in mind that the template is designed once, and that the user 'does not see it'.

The programmer should develop checking routines for the data. The following, which appear in the example, are interesting:

- function datatest.numrange (x1, x2) returns a function that checks whether a numerical value falls within a range. x1 and x2 are numerical values.

- function datatest.inset (t, f) returns a function that checks whether a value falls within a set of values. t is a homogeneous table with values (strings, numbers, etc.); f is a function to transform the target and the fields of t before the comparison (such as string.upper, math.abs, etc.). If f is not provided, no conversion is assumed.

These routines are included in the appropriate place in the Gems repository (as part of a complete example). Other similar datatest.* routines can be developed to check other entry types.

In Listing 1, we defined and used several variables (positive, purecolor, and rgbcolor) based on the above functions, because the code is clearer.

The routines set out in http://lua-users.org/wiki/LuaTypeChecking could also be useful for data checking (but be careful, as another box function is given there which has no relationship with ours).

The recursive character of the data structure allows a relatively simple process via a recursive function: datatest.main (template, data, label) verifies whether table `data` agrees with `template`. The argument `label` is used to display the table name if an error is detected. The function returns `true` and a void string `""` if all is correct, and `false` plus an error message otherwise. An outline of this function is shown in Listing 2. (In the repository, the library `datatest` is provided as a `module`.)

Justification and explanation

Although the ensemble `datatest.main/template` now appears somewhat simple, its development underwent several improvement stages. The first improvement, from the initial idea set out at the beginning of Section 17, consisted of a more advanced type checking through test functions. One possibility which was initially analyzed was to add an auxiliary table to these. However, some fields do not require more than a type checking (such as some text labels or unbounded numbers), and this is not convenient. Finally, the tests were added to the template as *control fields* (three initially, CONTAINS, VALUE and TEST).

After the idea of control fields was 'discovered', others were included. STRICT is of major usefulness: by means of this, errors in the field names are detected, since we can enforce their uniqueness at a given level in the template. This control gave rise to ALLSTRICT, which extended the same idea to all the sub-tables from a given depth.

However, the user should sometimes not be forced to give data for all fields. This was achieved by means of the control OPTIONAL. On other occasions, it is of interest for the program to give some values for optional, not provided fields in data. This was achieved using the control DEFAULT, which contains the default value.

For the sake of brevity, the explanation of `datatest.main`, following Listing 2, is simplified. The reader can explore the complete routine in the repository. The main characteristic of the routine is that it is a wrapper, which hides some necessary variables inside it, when treating the successive template levels.

In the first lines, the function prepares two containers for possible error messages and stores a pointer to the original table (to use it in default value assignment inside the recursive function that follows).

Then it defines the local function `maintest`, which actually does the work and calls itself if necessary. As arguments, it has: a template (or sub-template) `template`, the target table (or sub-table) `data`, a Boolean variable `allstrict` to indicate whether all branches of the target table could have more fields than the template or not, and finally the name of the field to process, `field`.

After the definition of `maintest`, the first invocation of it appears, with `nil` for the last two arguments. Finally, `datatest.main` returns with the appropriate messages if an error is detected.

We shall now describe the function `maintest`. At its beginning, some local variables are defined from the information in the control fields of `template` (VALUE, OPTIONAL, etc.). Also, a variable to store the error status of the execution and a label for displaying purposes are prepared.

```
function datatest.main (template, data, label)  -- the wrapper
  label = label or ""
  local cart, precart, torig = "", "", data

  local function maintest (template, data, allstrict, field)
    -- prepare some local variables:
    field = field or ""
    local ok = true
    local contains, value = template.CONTAINS, template.VALUE --etc.

    <<check if one (and only one) of CONTAINS and VALUE is present>>
    <<check if a field is not provided and it must be>>
    <<set the DEFAULT value if an OPTIONAL field is not given
      and put and adequate label in precart>>

    if value ~= nil then    -- terminal data
      <<check if type of value is correct>>
      <<check with TEST function>>
    else                    -- non-terminal data
      <<check if data is a non-void table>>
      <<check if contains has extra fields than allowed>>

      for key, val in pairs(contains) do
        local name = field .. (field == "" and "" or "." )
                           .. tostring(key)
        ok = maintest(val, data[key], allstrict, name)
        if not ok then return ok end
      end
    end
    precart = "" -- reset it after a DEFAULT field was analyzed
    return ok
  end -- of maintest

  local ok = maintest(template, data)
  return ok, cart == "" and "" or precart .. cart
end
```

Listing 2. Outline of `datatest.main`. Parts of the code summarized inside <<···>>.

Then the function checks CONTAINS and VALUE fields, which are incompatible, but one of which must appear. After this, the routine analyzes whether the field exists in the data table. If the field is not optional and is not provided, an error message is prepared and the error is returned. If the field is optional and is not given, but it has a DEFAULT field, this is assigned to the corresponding one in the original table torig. (We use setvar from http://lua-users.org/wiki/ SetVariablesAndTablesWithFunction in this part.) A message is placed in an auxiliary container (precart) to indicate the analysis of the default value (this might have been incorrectly input in the template). It is evident that an error in a template DEFAULT field is more a problem of programming than of the user: the latter could inform the developer of it. Nevertheless, the user should check the template with an extensive set of testing data before deployment of the program.

After that, the routine tests whether the item is terminal. If so, the data type is checked versus the one in the template. Then the corresponding TEST function is called to verify whether the value is valid, returning an error otherwise.

When data are not terminal, the field in data and template must contain tables. If this is so, the presence of more fields than allowed (if STRICT or ALLSTRICT are true) is analyzed, returning an error in that case. Otherwise all the fields in the sub-table are analyzed by recursively invoking maintest for each one with the appropriate arguments.

How to use

A driver for the above example is shown in Listing 3. Data processing is performed in a protected environment, which allows assignments, calling functions from the libraries math, string, table, and the ones defined in process (like box). This methodology is known as 'sandboxing'. The use of a protected environment is very important in the present case: it avoids undue use of some dangerous functions (like os.execute and os.remove) by the user.

Employing this method, variables can be included in the data file for their use in some parts of the data. For example, we can define a color:

```
reddish = {r = 0.8, g = 0.4, b = 0.4}
```

to be used subsequently, in a consistent way, in any place in which we need this color by putting color = reddish. If auxiliary variables are used, we also recommend strict.lua to avoid problems with the variables used and not defined by mistake.

On the other hand, as the data file is a chunk of Lua, we can program inside it. We can obtain some effects with loops and conditionals; for example:

```
for k = 1, 10 do
  w = k; h = 11-k
  if k ~= 3 then box{width = w, height = h, <<other fields>>} end
end
```

```
require "datatest"; require "template"

local process = {} -- to include other processes: isbn, text, etc.

function process.box (b)
  local ok, msg = datatest.main(template.box, b, "box")
  if msg ~= "" then print(msg) end
  if not ok then return end
  <<the appropriate code for make a box with 'b'>>
end

-- fname stores the name of the data file taken from argument #1
local fname = arg[1]
local proc, msg = loadfile(fname)
if not proc then
  print(msg); os.exit(1)
end

setfenv(proc, {math = math, string = string,
               table = table, box = process.box})

local ok, msg = pcall(proc)
if not ok then
  print(msg); os.exit(2)
end
```

Listing 3. A simple driver (in protected mode) for data processing.

In this case, we could also export pairs, ipairs, tonumber, tostring, and perhaps os.time and os.date by means of setfenv.

In the data file, we can also define functions to be applied to the data before processing them inside box (in the example). Any variable definition, whether local or global, used in the data file (using the driver shown above) remains internal in it and does not pollute other environments of the program.

Weaknesses and suggested improvements

The main weakness of the proposed system is that the user might define a substitution for the function box inside the data file, for example:

```
local function box (b) <<some code>> end
```

From this point on, our (correct) function box is no longer accessible inside the data file. This problem is impossible to overcome because a local variable can always be defined without limitations inside the data file[1]. However, this

---

[1]In contrast, a global table can be defined read-only with a metatable; see PIL2, p. 127.

problem is general in character: we cannot ensure the correctness of user input for every bit in the data. Actually, if we want the great versatility in inputting provided by the use of Lua chunks as data, we have to bear the potential misuses.

Another limitation of the proposed method (not of the datatest/template system, but of the use of functions like box) is that it is not possible to share pieces of tables, unless they have been previously defined as variables with values.

To avoid this, we can directly use assignments to tables instead of function callings. Security is also easily controlled by using setfenv to process the data file. In this case, different boxes can be handled as sub-tables; for example:

```
box[1] = {<<some data>>}
box[2] = {<<some other data>>}
```

This method allows the direct re-use of data, because we can do:

```
box[2] = box[1]
box[2].angle = 45
```

and the second box is equal to the first, except for angle. The checking of data is now:

```
local ok, msg = datatest.main(template.box, box[1], "box 1")
local ok, msg = datatest.main(template.box, box[2], "box 2")
```

With respect to enhancements, more control fields can be defined. We could add others similar to VALUE, STRICT, etc., bearing information related to the process of the actual fields. This obviously implies the subsequent modification of datatest.main. For example, a control field NOCASE could be added: if true, the program would not distinguish lower and upper cases in the field names (converting, for example, all names to lower case). Another possibility is to include a control field FIXED which assigns a fixed value to the corresponding data field, irrespective of user input (the corresponding field is even forbidden in the data file).

As described above, in the case of error datatest.main promptly returns control to the calling function or chunk, along with an error message. Therefore, if several errors are scattered in the data file, they will be spotted in successive runs of the program. This keeps error control simple. One possible (though difficult) improvement would consist in storing all error messages, returning them after the whole data table has been analyzed. In this case, however, some errors would interfere with one another, thus confusing the user, and we prefer the simple approach used here.

Conclusions

Sooner or later programmers using Lua are confronted with often complex data input, which is frequently not under their control (because other people use the program). A method that allows management of the data, with contents control and validation, is thus convenient.

This gem presented a solution to this problem, using table templates and combining these with a function that does the checking. The templates are tables with control fields placed at odd depth levels, whereas even levels are used for the proper data field names and values. The template is actually a qualitative-quantitative description of the input data to be treated.

Control fields are used to define characteristics of data fields: whether these are optional or not, whether they have default values, whether other fields not present in the template are allowed in the data, and to define data check functions.

From a programming point of view, the solution (mainly) uses a function that behaves as a wrapper and includes a recursive function that performs the checking of the data table level by level. The number of code lines is small due to the facilities provided by Lua: tables, recursivity, and the first-class character of functions (among other questions).

An example driver is included accompanying this main function. This works in an appropriate environment to protect the data processing from possible undue uses.

Finally, due to its versatility, this library can be used to neatly develop programs for user-friendly data input, adaptive configuration of programs and graphical user interface design, among other tasks.

18

Lua Implementations of Common Data Structures

Matthew M. Burke

In Lua, as with any programming language, one should learn the style and idioms that best take advantage of the language's features, rather than utilizing techniques from other languages. Jung and Brown state "[b]ecause of tables' flexibility, you often don't need a customized data structure. Just ask yourself how you most often want to access your data — usually an associative table or an array will do the job" [7, pg. 157].

Lua provides a single built-in data structuring mechanism, the "table," which combines the functionality of (re-sizable) arrays and hashes. Any of the fundamental data structures and their associated algorithms can be implemented using Lua tables, but it is not always clear how best to do so. After a brief discussion of how tables are implemented in Lua, this article describes implementations of several of the most important and common data structures: lists, stacks and queues, trees, graphs, and sets. Next, several specialized data structures, including dictionaries and multisets, are presented. Finally, a few tips are provided on how to structure data in concordance with the spirit of Lua.

Code examples

Good Lua practice dictates that the functions associated with a data structure be collected in a (meta)table associated with the data structure. Not only does this reduce pollution of the global namespace, but it allows one to program in an object-oriented style.

In order to focus on implementation techniques, the code examples in this article do not include error checking. More robust implementations of the data structures that follow Lua best practices can be found at the book's web site.

In discussing the data structures presented in this article, runtime characteristics of the implementations are noted. While these runtime characterizations are correct, they should not be taken too seriously for two reasons. First, although Lua is an interpreted language, Lua scripts are byte-compiled and run on a virtual machine that is quite fast. The VM is most likely fast enough for your purposes and, as Donald Knuth states, "premature optimization is the root of all evil" [8, pg. 268]. While proper programming technique suggests one choose effective implementations, it is the author's experience that Lua's speed is usually not a limiting factor. Second, in those cases in which Lua's speed is limiting, one is almost always better off extending Lua with a C library rather than worrying about optimizing Lua code.

Abstract data types and common functionality

The following sections discuss several common data structures. In each case the data structure is presented by means of its Abstract Data Type (ADT) definition. An ADT definition is a description of the functions which make up a data type's public interface.

All ADTs are assumed to have the methods presented in Table 1. These methods will not be repeated in the various ADTs.

isEmpty()	Return a Boolean indicating if the data structure is empty
size()	Return the number of items in the data structure

Table 1. Functions common to all ADTs.

One easily implements isEmpty as

```
function DS:isEmpty()    return (DS:size() == 0)    end
```

It is tempting to make use of table.getn for implementing size. But there are three points to consider: First, table.getn only returns the size of the array portion of a table. Not only does it not count entries in the hashed portion of the table, but if there is a gap in the sequence of integer keys, the indices following the gap are not counted[1]. Second, table.getn is $O(n)$. Finally, and, perhaps, obviously, implementations which use more than one table, particularly linked data structures, cannot be sized using table.getn.

For these reasons, it is preferable to store the size explicitly in the data structure. Doing so yields an $O(1)$ implementation, although care must be taken to ensure that this value is properly updated as the data structure is manipulated. Implementations will accompany the discussions of the various data structures in this article.

---

[1]This follows from the fact that non-sequential integer keys are stored in the hash part of the table.

Lua tables

Lua tables function as a combination of (adjustable-size) arrays and associative arrays depending on what kinds of values are used as keys. In this article, a Lua table that has exclusively integral keys is referred to as an array, provided the table also satisfies the condition that there are no gaps in the sequence of key values. Tables that do not qualify as arrays will be referred to as *mixed tables*, or simply, *tables*.

Lua table implementation

The implementation of tables in Lua 5.x is described in [3]. Of course, the full details are always available in the source code. The following is a brief exposition of the most important points.

Tables have a hash portion and an array portion, either (or both) of which can be zero bytes in size. Both portions are resized as necessary. Whenever possible, items with integer keys are stored in the array portion. This eliminates the need for explicitly storing the key and thus reduces memory requirements. The hash portion of tables is implemented using chained scatter table with Brent's variation [3, pg. 18]. This algorithm performs well even at 100 percent load.

Assigning a value to an array index is typically considered to be $O(1)$. But in the case of Lua tables, this is correct only if one is not performing insertions and deletions on the table. Insertions and deletions may cause the table to adjust the sizes of its array and hash parts. When one of these re-sizings occurs, memory is allocated and items are copied; this is not a constant-time operation. So, to be more precise, access has an *amortized* cost of $O(1)$.

The fact that table access does not have a hard upper bound can be significant if one has tight time constraints on individual actions. If it is assumed that a high startup cost is acceptable, one could create a table and prefill it with a number of entries whose values are some sentinel value.

Lists

There are two common ADTs for Lists. The first is the Array List[2], whose ADT is presented in Table 2. The second is the Node List with ADT in Table 3.

`get(i)`	Return the element of the list with index i
`set(i, e)`	Replace with e and return the element at index i
`add(i, e)`	Insert a new element e into the list to have index i
`remove(i)`	Remove the element at index i

Table 2. Array List ADT.

---

[2]which does not necessarily imply an array implementation.

first()	Return the first node
last()	Return the last node
next(p)	Return the node following node p
prev(p)	Return the node preceding node p
set(p, e)	Replace node p's current value with e
addFirst(e)	Insert a new first node with value e
addLast(e)	Insert a new last node with value e
addBefore(p, e)	Insert a new node with value e into the list before node p
addAfter(p, e)	Insert a new node with value e into the list after node p
remove(p)	Remove and return node p

Table 3. Node List ADT.

Array lists

Array lists are most easily implemented as Lua tables with integer indices. The functions in the Array List ADT are implemented below. The functions get and set have (amortized) costs of $O(1)$ and the costs of add and remove are $O(n)$ because elements must be shifted up or down.

```
List = {};   List.__index = List

function List:new()
   return setmetatable({ __size = 0 } , self)
end

function List:get(i)
   return self[i]
end

function List:set(i, e)
   self[i] = e
end

function List:add(i, e)
   table.insert(self, i, e)
   self.__size = self.__size + 1
end

function List:remove(i)
   table.remove(self, i)
   self.__size = self.__size - 1
end

function List:size()
   return self.__size
end
```

Node lists

Since variables store references to tables, it is easy to create linked lists using one table per node. Moreover, these linked lists can very easily be multiply-linked lists. Two example implementations follow. The first is a doubly-linked list. The second is an excerpt from an implementation of a Skip List. In these examples, a node's data is accessed with an index *value*. The other (string) indices are used for the links. The motivation for Skip Lists is outside the scope of this article. Interested readers should consult [2].

Note that using a doubly-linked structure makes implementing the Node List easier, although it can be implemented with a singly-linked structure.

```
NList = {};   NList.__index = NList

function NList:new()
   local l = { head = {}, tail = {}, __size = 0 }
   l.head.__next, l.tail.__prev = l.tail, l.head
   return setmetatable(l, self)
end

function NList:first()
   if self.__size > 0 then
      return self.head.__next
   else
      return nil
   end
end

function NList:last()
   if self.__size > 0 then
      return self.tail.__prev
   else
      return nil
   end
end

function NList:set(node, elem)
   node.value = elem
end

function NList:next(node)
   if node.__next ~= self.tail then
      return node.__next
   else
      return nil
   end
end
```

```lua
function NList:prev(node)
    if node.__prev ~= self.head then
        return node.__prev
    else
        return nil
    end
end

function NList:addFirst(elem)
    local node =
        { __prev = self.head, value = elem, __next = self.head.__next }
    node.__next.__prev = node
    self.head.__next = node
    self.__size = self.__size + 1
end
function NList:addLast(elem)
    local node =
        { __prev = self.tail.__prev, value = elem, __next = self.tail }
    node.__prev.__next = node
    self.tail.__prev = node
    self.__size = self.__size + 1
end
function NList:addBefore(node, elem)
    local new_node =
            { __prev = node.__prev, value = elem, __next = node }
    new_node.__prev.__next = new_node
    node.__prev = new_node
    self.__size = self.__size + 1
end
function NList:addAfter(node, elem)
    local new_node =
        { __prev = node, value = elem, __next = node.__next }
    node.__next = new_node
    new_node.__next.__prev = new_node
    self.__size = self.__size + 1
end
function NList:remove(node)
    node.__prev.__next = node.__next
    node.__next.__prev = node.__prev
    self.__size = self.__size - 1
end

function NList:size()
    return self.__size
end
```

The Skip List example below is included here to demonstrate the ease with which one can build structures with arbitrary linkages. A Skip List is implemented using several doubly-linked lists. Each list has copies of some of the nodes in the previous list. A node in a list points to its predecessor and successor in the list. It also points to its copies (if they exist) in the previous and next lists. Therefore, a node in a Skip List has four pointers: next, prev, below, and above. The example code shows an implementation of the find function.

```
function SkipList:find(k)
   local p = self.TopLeft
   while p.below do
     p = p.below
     while k >= p.next.key do p = p.next end
   end
end
```

Stacks, queues, and dequeues

Stacks, queues, and double-ended queues (dequeues) can be implemented quite simply with the insert and remove functions from Lua's standard table library. The ADTs for these three data structures are presented in Tables 4, 5, and 6. As mentioned before, if amortized costs are acceptable, one can rely on the automatic resizing of tables to relieve the need to explicitly manage memory.

push(e)	Insert element e as the new top of stack
pop()	Remove and return the top element of the stack
top()	Return the top element of the stack without removing it

Table 4. Stack ADT.

enqueue(e)	Insert element e at the end of the queue
dequeue()	Remove and return the object at the front of the queue
front()	Return the object at the front of the queue without removing it

Table 5. Queue ADT.

addFirst(e)	Insert element e at the beginning of the dequeue
addLast(e)	Insert element e at the end of the dequeue
getFirst()	Remove and return the object at the front of the dequeue
getLast()	Remove and return the object at the end of the dequeue
first()	Return the object at the front of the dequeue without removing it
last()	Return the object at the end of the dequeue without removing it

Table 6. Dequeue ADT.

Stacks

The default value for table.insert's position parameter is $n + 1$, where n is the length of the table. For table.remove, the default value for position is n. Thus, we can implement push as table.insert(stack, value). One implements pop as table.remove(stack). The cost of these functions is interesting because it depends on whether the table needs to be resized, whether getn compatibility was enabled when Lua was compiled, and whether the *sizes* table has been created (see getsizes in lauxlib.c). In some cases, these function calls may invoke the internal function luaH_getn in ltable.c, which costs $O(\log n)$, to determine the correct value for the insertion/removal position.

Queues and dequeues

Queues and dequeues are slightly problematic. While we could implement dequeue as table.remove(q, 1), this involves shifting all of the table elements down to fill the gap. Thus, this implementation has a runtime of $O(n)$. There are two ways to avoid this cost penalty. An implementation which explicitly tracks the left and right indices of the dequeue is discussed in [5] and sketched below. Alternatively, one can make use of the Node List ADT described above.

```
Dequeue = {};   Dequeue.__index = Dequeue

function Dequeue:new()
   seturn setmetatable({ __first = 0, __last = -1 } , self)
end

function Dequeue:addFirst(elem)
   self.__first = self.__first - 1
   self[self.__first] = elem
end

function Dequeue:addLast(elem)
   self.__last = self.__last + 1
   self[self.__last] = elem
end

function Dequeue:first()
   return self[self.__first]
end

function Dequeue:last()
   return self[self.__last]
end
```

```lua
function Dequeue:getFirst()
   if self.__first > self.__last then return nil end
   local result = self[self.__first]
   self.__first = self.__first + 1
   return result
end

function Dequeue:getLast()
   if self.__first > self.__last then return nil end
   local result = self[self.__last]
   self.__last = self.__last - 1
   return result
end

function Dequeue:size()
   return (self.__last - self.__first + 1)
end

require 'NList'

NDequeue = {}
NDequeue.__index = NDequeue

function NDequeue:new()
   local l = { nlist = NList:new() }
   return setmetatable(l, self)
end

function NDequeue:addFirst(elem)
   self.nlist:addFirst(elem)
end

function NDequeue:addLast(elem)
   self.nlist:addLast(elem)
end

function NDequeue:getFirst()
   local result = self.nlist:first()
   if result then
      self.nlist:remove(result)
      return result.value
   else
      return nil
   end
end
```

```
function NDequeue:getLast()
   local result = self.nlist:last()
   if result then
      self.nlist:remove(result)
      return result.value
   else
      return nil
   end
end

function NDequeue:first()
   return self.nlist:first().value
end

function NDequeue:last()
   return self.nlist:last().value
end

function NDequeue:size()
   return self.nlist:size()
end
```

Trees

The Tree ADT is presented in Table 7. In the case of binary trees, additional functions are typically implemented. These are described in Table 8. Trees are typically implemented in one of two fashions: either collections of linked nodes or arrays with a protocol for making use of entries. Lua works well for both implementations. Linked node implementations will be discussed first.

`root()`	Return the tree's root
`addRoot(e)`	Create a root node with value e
`parent(v)`	Return the parent of v
`children(v)`	Return a list containing the children of node v
`insertChild(v, i, e)`	Create a new node with value e and insert it as the i-th child of node v
`isInternal(v)`	Test whether node v is internal
`isExternal(v)`	Test whether node v is external
`isRoot(v)`	Test whether node v is the root
`replace(v, e)`	Replace with e and return the element stored at v
`remove(v)`	Remove the subtree rooted at node v

Table 7. Tree ADT.

`left(v)`	Return the left child of node v
`right(v)`	Return the right child of node v
`insertLeft(v, e)`	Create a new node with value e and insert it as node v's left child
`insertRight(v, e)`	Create a new node with value e and insert it as node v's right child

Table 8. Additional functions for binary trees.

Linked-node trees

A linked-node implementation of a Tree can be accomplished using the same techniques described above for Node Lists. Each node of the tree is represented by a table. This table has an entry with index *value* for the element and an entry with index *children* for the references to the node's children. The *children* entry is itself a table whose elements are references to the child nodes. For binary trees, a slight optimization is to have entries indexed with *left* and *right* to hold the references for the node's children. The following code implements the binary tree interface.

```
NTree = {};   NTree.__index = NTree

function NTree:new()
    return setmetatable({ __size = 0 }, self)
end

function NTree:root()
    return self.__root
end

function NTree:addRoot(elem)
    self.__root = { value = elem }
    self.__size = 1
    return self.__root
end

function NTree:parent(node)
    return node.__parent
end

function NTree:left(node)
    return node.__left
end

function NTree:right(node)
    return node.__right
end
```

```lua
function NTree:insertLeft(node, elem)
   local new_node = { value = elem, __parent = node }
   node.__left = new_node
   self.__size = self.__size + 1
   return new_node
end

function NTree:insertRight(node, elem)
   local new_node = { value = elem, __parent = node }
   node.__right = new_node
   self.__size = self.__size + 1
   return new_node
end

function NTree:isInternal(node)
   return node.__left or node.__right
end

function NTree:isExternal(node)
   return not self:isInternal(node)
end

function NTree:isRoot(node)
   return (node == self.__root)
end

function NTree:replace(node, elem)
   node.value = elem
end

function NTree:remove(node)
   local parent = node.__parent
   local i_am_left_child = (parent.__left == node)
   if i_am_left_child then
      parent.__left = nil
   else
      parent.__right = nil
   end
   self.__size = self.__size - 1
end

function NTree:size()
   return self.__size
end
```

Array-based trees

An array-based implementation of a Tree can be accomplished by numbering the nodes of the tree. For a binary tree this can be done as follows:

$$n(v) = 1 \qquad \text{if } v \text{ is the root node}$$
$$n(v) = 2i \qquad \text{if } v \text{ is the left child of node } u \text{ and } n(u) = i$$
$$n(v) = 2i + 1 \quad \text{if } v \text{ is the right child of node } u \text{ and } n(u) = i$$

More generally, we can number the nodes of a k-ary tree as follows:

$$n(v) = 1 \qquad \text{if } v \text{ is the root node}$$
$$n(v) = ki - k + j + 1 \quad \text{if } v \text{ is the } j\text{-th child of node } u \text{ and } n(u) = i, \ 1 \le j \le k$$

With this numbering scheme at hand, implementing a tree with an array simply requires storing node v at $n(v)$. Note that, with this implementation, it is not possible to store nil as a tree entry.

Implementations in other languages typically use zeroth array entry to hold the number of elements in the tree. This implementation, however, uses the index $size$ to store the number of elements in the tree.

```
ATree = {};   ATree.__index = ATree

function ATree:new()
   return setmetatable({ __size = 0 }, self)
end

function ATree:root()
   return self[1]
end

function ATree:addRoot(elem)
   self[1] = elem
   self.__size = 1
end

function ATree:parent(node)
   return math.floor(node/2)
end

function ATree:left(node)
   return 2 * node
end

function ATree:right(node)
   return 2 * node + 1
end
```

```lua
function ATree:insertLeft(node, elem)
   self[2 * node] = elem
   self.__size = self.__size + 1
end

function ATree:insertRight(node, elem)
   self[2 * node + 1] = elem
   self.__size = self.__size + 1
end

function ATree:isInternal(node)
   return (self[2*node] ~= nil or self[2*node+1] ~= nil)
end

function ATree:isExternal(node)
   return not self:isInternal(node)
end

function ATree:isRoot(node)
   return (node == 1)
end

function ATree:replace(node, elem)
   self[node] = elem
end

function ATree:subsize(node)
   if self[node] == nil then
      return 0
   else
      return 1 + self:subsize(self:left(node))
               + self:subsize(self:right(node))
   end
end

function ATree:remove(node)
   local count = self:subsize(node)
   self[node] = nil
   self.__size = self.__size - count
end

function ATree:size()
   return self.__size
end
```

Maps and dictionaries

The Map ADT is presented in Table 9. Maps are usually defined so that each object has a distinct key. Relaxing that assumption yields the Dictionary ADT, presented in Table 10.

get(k)	Return the value with key k
put(k, v)	Insert value v with key k
remove(k)	Remove the value with key k
keys()	Return a list of keys
values()	Return a list of values

Table 9. Map ADT.

find(k)	Return a value with key k
findAll(k)	Return a list of all values with key k
insert(k, v)	Insert value v with key k
remove(k, v)	Remove value v with key k
keys()	Return a list of keys

Table 10. Dictionary ADT.

Note that almost all of the Map ADT is already provided by Lua tables. Below are implementations of the functions keys and values. One can implement the Dictionary ADT by storing a table of values at each index in a Lua table. See the following implementation for details.

```
Dictionary = {}
Dictionary.__index = Dictionary

function Dictionary:new()
   local l = { __size = 0 }
   return setmetatable(l, self)
end

function Dictionary:find(k)
   local matches = self[k]
   if (matches == nil) then
      return nil
   else
      local _, match = next(matches)
      return match
   end
end

function Dictionary:findAll(k)
   return self[k]
end
```

```lua
function Dictionary:insert(k, v)
    local tab = self[k] or {}
    table.insert(tab, v)
    self[k] = tab
    self.__size = self.__size + 1
end

function Dictionary:remove(k, v)
    local tab = self[k]
    if tab ~= nil then
        for k, val in pairs(tab) do
            if val == v then
                tab[k] = nil
                self.__size = self.__size - 1
            end
        end
        if next(tab) == nil then
            self[k] = nil
        end
    end
end

function Dictionary:keys()
    local keys = {}
    for k, _ in pairs(self) do
        if k ~= '__size' then
            table.insert(keys, k)
        end
    end
    return keys
end

function Dictionary:size()
    return self.__size
end
```

Sets

The mathematical definition of a set is a collection of distinct objects. In particular, sets do not allow for duplicates, and there is no notion of order amongst the elements. In addition to functions that manipulate set elements, several binary operations are defined on sets. The most common of these operations are union (members of the new set are all objects that are members of either of the input sets), intersection (whose members are only those objects that belong to both input sets), and difference (all members of the first set that are not members of the second set). An ADT for a set is presented in Table 11.

add(e)	Inserts object e into the set
remove(e)	Removes object e from the set
member(e)	Returns a Boolean indicating whether e is in the set
union(A, B)	Replaces the set A with the union of A and B
intersect(A, B)	Replaces the set A with the intersection of A and B
difference(A, B)	Replaces the set A with the difference of A and B

Table 11. Set ADT.

An example use of sets follows. Suppose one wants to create an index of a collection of documents. This is easily accomplished by first generating a list of all distinct words that occur throughout the collection of documents. Then, for each word in this list, a set is created whose elements are the names of the documents in which this word occurs. These sets are stored in a table indexed by the words in the list.

The index is used as follows. Obviously, if one wants to find all documents containing a particular word, one simply retrieves the set stored at that word's index. Suppose, however, that one is interested in finding the set of documents containing several words. The desired set is the intersection of the sets for each individual word. If, however, one desires the set of all documents containing any one of several words, the desired result is the union of the sets for the individual words.

Lua tables allow for a straightforward implementation of sets. A set can be represented by a Lua table whose keys are the objects which belong to the set. The value stored at each key is the Boolean true. Thus, the functions for manipulating set elements are implemented as follows:

```
Set = {}
Set.__index = Set

function Set:new()
   return setmetatable({ __size = 0 }, self)
end

function Set:add(elem)
   local result = self[elem]
   self[elem] = true
   if not result then
      self.__size = self.__size + 1
   end
end
```

```lua
function Set:remove(elem)
   local result = self[elem]
   self[elem] = nil
   if result then
      self.__size = self.__size - 1
   end
end

function Set:member(elem)
   return (self[elem] or false)
end

function Set:size()
   return self.__size
end
```

The following implementations of the binary set operations are all destructive in that they modify the first set rather than return a new result set. They are all implemented by iterating over the keys of one set and modifying the entries of the first set as appropriate.

```lua
function Set:union(b)
   for k, _ in pairs(b) do
      if k ~= '__size' then
         if not self[k] then
            self.__size = self.__size + 1
         end
         self[k] = true
      end
   end
end

function Set:intersect(b)
   for k, _ in pairs(self) do
      if k ~= '__size' then
         if not b[k] then
            self.__size = self.__size - 1
            self[k] = nil
         end
      end
   end
end
```

```
function Set:difference(b)
    for k, _ in pairs(b) do
        if k ~= '__size' then
            if self[k] then
                self.__size = self.__size - 1
            end
            self[k] = nil
        end
    end
end
```

The run times of these three functions are all $O(n)$. Note that the implementation of these functions can be simplified by using the (functional programming) map. A non-destructive implementation can be achieved by copying the first set to a new set before proceeding with the rest of the operation.

Multisets

A common variation of a set is the so-called multiset (also known as a bag). A multiset discards the restriction that each contained object be distinct. One can easily adapt the prior implementation of set operations to multisets by storing an integer count, rather than the Boolean value true, at each key. The Multiset ADT has two functions in addition to the functions in the Set ADT. These functions are described in Table 12.

count(e)	Returns how many e objects are in the multiset
removeAll(e)	Removes all e objects from the multiset

Table 12. Multiset ADT.

Additionally, the semantics of the binary set operations are modified to take into account the possibility of elements occurring multiple times in a multiset. The Multiset ADT is implemented as follows:

```
MSet = {}
MSet.__index = MSet

function MSet:new()
    local l = { __size = 0 }
    return setmetatable(l, self)
end

function MSet:add(elem)
    self[elem] = (self[elem] or 0) + 1
    self.__size = self.__size + 1
end
```

```lua
function MSet:remove(elem)
   local current = self[elem] or 0
   if current > 0 then
      current = current - 1
      self.__size = self.__size - 1
   end
   self[elem] = current
end

function MSet:member(elem)
   return ((self[elem] or 0) > 0)
end

function MSet:count(elem)
   return self[elem] or 0
end

function MSet:removeAll(elem)
   local rcount = self[elem] or 0
   self[elem] = nil
   self.__size = self.__size - rcount
end

function MSet:size()
   return self.__size
end

function MSet:union(b)
   for k, v in pairs(b) do
      if k ~= '__size' then
         local bcount = v or 0
         self[k] = (self[k] or 0) + bcount
         self.__size = self.__size + bcount
      end
   end
end

function MSet:intersect(b)
   for k, acount in pairs(self) do
      if k ~= '__size' then
         local bcount = b[k] or 0
         self[k] = math.min(acount, bcount)
         self.__size = self.__size - math.abs(acount - bcount)
      end
   end
end
```

```
function MSet:difference(b)
    for k, bcount in pairs(b) do
        if k ~= '__size' then
            local acount = self[k] or 0
            local reduced = acount - bcount
            if acount >= bcount then
                self[k] = acount - bcount
                self.__size = self.__size - bcount
            else
                self[k] = nil
                self.__size = self.__size - acount
            end
        end
    end
end
```

Partitions

A *partition* of a set S is a collection of subsets of S with the following property: Each element of S is a member of exactly one set in the partition. For example, consider $S = \{1, 2, 3, 4, 5, 6\}$. One partition is the collection of singleton sets: $\{1\}$, $\{2\}$, $\{3\}$, $\{4\}$, $\{5\}$, $\{6\}$. Another partition consists of the following sets: $\{1, 2\}$, $\{3, 4\}$, $\{5, 6\}$. As an interesting aside, one can define an ordering on partitions where a partition A is a *refinement* of partition B if every set in B is composed of a union of sets of A. Note this is not a total ordering because it is possible to have two partitions, neither of which is a refinement of the other. An ADT for partition is presented in Table 13. An implementation of this ADT follows.

makeSet(x)	create a singleton set containing the element x
merge(A, B)	Merge the sets A and B, destroying the old B
find(x)	find the set containing x
get_set(x)	return the elements in the same set as x

Table 13. Partition ADT.

```
Partition = {}
Partition.__index = Partition

function Partition:new()
    local l = { __size = 0 }
    return setmetatable(l, self)
end

function Partition:make_set(x)
    self[x] = self.__size
    self.__size = self.__size + 1
end
```

```lua
function Partition:merge(a, b)
    local a_idx = self:find(a)
    local b_idx = self:find(b)
    for k, v in pairs(self) do
        if k ~= '__size' and v == b_idx then
            self[k] = a_idx
        end
    end
    self.__size = self.__size - 1
end

function Partition:find(x)
    return self[x]
end

function Partition:get_set(x)
    local idx = self:find(x)
    local res = {}
    for k, v in pairs(self) do
        if k ~= '__size' and v == idx then
            table.insert(res, k)
        end
    end
    return res
end
```

Graphs

A graph is composed of a set of vertices and a set of edges which connect the vertices. It is important to remember that a graph is a topological object rather than a geometric one, i.e., it is the connections between vertices that is important, not the precise picture used to illustrate a graph. Normally in a graph, if a node u is connected to a node v, this implies that node v is connected to node u. In a directed graph, however, it is possible for a node u to be connected to a node v while node v is not connected to node u. A good analogy to help understand the difference between directed and undirected graphs is to think of a road map. A directed graph is a network of one-way streets, whereas an undirected graph is a network of two-way roads. A graph, either directed or undirected, may have weights assigned to the edges. Again, if one considers the road map analogy, weights would correspond to the distances between cities.

There are two common representations of graphs: the adjacency matrix and the vertex list. Adjacency matrices are simple but waste space in the cases of non-directed graphs and sparse graphs. When using Lua tables, however, adjacency matrices, even for sparse graphs, are memory efficient. Therefore, the vertex list representation of graphs is not discussed in this article.

Although a directed graph with n nodes requires an $n \times n$ adjacency matrix, a non-directed graph only requires a triangular portion of the full $n \times n$ matrix. Lua tables can be used to store *shaped* multi-dimensional matrices. One can take advantage of this feature to reduce by half the storage requirements for non-directed graphs. The (undirected) Graph ADT is presented in Table 14. An implementation of undirected graphs follows. An implementation of directed graphs may be found at the book's web site.

vertices()	Return a list of the vertices of the graph
edges()	Return a list of the edges of the graph
incidentEdges(v)	Return a list of all edges where one endpoint is vertex v
areAdjacent(v, u)	Test whether vertices v and u are adjacent
insertEdge(v, u)	Make vertices u and v adjacent
removeEdge(v, u)	Make vertices u and v non-adjacent

Table 14. Graph ADT.

```lua
Graph = {};   Graph.__index = Graph

function Graph:new(n)
   local l = { __size = n }
   local vertices = {}
   for i = 1, n do
      table.insert(vertices, i)
   end
   l.__vertices = vertices
   local graph = {}
   for i = 1, n do
      table.insert(graph, {})
   end
   l.__graph = graph
   return setmetatable(l, self)
end

function Graph:vertices()
   return self.__vertices
end

function Graph:incidentEdges(v)
   local result = {}
   for i = 1,v-1 do
      if self.__graph[i][v] then table.insert(result, i) end
   end
   for i, _ in pairs(self.__graph[v]) do
      table.insert(result, i)
   end
   return result
end
```

```lua
function Graph:areAdjacent(v, u)
   return ( (self.__graph[v][u] or self.__graph[u][v]) or false)
end

function Graph:insertEdge(v, u)
   if u < v then v, u = u, v end
   self.__graph[v][u] = true
end

function Graph:removeEdge(v, u)
   if u < v then v, u = u, v end
   self.__graph[v][u] = nil
end
```

Text processing

Most books on data structures contain a chapter discussing text processing, particularly pattern matching and compression. This article does not cover these topics, but the interested reader is directed to read the documentation for Lua's string library [4][3], Reuben Thomas and Shmuel Zeigerman's rex library [13], and Roberto Ierusalimschy's LPEG library [6].

Augmented data structures

In many circumstances, an operation on a data structure can be made more efficient by including additional information. This technique is known as using augmented data structures. For example, threaded trees use additional pointers so that it is possible to find the pre-order successor to a given node in $O(1)$ time.

A particularly elegant example of an augmented data structure is the use of an augmented binary search tree to enable determination of k-th order statistics in $O(\log n)$ time. An implementation based on the discussion in [11] follows.

```lua
require 'NTree'

OrderTree = {}
OrderTree.__index = OrderTree

function OrderTree:new()
   local l = { }
   l.tree = NTree:new()
   return setmetatable(l, self)
end
```

---

[3]and, of course, refer to the source code.

```lua
function OrderTree:addRoot(elem)
   elem = { data = elem, subtree_size = 1 }
   return self.tree:addRoot(elem)
end

function OrderTree:increment_ranks(node)
   while (node ~= nil) do
      node.value.subtree_size = node.value.subtree_size + 1
      node = self.tree:parent(node)
   end
end

function OrderTree:decrement_ranks(node)
   while (node ~= nil) do
      node.value.subtree_size = node.value.subtree_size - 1
      node = self.tree:parent(node)
   end
end

function OrderTree:insertLeft(node, elem)
   elem = { data = elem, subtree_size = 1 }
   local new_node = self.tree:insertLeft(node, elem)
   self:increment_ranks(node)
   return new_node
end

function OrderTree:insertRight(node, elem)
   elem = { data = elem, subtree_size = 1 }
   local new_node = self.tree:insertRight(node, elem)
   self:increment_ranks(node)
   return new_node
end

function OrderTree:rank(x)
   local root = self.tree:root()
   return self:_rank(x, root)
end

function OrderTree:select(k)
   if k > self.tree:size() then
      error('Tree does not contain that many items.')
   end
   local root = self.tree:root()
   return self:_select(k, root)
end
```

```lua
function OrderTree:_rank(x, node)
   local key = node.value.data
   local left_child = self.tree:left(node)
   local right_child = self.tree:right(node)
   if x == key then
      return 1 + ((left_child and left_child.value.subtree_size) or 0)
   elseif x < key then
      if left_child then
         return self:_rank(x, left_child)
      else
         error('Key is not in tree.')
      end
   else
      if right_child then
         return  1 + self:_rank(x, right_child) +
                    ((left_child and left_child.value.subtree_size) or 0)
      else
         error('Key is not in tree.')
      end
   end
end
function OrderTree:_select(k, node)
   local left_child = self.tree:left(node)
   local right_child = self.tree:right(node)
   local left_tree_size =
                  (left_child and left_child.value.subtree_size) or 0
   if k == left_tree_size + 1 then
      return node
   elseif k <= left_tree_size then
      return self:_select(k, left_child)
   else
      return self:_select(k - 1 - left_tree_size, right_child)
   end
end
```

Homogeneous data structures

In Lua, values are typed, but variables are not. In other words, a particular variable, say my_variable, may refer to a string at one point during a program's execution, a table at a later point, and, perhaps, a number later on. Thus, the data structures discussed here are all heterogeneous, i.e., they can simultaneously store values of different types.

Often, however, it is necessary to restrict a data structure to values of a particular type. For example, suppose one is collecting a list of expenses with the intent of calculating an average expense. If a non-numeric value is inadvertently inserted, the result would either be an erroneous result or a run-time error.

One can easily modify the data structures presented here so that the insertion routines check the type of the value before inserting it into the structure. A simple approach would be to use the type function, although in many circumstances that is not sufficient. A more robust approach would be to make use of metatables, particularly since most object-oriented systems in Lua rely on metatables to implement classes.

Below is the implementation of a factory for creating functions to verify types.

```
function make_typechecker(spec)
    if type(spec) == "string" then
        return function(v) return (type(v) == spec) end
    else -- spec is a table
        return function(v) return (getmetatable(v) == spec) end
    end
end
```

One can use the type-checker factory as follows:

```
local isNumber = make_typechecker("number")
-- Stack which only holds numeric values
function push(stack, v)
  if not isNumber(v) then error("This stack only holds numbers!") end
  table.insert(stack, v)
end
```

Working with Lua

To paraphrase an anonymous saying, "any programmer can write a C program in Lua." For the most part, the data structures presented here were developed in response to the constraints of languages such as C and Fortran. In some circumstances, these data structures can be the best choice in Lua programs. Whenever possible, however, it is preferable to develop data structures that take advantage of the strengths of Lua. A few heuristics to aid one in this task follow.

1. Take advantage of table resizing.

2. Consider using values as keys (such as in the Set implementation).

3. Remember that objects of any type can be table keys (except nil).

4. Make use of both the array portion and hash portion of a table.

Resources

There are a number of resources available to Lua programmers to aid in the design of data structures. These include both existing libraries and reference material. Good texts on Lua programming include *Programming in Lua* [5], the *Lua Reference Manual* [4], and *Beginning Lua Programming* [7].

There are also several existing libraries which contain a range of data structures and algorithms. These include Reuben Thomas's stdlib [12] and Paul Chisano's Sano Library [1]. Thomas's work contains a number of useful extensions to Lua's standard libraries and has a particularly functional programming style. Chisano's library contains implementations of almost all the data structures described in this article.

Complete implementations of the data structures discussed in this article are available at the book's web site. And, of course, there are a number of examples of data structure implementations available at the Lua Wiki [9]. Finally, the Lua mailing list [10] has an excellent signal-to-noise ratio.

References

[1] Chisano, Paul. *Sano Library*. http://luaforge.net/projects/sano/.

[2] Goodrich, Michael T. and Roberto Tamassia. *Data Structures and Algorithms in Java*. 4th Ed. John Wiley and Sons, 2006.

[3] Ierusalimschy, Roberto, de Figueiredo, Luiz H. and Waldemar Celes. "The implementation of Lua 5.0," *Journal of Universal Computer Science*, Vol. 11, No. 7, 2005.

[4] Ierusalimschy, Roberto, de Figueiredo, Luiz H. and Waldemar Celes. *Lua 5.1 Reference Manual*, Lua.org. 2006.

[5] Ierusalimschy, Roberto. *Programming in Lua*. 2nd Ed. 1006.

[6] Ierusalimschy, Roberto. *lpeg*. http://luaforge.net/projects/lpeg/.

[7] Jung, Kurt and Aaron Brown. *Beginning Lua Programming*. Wiley, Indianapolis, IN, 2007.

[8] Knuth, Donald. "Structured Programming with go to Statements," *ACM Computing Surveys*, Vol 6, No. 4, Dec. 1974.

[9] Lua Community. *Lua Users' Wiki*. http://www.lua-users.org/wiki.

[10] Lua Community. *lua-l*. http://www.lua.org/lua-l.html.

[11] Ottmann, Thomas. http://electures.informatik.uni-freiburg.de/catalog/chapter.do?courseId=advancedAD2005&chapter=9

[12] Thomas, Reuben. *stdlib*. http://luaforge.net/projects/stdlib/.

[13] Thomas, Reuben and Shmuel Zeigerman. *lrexlib*. http://luaforge.net/projects/lrexlib/.

19

Tic-Tac-Toe and the Minimax Decision Algorithm

Rafael Moreira Savelli
and Roberto de Beauclair Seixas

We present a way to implement the minimax algorithm from scratch in Lua. First, we start with some game-playing concepts. Then, we explain how could tables handle with required data structures specifications such as trees and nodes, and present a Lua implementation of the minimax algorithm, showing how those tables are manipulated. Its performance is evaluated based on the worst case execution time defined by the game-playing concepts. In addition, in order to confirm the given approach, we also implemented the well-known tic-tac-toe and checkers games as case studies. At the end practical results are commented proving that, like many other languages, Lua can easily handle this sort of adaptive search problems.

Introduction

Humans started to play games a long time ago and just after the firsts civilizations have existed. The main purpose of them were basically for entertainment. Since then, more and more games have been created so that future generations still spend their time with game playing.

depth	nodes	time	memory
0	1	1 millisecond	100 bytes
2	111	0.1 seconds	11 kilobytes
4	11.111	11 seconds	1 megabyte
6	10^6	18 minutes	111 megabytes
8	10^8	31 hours	11 gigabytes
10	10^{10}	128 days	1 terabytes
12	10^{12}	35 years	111 terabytes
14	10^{14}	3500 years	11.111 terabytes

Table 1. Time and memory requirements for breadth-first search. The figures shown assume branching factor $b = 10$; *1000 nodes/second; 100 bytes/node.*

Adding this fact with computing, many of this games were inserted into computers and thus some artificial intelligence became indispensable. In fact, game playing is one of the oldest areas of endeavor in artificial intelligence, turning up around 1950 when computers just became programmable [3].

Search problems

In order to solve search problems we build a tree that is superimposed over the problem space and find a solution by searching node-after-node until reaching the desired goal node. However, in some cases, building such tree is not an easy task. Even a simple problem can generate a huge amount of data and, in this case, the resulting tree becomes intractable even when submitted to modern computers. This can be observed by looking at Table 1 which shows a hypothetical computer times and memories usage for a given number of tree depth.

Even with this exponential growth, the most common difficulties related to problem solving is finding a good strategy for searching among those trees. This is almost always the majority of work in the area of search problems. The strategy can be classified in term of four different criteria as presented on following:

Completeness. Is the strategy guaranteed to find a solution if one exists?

Time Complexity. How long does it take to find a solution?

Space Complexity. How much memory does it need to perform that search?

Optimality. Does the strategy find the highest-quality solution when there are several different solutions?

Games

An important consideration when designing games is to treat them as search problems. However, the presence of an opponent makes the decision problem somewhat more complicated when compared to simple search problems. The opponent introduces uncertainty, because one never knows what he or she is going to do. So, in essence, all game playing programs must deal with the contingency problem as well [1].

As mentioned before, the best way for solving search problems is to build a tree for that problem. Here, the idea is applied according to a generic two-players game as shown in the following:

- The *initial state* (root), which includes board position and an indication of whose move it is.

- A set of *operators* (transition), which defines the legal moves that a player can make.

- A *terminal set* (leaves), which determines when the game is over.

- A *utility function* (node values), which gives a numeric value for the outcome of the game. For example, we can assign to leaves the values +1, 0 or −1 respectively for winning, drawing, or losing the game.

In order to understand some of approaches used in this work, first we need to introduce some of Lua table concepts. In Lua, a table is a special type that implements associative arrays. An associative array is an array that can be indexed not only with numbers, but also with strings or any other value of the language (except nil). Moreover, tables have no fixed size. You can add as many element as you want to a table dynamically. The most surprising fact is that tables are the main and also the only data-structuring mechanism. We can use tables to represent ordinary arrays, symbol tables, sets, records, queues, and more [2].

In our case we used tables for storing trees nodes. Each node must have information of the current board position. For example, Figure 1 shows how a possible search tree for the tic-tac-toe game. For instance, the given left positioned block of code in Figure 2 illustrates how to build each node in Lua. The corresponding tic-tac-toe board situation appear on the right yet in the same figure. In addition, positions marked as "X" or "O" are both players while positions marked " " denote only empty position.

The minimax algorithm

Having defined the main game concepts and its data structure, we are now ready to understand the essence of minimax algorithm. The minimax algorithm is designed to determine the optimal strategy for one player at a time informing the best move for that player. The entire algorithm consists of four steps:

1. Generate the whole game tree, all the way down to the terminal states.

2. Evaluate the utility function to each terminal state to get its value.

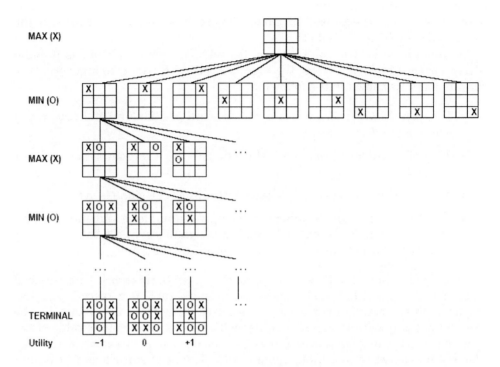

Figure 1. A partial search tree for the Tic-Tac-Toe game.

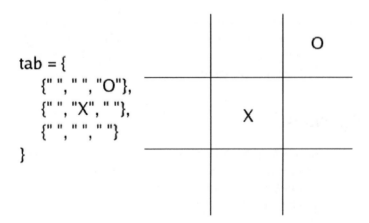

Figure 2. A partial search tree for the Tic-Tac-Toe game.

3. Recursively, use the evaluated utilities to determine the utilities of the nodes one level higher. To do that, apply minimal or maximal utility alternately until reach the root by taking a maximal utility for last. [XXX]

4. Finally, choose the move that leads to the highest utility value.

For programming purposes, imagine the computer playing CIRCLE and the human playing CROSS. The code in Listing 1 shows a Lua implementation of the minimax algorithm. The top function, MINIMAX_DECISION, starts the decision process and selects the computer best move from all legal ones, which are evaluated in turn by the MINIMAX_VALUE recursive function.

When computer's turn comes, the CROSS player leaves it a board with a given game situation. Then, MINIMAX_DECISION is invoked with the current game board as argument. After that, all legal moves are taken by using getLegalMoves. From the resulting table, every legal move must be played in separate boards and passed to MINIMAX_VALUE, which calls itself recursively until it reaches the maximum predefined hMax depth or when the game is over for that board state. In both cases, the recursion stops and the UTILITY function is evaluated. Otherwise, the recursive function continues alternating each player's turn, maximizing or minimizing the utilities.

Comparing Lua to other programming languages, such as C or Java, we can spot some particular differences. The first one is related to Lua tables. They are simple, easy to use, and avoid any additional memory management. As an example, take this line from MINIMAX_VALUE

```
newBoard = move( gameBoard, v )
```

This line means that a function move receives a game board (a Lua table) and a move v to play on this board. The resulting situation leads to a new game board named newBoard. If we were using C, one of the best ways would be treating boards as integer vectors. However, special memory managements would be required in that case because vector copying in that language is not as simple as copying tables in Lua. This will surely require user care and attention with pointers. And every programmer knows that just a single, small memory manipulation mistake can affect the whole application integrity. This sort of bug does not happen in Lua programs.

Case study

Up to this point, we have been using the tic-tac-toe game in our explanations. In fact, this game was chosen to be our case study for several reasons. First, it is a well-known and popular game with dismiss any rules explanations. Second, other games like checkers (also known as draughts) and chess are much more complex than tic-tac-toe. For instance, tic-tac-toe has a maximal branching factor of 9 while in chess the average is about 35. Moreover, tic-tac-toe has exactly 623530 nodes in its search tree but chess can easily achieve 35^{100}.

```
function MINIMAX_DECISION( gameBoard )
        local bestMove, newBoard, value
        local maxValue = -999
        local legalMoves = getLegalMoves( gameBoard, CIRCLE )
        for i,v in pairs(legalMoves) do
                newBoard = move( gameBoard, v )
                value = MINIMAX _VALUE( newBoard, 1, CROSS )
                if value > maxValue then
                        maxValue = value
                        bestMove = v
                end
        end
        return bestMove
end


function MINIMAX_VALUE( gameBoard, h, player )
        local legalMoves, newBoard, value
        local maxValue = -999, minValue = 999
        if gameOver(gameBoard) or h == hMax then
                return UTILITY(gameBoard)
        end
        legalMoves = getLegalMoves( gameBoard, player )
        if player == CIRCLE then
                for i,v in pairs(legalMoves) do
                        newBoard = move( gameBoard, v )
                        value = MINIMAX _VALUE( newBoard, h+1, CROSS )
                        if value > maxValue then
                                maxValue = value
                        end
                end
                 return maxValue
        else
                for i,v in pairs(legalMoves) do
                        newBoard = move( gameBoard, v )
                        value = MINIMAX _VALUE( newBoard, h+1, CIRCLE )
                        if value < minValue then
                                minValue = value
                        end
                end
                return minValue
end
```

Listing 1.

While implementing minimax in Lua, we have noticed how important and powerful a table is. Alone or combined with others tables, we can build complex data structures which make Lua easy to use and much better than many other programming languages. In this work, we used combined tables to form matrices. Those matrices were used to store tic-tac-toe boards which stands for valid game positions. This table was defined as shown in Figure 2.

However, the generic Lua algorithm described in the previous section works not only for simple games like tic-tac-toe but basically for every other two-player board games. The key is to know how to combine tables to form the desired game board. For example, if we wish to store checkers board information, instead of doing code shown in Figure 1, we simply store the necessary 32 dark squares of checkers board. By checkers rules, the pieces must remain only in these squares. So, a table for this game might be:

```
-- Defining valid board positions
local EMPTY = 0, CROSS = 1, CIRCLE = 2
local checkersBoard = {EMPTY, CROSS, CROSS, ... , CIRCLE}
```

Of course this is the main change, but not the only one. The functions `getLegalMoves`, `move`, and `gameOver` must also be adapted to match with checkers rules. Once these changes are made, the main algorithm structures are still valid and solve the search problem now for the checkers game.

Conclusions

The first conclusion is that implementing the minimax strategy in Lua is an easy task. The Lua combine tables facility to form matrices speeds up users implementation skills keeping the source code simple and clear. The memory manipulation abstraction also contributes to make Lua an easy programming language.

Another important Lua approach consists in collecting any memory garbage with frees programmers from this responsibilities.

Yet Lua is a powerful programming language and also provides extensions.

One future work could be implementing other games concepts such as alpha-beta pruning. Alpha-beta pruning is a technique where a large amount of nodes are securely removed from search tree and for this reason they are not processed. Avoiding unnecessary processing means increasing the computer answer velocity.

References

[1] J. D. Funge. *Artificial Intelligence for Computer Games*. Peters Corp., 2004.

[2] R. Ierusalimschy. *Programming in Lua*. Lua.org, 2006.

[3] S. Russel and P. Norvig. *Artificial Intelligence: A Modern Approach*. Prentice-Hall, 1995.

Part IV

Game Programming

20

Using Lua in Game and Tool Creation

Konstantin Sokharev and Vadim Groznov

Nowadays, when development costs are skyrocketing, selection of tools and instruments for creating and designing your game is of utter importance. This article discusses the use of Lua as a language for writing game and its game play, and as a platform for the creation of a game editor. Writing high quality code is impossible without a good convenient IDE. In this article we discuss struggle for higher performance and lower memory consumption, and issues of readability that arise when the volume of Lua code grows significantly.

Programmable access via Lua

Our earliest architectural solutions used Lua to script events in game missions, allowing designers to realise a lot of ideas and make missions sufficiently diverse. Usage of Lua also allows to differentiate tasks between scripters and programmers (in spite of scripter being a programmer too — but a programmer of less complex constructions), which is extremely useful from the production process viewpoint (Listing 1).

Actually, this approach allowed quick prototyping and production of missions (of an RTS/Action game in production at that time). Later, we researched Lua's capabilities further and understood that usage of such architectural features as tables allowed for a convenient storage of game structures. Here is an example of our organisation of structured database of game entities (Listing 3).

It can be seen that we are creating a table named `Prot.Characters` with sub-tables named `Defaults`, where default properties of an object are stored — like its radius (space it occupies on terrain in game), HP (health points), ability to cast and receive shadows, physic characteristics (information used by a physics engine), material type (for drawing hit effects etc.). All the actual game characters follow, also in sub-tables (such as `TestCharacter1`), where model for its representation, class and other individual characteristics are indicated. Previously, we used XML for these, and it was quite handy, but Lua syntax turned out to be simpler and easier understand and it does not require knowledge of XML markup. Also, while using XML, one will need to find a parser with required functionality and optimal speed. Lua parser is very fast (comparable with the fastest XML parsers such as tinyxml and pugxml). If need be, Lua database can even be compiled to Lua bytecode for instant loading.

Early successes led us to the idea that all game logic can be written in Lua (this beauty and convenience fooled us, as will be described later in the "Excessive flexibility of Lua" section). This way, game entities' classes (for example, base functions of a main hero, `mainhero_class.lua`), Finite State Machine of a game class (`mainhero_behaviours.lua/mainhero_goals.lua`), Events Management System (Listing 2) were fully transferred to Lua, while C++ retained only low-level functions such as pathfinding. As can be seen, Object Oriented programming paradigm is used here. (It can be added that later, during the development of a third person shooter game, a system for management of multi-axis blending of animations was also written in Lua.)

Lua has a built-in system of threads/coroutines and their management. We first thought to use this feature of Lua and wrote a test system, but realised that for an RTS game usage of FSM is more important, and debugging of such system will be too difficult.

IDE (debugger)

Soon we understood that, with all the convenience and flexibility of Lua, at large volume of code (over 10 Lua files at several thousand lines each) means of debugging are lacking, so we decided to write full-featured Lua script debugger. Such a debugger was written and built into the game. It has a convenient IDE with game files navigation tree, search, multitabs, syntax highlighting, and all the functionality for debugging: breakpoints, step in, step out, edit and continue, watches, expressions. It significantly simplified and sped up development, because earlier we had to debug code by logging.

It is worthy of note that for text representation we used Scintilla middleware, while Lua middleware has all the functionality for the creation of a good debugger (i.e., we didn't have to change anything in Lua source code), so the creation of a debugger took only one man-month.

Excessive flexibility of Lua

Despite seeming simplicity and beauty of code, Lua conceals some dangers. A sudden problem arose — excessive flexibility of Lua. For example, access to any member of any object at any place in the script (as an example) is a straight way to "hacks" — often forgetting to write "local" inside a function you create a global. A conclusion that can be made — strict coding standards are a must, i.e.:

- All structural definitions must *always* have the same format (Lua allows to do one thing by several means). For example, function declaration: `function Running()` or `Running = function()` — you must choose most convenient.

- Names of different entities must be created by one mnemonic rule — or the code will become very difficult to understand. For example, signal enumerator: `SGN_USE1`, `SGN_CAMERA_ROTATE`, `SGN_MOVE`.

- Despite Lua being a type-less language, type shall be pointed in variable name. For example, `vPos` (Vector), `fRadius` (float), `blsCovered` (boolean).

To conclude this topic, good advice: frequently make a code review to solidify structures (we advise to include it into the weekly development cycle).

Performance issues

One of the most important questions with script language usage is "Will it be fast enough?". We conducted preliminary synthetic tests and found that performance was sufficient even with several hundred units operating simultaneously in game. In reality, it turned out to be slower — in massive combats with many game entities (30–60 fighting units on-screen), the game began to lag significantly. An important conclusion was made: game designers' vision of battles in game and other scripted events happening simultaneously on the map must be taken into account beforehand. Then most critical (performance-wise) stuff must be exposed and it should be decided whether to keep it in C++ or transfer it to Lua. Regrettably, we made this too late, so we had to fix these problems during production. We decided to integrate a Lua profiler (from the Kelper project), which did its job well and showed up bottlenecks, and did it in runtime, without stopping game in needed game situations, which is very important. That way we found out that significant amount of processing time was consumed by Lua-to-C++ data transfer (we will elaborate on that later), and `next` function used for looking through table elements. A conclusion can be made: thoroughly plan structure of data that you will store in script (use massives extensively and tables where you really need them.) Remember that performance impact when looking through larger number of elements is significantly heavier in Lua then in C++. Also, there is sense in using custom containers, exported from C++, with faster look through elements.

Later we stumbled upon a problem of excessive memory allocation — the fact that Lua automatically manages memory is very useful and actually simplifies coding, but several things must be remembered.

Profiling showed that excessive memory allocation had to do with Lua hash tables (i.e., if your game entity has 129 elements in table, this table will be of 256 element size — which is a substantial overhead). Regrettably, this problem was solved only partially by code review and better architecture.

Also you need to remember that table element of type "byte", that would take 1 byte in C/C++ will take 40 bytes in Lua (not counting the table itself).

Another problem connected with memory was the garbage collector — as we used Lua 5.0.2, we did not have many alternatives. Mixed approach such as reference counting + garbage collection can be used — this can be a good solution (LuaRC can be used as a foundation). Or, if you have little amount of runtime data, make garbage collection every frame. Today, Lua 5.1 has incremental garbage collection, which is more progressive and has wide functionality for management and budgeting of memory, but can't solve all the problems, because it has a substantial overhead at large volumes of data. Perhaps, fine tuning and low volumes of game data may provide the needed result. Also, an integration of a custom memory manager (Lua allows this to be done easily) may help. Such manager can be adapted for size and quantity of memory chunks allocated by Lua code.

As a conclusion, these are several useful solutions that have to do with Lua being used as a game script. The most used types (Vector, Quaternion, Matrix) can be made native for Lua — this significantly increases performance. If Lua execution speed is not enough (event though it is higher than in other script languages such as Python, Perl, and Ruby), you can try to use LuaJIT. We tested it — LuaJIT actually speeds program several times in certain circumstances and brings execution speed closer to native C.

Lua–C++ data transferring

One of the important moments in integration of C/C++ code and Lua is data transfer and class exporting. For this we first used a proxy class that made Lua and C++ integration less solid and allowed usage of another scripting language, but profiling showed that significant memory overhead and excessive calls happened. Our latest solution is based totally on #defines and works directly with Lua stack. See Listing 4. You can see pseudo-C++ code where we have bindings macros part, example Obj class method (GetAnimations) and so called "exportmap" below separated by comments.

Lua and .NET

Our second case of Lua usage was as a script language for creation of tools in a game editor. It was decided to use .NET platform because of its capabilities and flexibility. As a link, we used the fantastic LuaInterface, which we used as a foundation and wrote our own link in C++ for Lua and .NET. That decision allowed us also to export needed methods of engine and import them into .NET, so Lua became a sort of glue between our code and Managed. Problematic were two garbage collectors (.NET and Lua), which began to conflict each other at large volumes of data and executed operations. The solution was to force .NET garbage collection every frame.

For interface and controls we used weifenluo.dll. That way, after we added ability of comfortable editing and edit and continue, we got a powerful tool for rapid prototyping and realisation of handy editing tools.

Conclusion

Our experience showed that utilization of Lua as a convenient database and a means for rapid creation of game entities is quite possible, provided you have a convenient IDE for debugging and navigation of code.

Well thought-out architecture of Lua allowed for good integration with .NET and usage of Lua as a tool for creating plug-ins for a game editor.

When using Lua, one should consider memory consumption, execution speed and "excessive" flexibility of Lua code — overlooking these peculiarities you may hinder all your efforts to improve your system.

```lua
function MapLogic:LocationSubscription()
  local loc

  g_Player:GetActiveTroop():Subscribe("Die", self, "OnActiveTroopDie")

  loc = getObj("loc_street_enter" )
  if ( loc ) then
    loc:Subscribe("GE_OBJECT_ENTERS_LOCATION", self,
                                  "OnUnitEnterLocationStreetEnter" )
  end

  loc = getObj("loc_yard_enter" )
  if ( loc ) then
    loc:Subscribe("GE_OBJECT_ENTERS_LOCATION", self,
                                  "OnUnitEnterLocationYardEnter" )
  end
end

function MapLogic:OnUnitEnterLocationStreetEnter(Sender, UnitId)
  if ( not self:IsOurUnit(UnitId) ) then
    return
  end

  local pos
  local index = 1
  for _, pos in self.Constants.StreetPos do
    local obj = self.ProtEnemy[index]()
    index = index + 1

    if index > table.getn(self.ProtEnemy) then
      index = 1
    end

    if ( obj ) then
      obj:SetPosForced(pos)
      obj:SetBelong(1002)
    end

  end
end
```

Listing 1.

```
-- PostEvent member

function g_ProcessManager:PostEvent(Recipient, EventName, SenderId, Params)
  local CurEventsQueue = self.EventsQueue[ self.EventsQueueNum ]
  CurEventsQueue[ self.EventsQueueCurIndex ] =
                                  { Recipient, EventName, SenderId, Params }
  self.EventsQueueCurIndex = self.EventsQueueCurIndex + 1
end


-- ProcessEvent member
-- Calls recipient ( if object) with OnEvent( EventName, SenderId, Params )
-- Calls function by itself with ( EventName, SenderId, Params )

function g_ProcessManager:ProcessEvent( Evn )
  local Recipient = Evn[1]
  if type( Recipient ) == "function" then
    Recipient( Evn[2], Evn[3], Evn[4] )
  else
    -- Exception handler
    local obj = getObj( Recipient )
    if not obj then
      LOG( "warning: attempt to deliver event "..Evn[2]..
           " to non-exist object with ObjId="..tostring(Recipient) )
      return
    end

    if obj.OnEvent then
      obj:OnEvent( Evn[2], Evn[3], Evn[4] )
    end
  end

end
```

Listing 2.

```
Prot.Characters = {
Defaults = {
  PhysicAnimDeath = true
  HP = 500
  Material = "FleshDead"
  FullInstanceCopy = true
  StandAnimationCount = 1
  Radius = 0.5
  HardRadius = 0.5
  RunSoftRadius = 1
  StandSoftRadius = 1
  TimeBeforeRemove = 10
  EngineProperties = {
    CastShadow = false
    ReceiveShadow = true
    DynamicShadow = true
  }
}
TestCharacter1= Prot {
  Class = Obj
  ModelFile = "data/Models/NPC/Women/Pols_1/model.xml"
  Material = "FleshAll"
  RotationSpeed = 2 * math.pi / 3
  HP = 2000
  Damage = 70
  CaptureTargetRadius = 20
  AttackRadius = 2
  AttackAngle = math.pi / 4
  AttackEnergy = 10
  MaxEnergy = 50
  RestoreEnergyPerSecond = 7
  EmaciationTIme = 3
  DamageTimeInAttackAnimation = 0.4
  MoveInUpdate = true
  EngineProperties = {
    DefaultAnimationSpeed = 0.78
    CastShadow = true
    DefaultPhysicState = "STATIC"
    Physic = {
      ObjectWeight = 7500
      RigidBodyWeight = 3000
      DynamicTimeout = 10
      NoSleepingCheckTimeout = 10
      DynamicSleepingTimeout = 10
    }
  }
}
}
```

Listing 3.

```
//Bindings stuff

/**
The types of exports supported by the binding system.
*/

enum eExportType
{
   METHOD,
   NATIVE_METHOD,
   PROPERTY,
   //CONST_INT,
   //PROP_INT,
   //PROP_FLOAT,
   //PROP_BOOL,
   //PROP_VECTOR,
};

/**
Information about a class entry point.
*/

struct ExportInfo
{
   const char* name; // The name of the entry point
   eExportType type; // METHOD, NATIVE_METHOD, etc.
   void* addr1; // The memory address of the entry point.
   void* addr2; // A second address, used by properties
   /// these are optional export descriptors
   const char* returns; // e.g. "void" or "int"
   const char* params;  // e.g. "int a, const CStr& s"
   const char* desc;    // e.g. "returns number of chicks avail"
};
```

Listing 4.

```
//Bindings stuff (continued)

#define RETURNS_TABLE int retCount = 1; _Lua_pushTable( L,

#define CLASS_METHOD(className, method, returnType) \
static int _export_##className##_##method( lua_State* L ) { \
className* _this = (className*)_Lua_popObject(L, 1, RT_CLASS_LOCAL(className)); \
returnType( _this->method(

#define METHOD_DESCRIBED(className, method, returnsDesc, paramsDesc, shortDesc) \
{ #method, ::engine::METHOD, \
(void*)_export_##className##_##method, 0, returnsDesc, paramsDesc, shortDesc },

#define BEGIN_EXPORT_MAP(className) \
static ::engine::ExportInfo _exports_##className[] = {

#define END_EXPORT_MAP {0}};

//Example Function( in c++ )

Lua::Table Obj::GetAnimations()
{
   Lua::Table tbl;
   for ( int i = 0; i < this->GetNumAnimations(); i++ )
   {
      tbl.SetNum(float(i + 1), sArg::FromS(this->GetAnimationName(i)));
   }
   return tbl;
}

//Begin export stuff

CLASS_METHOD(Obj, GetAnimations, RETURNS_TABLE ) END_METHOD
BEGIN_EXPORT_MAP(Obj)
METHOD_DESCRIBED(Obj, GetAnimations, "", "", "" )
END_EXPORT_MAP
```

Listing 4. (continued)

21

Leveraging Lua and C++ to Create a Dynamic and Flexible Event System for Script-Driven Games

Robert Oates

Lua boasts several features that make it an attractive option for use in event-driven applications such as video games. These programs are made much easier to program through judicious application of the *subscriber* pattern, and can be given a lot of runtime flexibility through the *strategy* pattern. In this article I will explain what these patterns are, how they are beneficial to game development, and finally how we can implement and optimize these patterns easily with Lua.

The subscriber

The subscriber pattern is absolutely integral to event-driven programming. Objects will *subscribe* to events through an *event manager*, and the event manager notifies the subscribers when the event occurs. There is a lot of room for creative implementation with this pattern, so let's step back a moment and consider the requirements we have for our application and see if that helps narrow down the possibilities.

Since we're going for an event-driven application here, most of our objects need to be able to subscribe to and receive events. Characters, UI components, even entire systems must have a consistent way of interacting with event managers. The goal here is for objects of any type to subscribe to events from multiple event managers and handle them in one place. We can accomplish this goal by leveraging Lua's *first-class functions*. To illustrate the usefulness of such functions, let's look at some example code for an imaginary game:

```
function LeftPlayerKeyHandler(receiver, eventData)
    if eventData.key == "A" then
        --move receiver left
    elseif eventData.key == "D" then
        --move receiver right
    end
end

function RightPlayerKeyHandler(receiver, eventData)
    if eventData.key == "J" then
        --move receiver left
    elseif eventData.key == "L" then
        --move receiver right
    end
end

local Player1 = ThisLevel:NewActor("PlayerPrototype")
local Player2 = ThisLevel:NewActor("PlayerPrototype")

Player1:Subscribe("OnKeyPress", LeftPlayerKeyHandler)
Player2:Subscribe("OnKeyPress", RightPlayerKeyHandler)
```

The first thing we did here was define two slightly different functions to be used as event callbacks. Second, we created two instances of some predefined "Player" object. These instances then subscribed to the *same event with different callback functions*. Player1's OnKeyPress callback will cause it to move left and right when the 'A' and 'D' keys are pressed. Player2's OnKeyPress callback uses the 'J' and 'L' keys instead. We can see that regardless of what our object, event, and callback functions are the act of subscribing to an event will be consistent with this interface. But the use of callbacks in event systems is certainly not groundbreaking and definitely not Lua-exclusive, so what's the big deal? The "big deal" is a combination of things. While callback functions are not exceptional on their own, when they also happen to be first-class functions it opens up some interesting possibilities.

Subscribers can define simple callbacks inline:

```
Player1:Subscribe("OnDeath", function()
    error("Player Died!")
end)
```

We can take full advantage of Lua's *closures*:

```
local counter = 0
function DoStuff()
     --do stuff
     counter = counter + 1
     print("DoStuff has been called " .. counter .. " times.")
end
Player1:Subscribe("OnDeath", DoStuff)
--the variable "counter" will be properly incremented when
--DoStuff is called by the event handling system even though
--it's not defined in the function. Powerful!
```

We can create data that is used to quickly subscribe an object to events common of its prototype. This creates a more data-driven approach.

```
--In the player prototype data somewhere
DefaultPlayerEvents = {
     OnCreate = PlayerPrototype.PlayerCreateFunc,
     OnKeyPress = PlayerPrototype.LeftPlayerKeyHandler,
     OnKilled = PlayerPrototype.DrawFrownyFace,
}

--In the NewActor function somewhere
for event, callback in pairs(PlayerPrototype.DefaultPlayerEvents)
do
     somePlayer:Subscribe(event, callback)
end
```

The other reason why callbacks in Lua are so useful is highlighted in the "inline callback" example above. Since Lua discards arguments if passed into a function that does not expect them, we can use callback functions that do not take a receiver or event data table. Notice also that we have not specified a return type for our callbacks. In general Lua's type flexibility sets our event system apart from similar systems in languages like C++ where all callback functions would be required to match a specific function signature. Callbacks in C# for different event types frequently have *different* function signatures! In our Lua-based system we can use the same callback to subscribe to several very different events and, as long as the event data table contains the entries expected in the callback function, everything will work out great. We can even create a callback function that will describe the event data of any event we subscribe to!

```
function EventDataWriter(receiver, eventData)
     for key, val in pairs(eventData) do
          print(key .. " - " .. val)
     end
end
```

```
MyGame:Subscribe("OnKeyPress", EventDataWriter)
MyGame:Subscribe("OnWindowResize", EventDataWriter)
MyGame:Subscribe("OnUDPRecv", EventDataWriter)
MyGame:Subscribe("OnKilled", EventDataWriter)
```

Now that we have a subscription and callback interface that satisfies our requirement for consistency and flexibility, we must turn our attention towards posting events and the interface thereof. To get the most out of our event manager we will need an equally flexible interface for sending events as we created for receiving them. Here again we will take advantage of Lua's flexibility with respect to data types. Consider the following call to send an event:

```
PostEvent("OnKilled", someEventDataTable )
```

All we've done here is tell some nebulous event managing system that the OnKilled event has fired and whatever is in the event data table should be passed along to any objects subscribed to that event. What's wonderful about this system is that there's no need for predefined events or event data types. We can post an OnKilled event without any object ever being subscribed to it, and we can put whatever we want in the event data so long as the subscriber's callback function handles (or ignores) it. Most importantly, the call to post an event looks the same no matter what the event is, who's getting it, or what data is associated with the event.

All that's left is to decide how the internals of our event manager should work. What happens when we subscribe to an event? What happens when we post one? In general, an event manager needs to keep a list of subscribed objects and their callbacks for each event. Such a structure could be visualized in a manner similar to picture below:

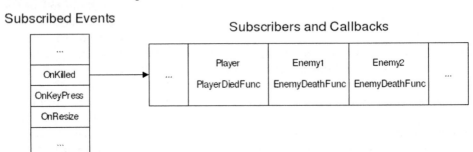

Let's examine how the subscription and posting of events works in better detail to provide some insight. Subscribing to an event would add it to the list of subscribed events above. Once the event name has been found or added, the subscriber and callback are inserted into the corresponding list as shown below:

```
function Subscribe(self, eventName, callback)
    table.insert( EventManager.Events[eventName],
                 { Subscriber = self, Callback = callback } )
end
```

This is event subscription at its simplest. A more robust system would need to add functionality for unsubscribing from events, as well as error checking to avoid duplicate registrations and similar cases. We must also consider events that add/remove other events, iterator invalidation, and all of the headaches that brings. The simplest way to handle these issues is with "pending queues". Rather than inserting new event handlers immediately when the function is called, it should add them to a separate list that is added en masse at the end of the frame. Removing events should flag them for deletion at the end of the frame.

Posting events is also remarkably simple. If the list of subscribed events contains the event being posted, then we iterate over the associated list and execute the callback for each subscriber. This example too eschews robustness for brevity:

```
function PostEvent(eventName, eventDataTable)
        for _, pair in ipairs(EventManager.Events[eventName]) do
                pair.Callback(pair.Subscriber, eventDataTable)
        end
end
```

Strategy

I mentioned earlier that one of the great things about Lua is that its functions are first-class. This language feature immensely facilitates the *strategy* design pattern. The strategy pattern creates differences between objects at runtime by changing their function references. We can leverage the event manager we created above as a way to implement strategy in our application by specifying different callbacks for different objects (as in the very first code example), but we can also override functions directly when it suits us. Consider the code below:

```
function Fly()
        --Do stuff
end

function Walk()
        --Do Stuff
end

local enemy1 =  ThisLevel:NewActor("BlobMonster")
local enemy2 =  ThisLevel:NewActor("BlobMonster")

enemy1.MoveFunc = Fly
enemy2.MoveFunc = Walk
```

Now if we have a list of similar enemies we can simply iterate through it and call MoveFunc for each one. This is similar to inheritance, with the exception that you can actually alter the behavior during runtime.

```
function Icarus(receiver, eventDataTable)
    --If we're flying right now then this is bad news. :-(
    receiver.MoveFunc = Walk
end
enemy1:Subscribe("OnTooCloseToSun", Icarus)
```

Now when our flying enemy gets too close to the sun, his movement function is changed to make him a walking enemy instead.

Extra credit

Serialization of this event data is very straightforward, and even allows us to leverage our existing event system for sending network messages. Consider the following example:

```
local MyChatWindow = GUI:NewWindow("ChatWindow")
MyChatWindow:Subscribe("OnNetChatMessage", NetChatMsgFunc)
```

Where will the "OnNetChatMessage" event be generated? From the other computer we're connected to, of course! What we need to do to make this work is create a method for remote systems to tell our event manager to broadcast the OnNetChatMessage event — with proper data and all. This gets a little involved, but it's definitely worth it. This section was written with winsock and C++ in mind, but the theory should apply to any network API you can use through Lua.

The remote system wants to send an event to our system. The data will need to be serialized into a stream of bytes by the remote system, sent across the network, and then deserialized into a meaningful event on our system. How should we approach this given that we do not predefine event templates? With a little trickery, of course! We will give events a predictable header that tells the receiver how to decode them on the fly. So what sort of information do we need to send so the receiver can decode our byte string?

- We should send the length of the serialized data as the first integer.
- We will need to store the name string of the event.

    - All strings will require an integer prefix to describe their length.

- We need to define the event table data.

    - We should consider adding a "sender" member to the table with our IP address or a connection ID, so the receiver knows who sent this message.
    - For all tables we need to specify the table size, along with each element's type.
    - We need to differentiate between (string) keyed tables and array- type tables.

· For keyed tables, we will need to store each key string as well as its value.

Taking all of this into consideration, a call and viable serialization might look like this:

```
SendNetEvent("PlayerData",
{
        Name = "Robert Oates",
        Age = 23,
        Single = false,
        Color = {255, 0, 0},
})
```

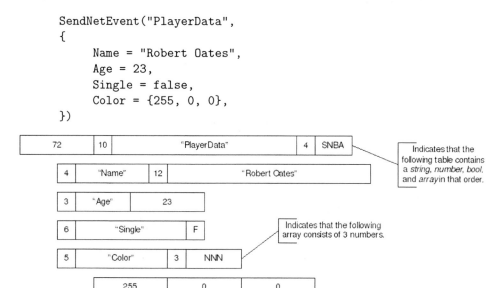

- Line 1 (header):

    - byte unsigned integer for the buffer length in bytes
    - 1 byte for size of event name string
    - 10 bytes for event name string (no null terminating character)
    - 1 byte for number of parameters in the event table
    - 4 bits to describe type of each value in event table (×2 = 2 bytes in this case)

- Line 2 (first event table entry):

    - 1 byte for key string length
    - 4 bytes for key string (Name)
    - 1 byte for value string length
    - 12 bytes for value string (Robert Oates)

- Line 3 (second event table entry):

    - 1 byte for key string length
    - 3 bytes for key string (Age)
    - 4 bytes for float number (23)

- Line 4 (third table entry):

    - 1 byte for key string length
    - 6 bytes for key string (Single)
    - 1 byte for Boolean (false)

- Line 5 (fourth and last event table entry)

    - 1 byte for key string length
    - 5 bytes for key string (Color)
    - 1 byte for number of elements in array
    - 4 bits to describe the type of each element in the array (3 numbers × 4 = 12, which rounds up to 2 bytes in this case)

- Line 6 (members of Color array)

    - 4 bytes for number (255)
    - 4 bytes for number (255)
    - 4 bytes for number (255)

Now that our data has been serialized, it is ready to be streamed across the internet to the waiting event handler on some other computer. The benefit to self-describing data such as this is that the receiver does not need to know about an event in order to receive and decode it.

As you can see, this setup allows for the nesting of tables and all sorts of other neat stuff. The drawback it suffers is bloat from all of the strings used to describe the various bits of data. Fortunately if the format of our event data is not going to change much, we can take advantage of caching. Once this message has been successfully sent, both sides can remember "Ok. There's an event called PlayerData, and its event structure looks a certain way." The event information will then be cached and assigned a unique number for future use. Next time the event gets sent across the network, it only needs to supply the values and none of the description data (keys, type info). The example I'm about to show makes the assumption that types will remain consistent even inside of nested tables. Your implementation may vary. In the event that I needed to send my player data again the serialized version would now look like this:

Notice that the buffer length in picture below is now a negative number, which I've decided to use as a flag to indicate that this is a cached message type. The following byte (you may wish to use a short or uint instead) with value 1 is the unique cached message type number. With the type information cached, we're able to send only the value data and reduce subsequent messages from 72 bytes to 35 bytes — cutting the message length by more than half while preserving the ability to send events over the network as easily as we send them to objects in our own game. When the PlayerData message is received on the other side, it will be reconstructed and then sent to an event handler which will then forward it to any objects (such as the game object, a level, a user interface, or an enemy) that have subscribed to the message.

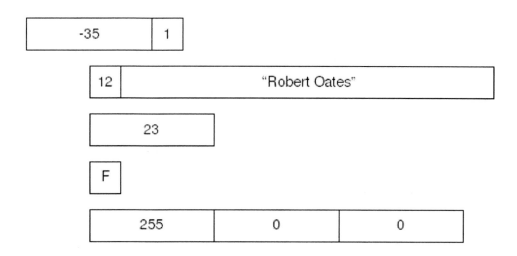

Closing

Hopefully the simple examples I have provided are adequate to illustrate the power and flexibility of these patterns. When combined with Lua's advanced features (closures, first-class functions) they can be used to build a solid foundation for any script-driven game.

22

Lua for Game Programming

Steve Gargolinski

The goal of this article is to describe a breadth of ways that Lua can be used to supplement a traditional (C++) game engine. The three areas that we will take a look at specifically are data representation, adding an extensible structure for providing dynamic in-game challenges to the player, and supplementing our game world with Lua-driven artificial intelligence.

When video games were young, all pieces of a typical game were coded directly into the engine. Maps, sprites, the user interface, game logic, and AI were all represented in assembly code or C, and later C++. This approach was cumbersome and inflexible, requiring a build step in between changing any sort of game data and being able to view it in the game. Before long, the concept of separating the game engine from its external components became possible. Maps are now created by editors as external files, Non-Player Character (NPC) dialogue is stored in a text file rather than C++ code, and sprites are stored as textures. It is no longer necessary to perform a costly build step after changing one line of NPC dialogue.

After moving game assets out of the engine and into data, the next step is to create a separation between our engine code and game logic, which can be achieved by exposing select areas of the game engine to a scripting language such as Lua. This separation allows programmers to define clean interfaces between select areas of the game and the chosen scripting solution. Also, less technically proficient designers can work at a higher level and tinker with game systems without needing to write actual C++ code, compile, or fully understand the engine. Much of the game experience can be tweaked and tuned without requiring the game to be rebuilt or even restarted.

Keep in mind that games are performance-intensive applications. It is necessary to make careful choices about which layers are implemented in script and which layers stay in the (faster) C++ game engine. It's up to the game programmers to decide just which areas of the engine will provide maximum advantage when exposed to a scripting solution.

In this article we will discuss several potential high-leverage areas ripe for Lua exposure. Lua is a particularly strong choice for a scripting solution in any game engine. It is fast and lightweight. It is open source—in case you decide it needs to be extended—and also completely free. It has a reasonably simple syntax while remaining powerful. This will come in handy considering that designers who do not write code every day for a living will often be the ones to use Lua scripts.

Example game

To clearly illustrate the goals of this article, we will refer to a sample game. Hopefully you all remember the classic game Adventure (or Zork). The framework game we are going to use is a very simple version of these "text adventures".

In this sample game there is a World made up of Locations. Locations are connected to each other in a sparse graph. There are Items in this World which can either be at a Location or in the possession of an Actor who can be either the Player or an NPC. Actors are able to pick up items, drop them, and move between connected Locations in the World. It is as simple as that.

Note that this article assumes an existing C++/Lua binding solution. A description of the different available techniques is beyond the scope of this article, but Celes et al.[1] provide a solid discussion.

Data representation

Games use huge amounts of data. In a typical game there are models, animations, maps, entities, and sounds, each with its own data format. Figuring out the best way to represent this data is an involved decision with many implication details including: platform-specific issues, memory limitations, and designer/artist workflow patterns.

Lua can be used to efficiently and flexibly handle loading designer-defined data. Assume that in the realm of our example game, designers are in charge of creating each Location in the World. The code in Listing 1 describes a way to load in two Locations by defining them as a Lua table.

LoadAllLocations is responsible for building up a `locationTable` and passing it along to LoadLocationsFromTable where the information is extracted and used to add Locations to the World through a minimal number of exposed C++

---

[1]W. Celes, L. H. de Figueiredo, and R. Ierusalimschy, "Binding C/C++ Objects to Lua", *Game Programming Gems 6*, Charles River Media: pp. 351–355, 2006.

```
function LoadLocationsFromTable(locationTable)
  local world = LPGWorld.GetInstance()
  for i = 0, table.getn(locationTable) do
    world:AddLocation(locationTable[i].name, locationTable[i].desc)
  end
end
function LoadAllLocations()
  local locationTable = {}
  local index = 0
  locationTable[index] = {}
  locationTable[index].name = "FOREST"
  locationTable[index].description = "A lush forest."
  index = index + 1
  locationTable[index] = {}
  locationTable[index].name = "SWAMP"
  locationTable[index].description = "A dark swamp."
  LoadLocationsFromTable(locationTable)
end
```

Listing 1.

functions. Allowing game data to be defined this way is very flexible; it's easy to cut and paste, add, and delete Locations with just a few clicks. In the real world of game development, however, game data is far more complicated than simple Locations with names and descriptions. Specifying our data explicitly in a Lua table is not optimal. It is important for designers to have the power to organize data in a cleaner way — in spreadsheet form, for example. No matter which external format we decide to use, the result will be a locationTable passed to LoadLocationsFromTable. Whenever designers want to use an external data format (.xml, .csv, etc.) we need to write a bit of code to turn this data into a properly formatted locationTable. Lua has a decent set of string manipulation utilities which makes writing these functions easy. If we want to represent our data above in a spreadsheet, we will end up needing to parse a .csv (comma separated value) file, as follows:

```
FOREST,A lush forest.
SWAMP,A dark swamp.
```

Extracting this data into a locationTable equivalent to the one defined as an explicit Lua table above can be done with a simple bit of code (Listing 2).

We can now update our loading process to read in a .csv file:

```
LoadLocationsFromTable(BuildLocationTableFromCSV("map.csv"))
```

Loading data in this fashion allows us to store the actual data in any format we want, while still passing through a common function (LoadLocationsFromTable) during the loading process. This allows load-time designer defined validation of

```
function BuildLocationTableFromCSV(csvFile)
  local locationTable = {}
  local index = 0
  for csvEntry in io.lines(csvFile) do
    local _, _, locationName, locationDesc =
                             string.find(csvEntry, "(.+),(.+)")
    locationTable[index] = {name = locationName, desc = locationDesc}
    index = index + 1
  end
  return locationTable
end
```

Listing 2.

data on top of the constraints implemented in our game engine. We can expose
this functionality by adding a single line:

```
function LoadLocationsFromTable(locationTable)
  local world = LPGWorld.GetInstance()
  for i = 0, table.getn(locationTable) do
    ValidateLocationData(locationTable[i]) -- ***
    world:AddLocation(locationTable[i].name, locationTable[i].desc)
  end
end
```

ValidateLocationData becomes an opportunity for designers to define validation requirements for the data they are specifying. A designer could decide
that Locations should always specify a description that is not an empty string.
It would be simple to add this check without requiring any change to the game
code. This is most useful for designer-desired guidelines, with more strict requirements enforced in the engine:

```
function ValidateLocationData(loc)
  if string.len(loc.desc) == 0 then
    print("DATA ASSERT - Empty description for location: " .. loc.name)
  end
end
```

With this structure in place, it is simple to expose the ability to add Locations
at run time. All that we need to do is add a Lua function to build up a
locationTable to pass through the same loading procedure used above. Hooking
a game debug console into this function allows designers to modify the game's
data easily at runtime, giving them the ability to test out new Locations without
even needing to restart the game.

```
function AddSingleLocation(locationName, locationDesc)
  local locationTable = {}
  locationTable[1].name = locationName
```

```
    locationTable[1].description = locationDesc
    LoadLocationsFromTable(locationTable)
end
```

Dynamic challenges

The goal of this section is to add a mechanism to present the player with challenges — focused, mix-in situations with risk/reward structures to drive and control the overall flow of the game. We will be creating a simple example challenge called "Water The Forest", in which the player must bring the "Water Jug" Item to the "Forest" Location in the World. This is a very simple challenge based on our example game, but the mechanism is powerful and can be applied to many different types of games. The idea here is that high-level control of the challenges (initialization, updating, etc.) is handled in the game engine, but the content is completely controlled through Lua scripts. Each challenge is defined in terms of a single Lua file. For the purposes of this article we will keep things very simple — Lua file only needs to implement four functions: EvaluatePreReqs(), Update(), Success(), and Failure(). EvaluatePreReqs() is responsible for controlling when a particular challenge is given out. This function returns a boolean value indicating true whenever the pre-requisites for this challenge are met, and false otherwise. We will use the results of EvaluatePreReqs() when deciding which challenge to present to the player. Here is some simple example (engine level) pseudocode for using EvaluatePreReqs() to choose a valid challenge based on the current game state:

```
Array<Challenges> validChallenges;
for i = 1; i < allChallenges.size(); ++i
{
  if (allChallenges[i]->TriggerEvaluatePreReqs() == true)
    validChallenges.push(allChallenges[i]);
}
activeChallenge = validChallenges[RandInt(0, validChallenges.size)];
```

This piece of code will loop through all of our challenges, building up an array of the ones which pass our EvaluatePreReqs() test. We then set our active challenge to a random entry in this array. Something important to note here is how the allChallenges array gets filled in. Since each of our challenges is contained within a Lua file, we can simply iterate on all the .lua files in a specified challenges directory, adding each one to the allChallenges array. This discovery mechanism is a very useful property since it does not require a list of challenges to be stored anywhere. Adding a new challenge only requires the addition of a new file. If we decide to release an expansion pack, downloadable content, or some combination of the two, there is no need to coordinate an index file of challenges between these permutations. Each expansion pack simply needs to drop a few files in the challenges directory. After the engine has chosen an active challenge, the next responsibility of the engine is to trigger an update on this challenge. The result of an update can either be success (1), failure (−1), or no resolution (0).

```
int challengeResult = activeChallenge->triggerUpdate();
if (challengeResult == 1)
{
  activeChallenge->TriggerSuccess();
  completedChallenges.push(activeChallenge);
  activeChallenge = NULL;
}
else if (challengeResult == -1)
{
  activeChallenge->TriggerFailure();
  failedChallanges.push(activeChallenge);
  activeChallenge = NULL;
}
```

These lists can be used to present the player with a history of the challenges they have attempted, or to filter allChallenges to prevent giving the player a challenge they have already completed. For our example challenge these functions are simple. The goal of "Water the Forest" is for the player to bring the Water Jug into the Forest. We do not want to give out this challenge unless three preconditions are met:

- The Water Jug Item exists somewhere in the World.

- The Forest is a Location in the World.

- The Water Jug is not already in the Forest.

The EvaluatePreReqs() implementation is very simple. As long as these three conditions are satisfied, we want to give out the challenge. Here is some example code to handle evaluating the prerequisites (assume that the world and itemManger are passed into EvaluatePreReqs() by default):

```
function EvaluatePreReqs(world, itemManager)
  local forest = world:GetLocationFromIDString("FOREST")
  local waterJug = itemManager:GetItemFromIDString("WATERJUG")
  if (forest == nil) or (waterJug == nil) or (forest:HasItem(waterJug))
  then
    return false
  end
  return true
end
```

In Update() we only need to perform one check: Does the Forest currently contains a Water Jug? When it does, we provide feedback for the player indicating that the challenge has been completed. In a full game we would also give out some gold or experience points. Here is an example Update() function for our challenge:

```
function Update(world, itemManager)
  local forestLoc = world:GetLocationFromIDString("FOREST")
  local waterJugItem = itemManager:GetItemFromIDString("WATERJUG")
  if forestLoc:HasItem(waterJugItem) then
    return 1
  else
    print("Still waiting for that Water Jug.")
  end
  return 0
end
```

When the player drops the Water Jug in the Forest, our Update() function will return 1, causing this challenge's Success() function to trigger. In this simple case we will print some feedback for the user, but in a more complicated example it could display some fancy UI, update the hero's experience points, or give out some gold pieces. In this simple example there is no failure case.

```
function Success()
  print("Successfully brought the Water Jug to the Forest!")
end
```

The above example displays a very useful pattern. We've created a fully data-driven challenge system. Each challenge is contained completely within a single Lua file. Aside from the C++ function exposure, the only responsibility of the game engine is to decide which challenge to run, and to know which script functions to call when updating. The rest of the logic is contained completely within the Lua code.

AI and state machines

AI programmers have long used Finite State Machines (FSMs) in all (ok, most) of your favorite games to successfully create the appearance of enemy/opponent intelligence. There are a number of ways to implement an FSM structure with Lua. It can be done completely in Lua code (and for certain situations this might make sense), but for this example we're going to stick with the pattern of supplementing a traditional FSM structure with Lua instead of moving over the entire implementation. This gives us the power to set breakpoints and monitor variables in C++ while retaining the flexibility of Lua.

It can make a lot of sense to expose your FSM functionality to a scripting solution such as Lua. This choice carries with it a lot of familiar benefits/drawbacks of exposing a game system to scripts. A data-driven AI solution can provide some serious power. With script-controlled game agents, it is quick and easy to make widespread changes. New AI logic can be quickly tested and iterated on. After exposing the necessary sections of the AI system to Lua, it is possible to hand off the state machine implementation to designers — allowing them complete control over the characters in game with no C++ knowledge required. However, with this amount of power comes the natural ability to screw things up big time. FSMs can become complicated, assuming control over a huge number of rich character behaviors. Designers (or programmers) unfamiliar with the subtleties of FSM design may have trouble keeping full view of the 'big picture' when modifying the AI. Changes in one state may have undesired side-effects on other states in the machine. These state to state relationships are not always obvious, and exposing them to more people (instead of just AI programmers) is a risk increase. Performance is another important factor to keep in mind when implementing a FSM solution. State logic implemented in Lua will never be as fast as state logic implemented in C++. Make sure that the majority of expensive calculations are taking place on the C++ side and develop metrics to keep an eye on where processor cycles are being used up in your game AI. As your FSMs near completion, consider moving the more expensive states into C++ code, trading flexibility for performance.

Here is the basic skeleton of our FSM:

```
class FSMMachine
{
  void UpdateMachine();
  void ChangeState(FSMState* newState);
  void AddState(FSMState* newState);
  FSMState* m_currentState;
}
```

FSMMachine is responsible for aggregating the states in our FSM. It keeps track of the active state, provides a mechanism for switching states, and is the entry point for updating our FSM.

```
class FSMState
{
  void Begin();
  void Update();
  void End();
}
```

Each FSMState requires three functions: Begin(), End(), and Update(). Begin() is called whenever the state machine transitions to this state, End() is called whenever the state machine transitions away from this state, and Update() is called each tick on the active state. This functionality is captured in the engine as FSMMachine::ChangeState(), which looks like this:

```
void FSMMachine::ChangeState(FSMState* newState)
{
  m_currentState->End();
  m_currentState = newState;
  m_currentState->Begin();
}
```

The base class FSMState can be extended to implement a specific state in C++ code. For example, we could add a new state FSMStateHunt, which extends

FSMState and implements the logic necessary to send an NPC out on a hunt. In order to facilitate a Lua-driven FSM, we're going to provide the LuaFSMState class:

```
class LuaFSMState : public FSMState
{
  LuaFunction m_beginFunc;
  LuaFunction m_updateFunc;
  LuaFunction m_endFunc;
  void Begin();
  void Update();
  void End();
}
```

This class replaces arbitrary C++ logic in Begin(), Update(), and End() with Lua function calls in this fashion:

```
void LuaFSMState::Begin()
{
  CallLuaFunction(m_beginFunc);
}
```

Our FSMMachine is now free to mix and match Lua driven states with C++ driven states.

Now that we've got the basic transition structure of state machine logic set up, how do we actually use it? First we need to define the state machine of an NPC. We'll expose a LuaFSMState factory function, and provide a startup method for each NPC to seed their state machine.

```
function SetupFSM(fsm)
  local idleState = LuaFSMState.Create("Idle", "npc0.lua",
  "Idle_Begin", "npc0.lua", "Idle_Update", "npc0.lua", "Idle_End")
  local wanderState = LuaFSMState.Create("Wander", "npc0.lua",
  "Wander_Begin", "npc0.lua", "Wander_Update", "npc0.lua", "Wander_End")
  fsm:AddStateToFSM(idleState)
  fsm:AddStateToFSM(wanderState)
  fsm:ChangeState("Idle")
end
```

This block of code starts off by creating "Idle" and "Wander" states, specifying which Lua functions to call for the Begin(), Update(), and End() of each. It then adds these states to our NPC's FSM, and finally starts him off in the "Idle" state. Note that it is possible to follow the pattern we defined in the "Data Representation" section to move this data into a .csv file.

For this example, we only need to define the Update() functions for our two FSM states (Assume that the FSM, the player, and our NPC are passed into these functions when called from the engine):

```
function Idle_Update(fsm, player, self)
  if player:GetLocation() == self:GetLocation() then
    fsm:ChangeState("Wander")
  end
end

function Wander_Update(fsm, player, self)
  if rand() < 0.5 then
    fsm:ChangeState("Idle")
  end
  self:SetLocation(GetRandomConnectedLocation())
end
```

This code will cause the NPC to hang out in the Idle state until the player comes onto the same location as him, which triggers a transition into Wander. This NPC will spend the next few updates wandering randomly through the world before returning to Idle.

We're not doing anything in the Begin() or End() functions in a simple example like this, but we can show some useful trace code here:

```
function Idle_Begin(fsm, player, actor, world)
  print(actor:GetName()..": Let's hang out here for a while.")
end

function Idle_End(fsm, player, actor, world)
  print(actor:GetName()..": Time to move!")
end
```

This is a simple example that shows the basic structure behind a flexible and powerful FSM. We've given developers the option to move any or all AI decision-making code into Lua, separating it completely from engine code. We retain the option to implement each state in either Lua or C++ as we see fit. We can define and iterate on many states quickly in Lua, while preserving the ability to implement states in C++ when speed is a priority or the potential exists for significant debugging.

Generic Lua function exposure

A powerful and simple use of Lua in a game engine is to expose arbitrary Lua script execution at run time via your game's command console or debug tools. All that you need to do is give the development team access to something as basic as: `runluascript file.lua function`.

This simple addition will be beneficial for everyone on the development team from programmers to artists to designers to QA. The ability to quickly, easily, and repeatedly run a set of actions contained in a script has advantages on many different levels. Designers can force situations they want to mess around with in game to see how they play out, QA can attach a Lua script to a bug report to provide more accurate reproduction, and programmers can use the script for anything from general code testing to performance evaluation.

Making generic Lua function execution available has the added benefit of increasing the development team's exposure to your chosen scripting solution. The more comfortable your team gets with Lua, the more use you will get out of it.

Conclusion

Hopefully this article has given you some ideas on how to supplement your game engine by exposing key areas to a Lua scripting solution.

The techniques discussed here barely scratch the surface of potential uses of Lua for game programming. Before you delve in, analyze the problems that your particular game is trying to solve and identify areas which lend themselves well to a data-driven, scripted solution.

23

Designing an Efficient Lua Driven Game Scripting Engine

Nicolas Peri

When designing a modern game engine, able to handle hundreds of "intelligent" objects with various complex behaviors, you need to deal with two major issues: runtime speed and ease of development. Using traditional C/C++ programming to define your objects behaviors implies recompiling your game code each time you make a modification in order to test it, which is a big time wasting. On the other hand, using a script driven game code will offer you a huge gain of development time, allowing you to perform "in game programming", but a bad integration can quickly result in poor runtime performance. The ease of use and the execution speed of Lua are not to prove anymore. However, a well-done integration is not an easy thing to do, if you do not understand exactly how Lua works and how to use it efficiently. This article explains how to take advantage of Lua to design a powerful and flexible game engine with autonomous object behaviors, using scripted event handlers, and how to avoid the common performance pitfalls.

The problem — motivation and statement

We can consider a game as a collection of scenes, also known as levels. Each scene represents an area in the universe, containing objects like flowers, trees, birds, and so on. Many objects do not need to have an artificial life, like flowers or dead trees, but some must have particular dynamic behavior, like birds flying from tree to tree or evil monsters trying to attack you. When designing a game engine, you must provide your future users an easy and flexible way to define those behaviors. Nowadays, scripted artificial intelligence is the best solution to do that. The problem is that scripts will always be slower than native code; that's a fact. When making a game engine, performance is one of the most important constraints. We thus must find a way to reduce the CPU cost of scripts execution, to stay under an acceptable threshold.

The solution — description

Use an object local solution

Every "intelligent" object in the scene must have its own behavior. We will call an AIModel the data structure defining an object's behavior: it can be compared to a C++ or Java class, with the main difference that all the code is written in Lua. An AIModel basically contains member variables and functions. Each instance of an AIModel has his own set of member variables, with or without initial values, allowing every instance to be independent and quite different from others. Each object will have one or more AIModel instances controlling it. For example, an object representing a soldier could have an AIModel dedicated to the path finding and another one to the attack.

Use frame-by-frame execution

Ideally, autonomous behaviors should be done by using one thread for each AIModel instance. For performance reasons, this is just impossible in a game engine. The execution of each AIModel instance must thus be designed frame by frame, with the aim to emulate multithreading: each AIModel must for example implement a runOneFrame function, written in Lua, that will be in charge to step for each frame the desired behavior. In pseudo code, the engine loop would basically be:

```
while ( gameIsRunning )
do
   for each Object o in the Scene
   do
     for each AIModel instance ai controlling o
     do
       ai.runOneFrame ( )
     done
   done
   scene.draw ( )
done
```

Member variables are used to maintain the state of an AIModel instance, frame to frame. Nothing remains at the end of the frame but those.

```
while ( gameIsRunning )
do
  for each Object o in the Scene
  do
    for each AIModel instance ai controlling o
    do
      if ( ai.isTimeToRunOneFrame ( ) )
      then
        ai.runOneFrame ( )
      end
    done
  done
  scene.draw ( )
done
```

Listing 1.

Allow different update rate for the AIModel instances

Some behaviors do not need to be updated every frame: consider for example a radar that has to check at a regular time interval if there are ships around. It would thus be useful to provide to the user a way to specify that an AIModel only needs, for example, to be updated every second. This will avoid Lua to execute a script that spends, in average, most of its time in a waiting code. Because of the object local and frame-by-frame design, it will be possible to pause the execution of any AIModel instance when it is required. Our engine loop, in pseudo code, would now look like Listing 1.

Use an automatic activation process

Big scenes can contain thousands objects with one or more behaviors each. To limit the number of simultaneous running AIModel instances, we have to use an automatic mechanism dedicated to identify if, for a given frame, an object really needs to be updated. A fairly simple but good criteria would be to consider the distance to the camera: far objects, which are not even visible, certainly do not need their behavior to be updated. By limiting only nearest objects to be active, we will only execute Lua calls for a little subset of the objects in the scene. Our engine loop, in pseudo code, would then look like Listing 2.

Use an event based communication schema between AIModel instances

Now that we have autonomous behaviors for our scene objects, we would like them to be able to communicate with each other. We will add to AIModels some sort of public functions called "event handlers", and give to the user a way to

```
while ( gameIsRunning )
do
  for each Object o in the Scene
  do
    if ( o.isActive ( ) )
    then
      for each AIModel instance ai controlling o
      do
        if ( ai.isTimeToRunOneFrame ( ) )
        then
          ai.runOneFrame ( )
        end
      done
    end
  done
  scene.draw ( )
done
```

Listing 2.

send "events" from an AIModel instance to another one. A solution will be to provide a function similar to the following one:

```
object.sendEvent ( hObject, "Pathfinder", "Goto", x, y, z )
```

This function takes at least three parameters: an identifier of the object, the name of the AIModel instance and the name of the event we want to send. All optional remaining parameters will be passed to the event handler onGoto, of the instance of the AIModel Pathfinder, that is controlling the object represented by hObject. By this way, objects in the scene will have their own local behavior and will be able to send or receive stimuli from others, thus taking some decisions or just changing their state. In addition, this schema guarantees that no objects will be strongly dependent of another one: if an object is not active, it will simply not react to incoming events.

Use high level function packages

Written in C/C++ and accessible from the Lua code, it is recommended to provide high level dedicated packages of functions, avoiding long calculations to be done in script. As an example consider a simple object behavior: the object must always look at the camera. This requires tens of multiplications and additions. If there are tens of active objects running, this will result in hundreds of arithmetic operations per frame to be done in Lua. We thus must provide a function to do this in one Lua call, all the calculations being done in C/C++ compiled and optimized code. In our case this could be something like:

```
object.lookAt ( hObject, x, y, z )
```

where hObject would be an identifier of the object we want to control, and x, y, and z the coordinates of the point to look at. In a game engine it would be a good idea to provide, in addition of common packages like math or system, a dedicated function package for each domain of application: animation, dynamics, navigation, sound, sfx, . . .

Use handles to exchange data structures between Lua and C/C++ runtime

Lua provides an easy way to access your C/C++ data structures through the lightuserdata type. This is nothing but a pointer, that cannot be used directly from script, but that should be used like that:

```
-- Always look at the origin of the scene.
function MyAIModel:runOneFrame ( )
  local hObject = self.getObject ( )
  if ( hObject ~= nil )
  then
    object.lookAt ( hObject, 0, 0, 0 )
  end
end
```

In this example that defines a simple behavior, the self keyword is the Lua sugar that represents the current AIModel instance that is executed: its members are set up by the C/C++ just before calling the Lua function. It allows to get a handle to the object controlled by this AIModel instance. Once we get this handle, it will be possible to use it in every high level functions that take an object handle in parameter. A more complex behavior using could be for example:

```
-- If the user pressed the space key, then jump.
function MyAIModel:runOneFrame ( )
  if ( input.isKeyPressed ( input.kKeySpace ) )
  then
    local hObject = self.getObject ( )
    if ( hObject ~= nil )
    then
      dynamics.addImpulse ( hObject, 0, 100, 0 )
    end
  end
end
```

In this example, input and dynamics are Lua function packages, dedicated to input devices management (keyboard, mouse, gamepad...), and dynamics subsystem access.

Limit the use of complex types

Strings, tables, or metatables used for temporary variables are not recommended, because they will fire the memory allocator. Prefer using simple types like booleans, numbers, or lightuserdatas. For example using a vector class implemented in Lua with metatables will surely be very elegant, but not encouraged if you are looking for the best performances. In general all syntax sugars are not good for speed, or must be preprocessed. So for example to perform a dot product between two vectors, prefer using this solution:

```
local x1, y1, z1 = 1.0, 0.0, 0.0
local x2, y2, z2 = 0.0, 1.0, 0.0
local dot        = math.dotProduct ( x1, y1, z1, x2, y2, z2 )
```

Than this more elegant but slower one:

```
local v1  = Vector3:new ( 1.0, 0.0, 0.0 )
local v2  = Vector3:new ( 0.0, 1.0, 0.0 )
local dot = v1:dotProduct ( v2 )
```

Separate values of the first version will be stored on top of the Lua stack, but tables used for the syntax sugar of the second one, will require at least two memory allocations. Multiplied by the number of such operations needed to represent your behavior, and then by the number of active AIModel instances at a time, those two versions of the same code will have a small but sometimes not negligible difference, in term of execution speed.

Encourage the use of local variables

When using multiple times an AIModel instance member variable, you can obtain a significant performance gain by storing it in a local variable. Lua local variables reside in registers, and are accessible by index, as opposed to global variables, that reside in a table, and are accessible by a hash lookup. Here is an example of a local variable usage:

```
function MyAIModel:runOneFrame ( )
  local hObject = self.getObject ( ) -- Store the global into a local
  if ( hObject ~= nil )
  then
    dynamics.enableGravity    ( hObject, true )
    dynamics.setLinearDamping ( hObject, 0.5 )
    dynamics.addImpulse       ( hObject, 0, 100, 0 )
  end
end
```

Use preallocated memory pools

Lua allows you to define your own memory allocation functions. If you do that, you will see that Lua allocates a lot of small temporary buffers that will be freed at the next garbage collection. All of this will fragment your system memory and will also be time consuming. In an embedded environment or a gaming console, with a limited and fixed amount of memory, it is vital to avoid as much as possible dynamic allocations at runtime. A solution is to use a preallocated pool of small buffers (16, 32, and 96 bytes are good values, but it should depend on your implementation) that will be dedicated to the Lua runtime. Bigger or unpredictable allocations are done through your main allocator.

Explanation and justification

Taken one by one, each of the recommendations done just before can look negligible, but if all are respected, the speed improvements will make it possible to use Lua as a runtime language for fast applications such as games. Indeed, we passed from a naive solution to an optimized one by reducing Lua runtime intrinsics, scripts execution, C/C++ communication and the number of calls.

Weaknesses and suggested improvements

Even with all of that, the same work done with C/C++ compiled behaviors will always be faster. A solution would be to allow Lua code to be translated to C/C+ code then compiled, at product releasing time, scripting being used just for development time. If you follow the recommendations written in this gem, and strictly use nothing but Lua simple types and loops, this should be a quite easy thing.

Conclusion

Making a well done integration of Lua in your game engine finally implies two major things: finding a way to execute only the scripts that are really needed (but every engine should already do that for all other sub systems like animation or dynamics, so doing it for AI should not be a big deal), and reducing the overheads of Lua execution by avoiding time consuming operations and providing high level dedicated function packages. Lua scripted behaviors would also be useful for remote programming and debugging: it is possible to change the behavior of one object in a game running on a game console, by simply uploading a string containing the new script, which will automatically be taken in account at the next frame.

Part V

Embedding and Extending

24

Enhanced Coroutines in Lua

Patrick Rapin

This article describes a method to increase the power of coroutines by using preemptive native threads together with standard collaborative Lua threads. This way coroutines are able to perform blocking operations, like reading data from a opened pipe, without freezing all the other coroutines. This is done by having a dynamic pool of preemptive threads executing commands on the background, while the associated coroutine is suspended from the Lua point of view.

History

Our company, Olivetti, is active in the ink-jet printer industry. We have always written specific programs in order to drive our printers for testing and production. The most recent one is a very powerful tool, called LuaDura, based on Lua 5.1. This program can send low level commands to the printer, through a dedicated communication channel. The protocol used here is similar to the Mass Storage Class of USB: the host sends a binary command, optionally followed by data; the printer always sends back a status, along with additional response data. Several communication channels can be used for this task: USB, serial port, Ethernet. Other ones may be added in the future, like Bluetooth or WiFi.

We wanted to be able to drive several printers simultaneously within a single Lua script, for example in a mass production test board. The problem is that all input/output commands through the preceding channels are blocking: it is therefore difficult to drive several printers in a single thread. This is why we need some form of true multithreading for our application.

Multithreading models

In the book "Programming in Lua" (second edition), Roberto Ierusalimschy explains in chapter 30 that Lua supports two models for multithreading. The third model is the one we will describe.

Lua collaborative threads with memory sharing

In the first model, there is only one Lua state, but several coroutines running sequentially inside it, by explicit yielding and resuming. As they run in the same state, all these threads can access the global variables and the registry, so it is easy to share data between them. However, the operating system has no knowledge about this mechanism. If one collaborative thread performs a blocking I/O operation, all other coroutines are stopped during that time. Consequently, this model does not fit our requirement. An option could be to use asynchronous input/output, as they are available on most operating systems. Unfortunately, this has several drawbacks: it is hard to implement, not portable across platforms, and not all operations can be done that way.

Preemptive threads in separate Lua states, sharing no memory

In the second model, several Lua states are created, each running in a different native preemptive thread. Because there is no connection between separate Lua threads, C code must be added in order to share data between the interpreters. This could be a solution for our application: we could imagine a C function, taking as parameter a function to execute, that would create a preemptive thread, which in turn would create a new Lua state and run the function until it exits. A blocking command only stops that specific thread. While possible, we don't like this option, as it would be hard for the main script to monitor the simultaneous processes without heavy intervention of C code and OS semaphores.

Preemptive threads associated with coroutines

The third model is essentially an enhanced version of the first one. There is only one Lua state, and several coroutines running inside it. Therefore the threads can easily share data between them. The key trick is to enable a native preemptive thread to executes the input/output commands instead a Lua coroutine. It works like this: the coroutine calls a C function when it has to perform a blocking operation. That function checks if there is an idle native thread from the pool, or instantiates a new one. It then sends a message to it, and yields. Lua interpreter will switch to another coroutine, while the command really starts executing in the background. To prevent memory corruption, the native thread has no access to the Lua state: all its input arguments, output results and error messages must be passed through the message structure.

Later on, the coroutine will be resumed, and if the command has finished executing, output result is pushed onto Lua stack, or an error is thrown.

Implementation

The annexed file `thread.c` implements this third solution for multithreading. It is partly based on the source code of LuaDura, but with all references to printer communication removed. Instead, it exports some simple tasks, which are widely available and used. The implementation is aimed to be both an example program and a startup file in which you can add features for your application.

The code supports both Windows and POSIX preemptive threads. To minimize the number of compilation switches, the following POSIX functions are implemented under Windows using native objects: `sem_init`, `sem_post`, `sem_wait`, `sem_destroy`, `pthread_create`, and `pthread_cancel`. With a simple similar interface, it should be possible to run the example on other operating systems as well.

The implementation does not need any change in Lua 5.1 sources. Like all standard Lua libraries, this code only uses the official API. And like Lua itself, it is written in clean C, thus should compile unmodified in both C and C++ languages.

A pool of C threads is maintained in the form of four lists, all initially empty. When a coroutine ask for a blocking operation, we look at the idle list of threads and take one from that list. If the list is empty, a new native thread is allocated and initialized. A table placed in Lua registry is used to keep track of which coroutine is using which C thread at any time.

Like with the coroutines, there is no need to explicitly close the threads. They will be collected like any other objects. If you are low in system resources, you can force a garbage collection by calling `collectgarbage` explicitly. For this purpose, a second table is present in the registry. Each time a thread is taken from the pool to execute a command, a userdatum is created and placed in the table. When the thread becomes idle again, the table entry is set back to nil. Because this userdatum is bound to a metatable of which the `__gc` method is overridden, the unused operating system resources can be freed when a garbage collection occurs.

The module exports one global `thread` table with a few functions. Four user functions are exported into that `thread` table. They were chosen because they are blocking functions, are simple and are available on most platforms. They only pretend to be examples for user needs, although they may be useful as is.

- `thread.sleep(milliseconds)`: a delay function, implemented with `Sleep` on Windows and `usleep` on Unix.

- `thread.system(command)`: calls the ANSI `system` function, which in turn starts a command interpreter: `sh` on Unix, `cmd.exe` on Windows NT.

- `thread.gets([maxbytes])`: reads a line of text from the standard input. It is implemented using the ANSI `fgets` function.

- `thread.wget(hostname, filepath, [port])`: a very minimal HTTP client, like the Unix command line utility `wget`.

All functions follow the same scheme. They do not execute directly their associated base function. Instead, each one fills a message structure with input parameters from the Lua state. Necessary checks on the parameters are done at that time. The message is then passed to one native thread for execution. And the function should yield until the message finishes executing.

Here we face the major difficulty. It is impossible in the standard Lua implementation to yield inside a C function: only Lua functions can yield. Although there are non-portable patches that allow this, we will stay with the standard distribution and thus avoid yielding inside C code. Therefore, it is necessary to use the following idiom, just after having sent the message to the thread:

```
return lua_yield();
```

The `lua_yield` function will register the yelded status into the Lua state, and return –1. The net effect is that the calling Lua function will yield just after the C function ends. When the coroutine is resumed, it would go ahead after the call as if the command was successful. Because it is not the case, the C function must be called again. The second time, the input parameters are useless, but we will suppose that they are the same as before, to simplify the coding. If the native thread has now finished executing the command, either the output data is copied from the message back into the Lua state, or `luaL_error` is called with the error message. If the command is still executing, we again return `lua_yield()`.

So we have to call any of the four user functions inside a loop, necessarily written in Lua language. As we wish to hide this complex mechanism from the user scripts, the initializing function `luaopen_thread` runs the following Lua chunk just after having registered the user functions into the thread table:

```
for name,fct in pairs(thread) do
  thread[name] = function (...)
    local result
    repeat
      result = { fct(...) }
    until result[1] ~= thread
    return unpack(result)
  end
end
```

With this mechanism, each C user function is overridden with a Lua closure that calls the underlying C function inside a loop until it does not yield, and returns all its result values. The original user function is stored inside a non-local variable, so it is inaccessible to user scripts. The loop test condition may be quite surprising. Remember that when resuming a previously yielded C function, its apparently returned values are in fact the parameters passed to `coroutine.resume`. We just decided that the main scheduler function will pass the global `thread` table as parameters for `coroutine.resume`. With this arbitrary but unique value, the above loop is able to know if the C function has previously yielded or not.

In order to avoid for the scheduler to do an active polling on working threads, which would waste CPU time, a `thread.wait` function is exported in the library. It will wait for an event and return the first coroutine from the finished list.

Coding

Now let's take a closer look into the C implementation. Each C thread has a state variable associated with it for the synchronization mechanism. The four states used by the state machine are as follows:

- `IDLE`: Lua can send a command to the native thread.

- `REQUEST`: A command has been sent, execution can start. Lua coroutine yields.

- `WORKING`: A command is in execution in native thread. Lua coroutine also yields.

- `FINISHED`: A command has finished execution, Lua can read back results.

There are four double linked lists of threads, one for each state. Each time a thread state changes, its item is removed from one list and placed into the next one. A shared semaphore assures that operations on these list cannot be interrupted by other threads. Also to avoid any real time problem, Lua is only allowed to exchange data with the thread during `IDLE` state for the command, and during `FINISHED` state for the output read back.

An important helper function is `retrieve_thread_data`. Given the Lua coroutine represented by the current `lua_State` parameter, it returns a pointer to a C thread structure. Four situations can occur:

- If called from the main Lua thread (`lua_pushthread` returned 1), simply returns nil.

- If a command is already started for the coroutine, uses the mapping table to return the associated thread.

- If the list of idle threads is not empty, returns its first element.

- Otherwise, allocates a new structure and fills it with a C thread and two semaphores. The mapping table is updated accordingly.

The central function in the code is `exchange_with_thread`. After having got the native thread structure from current coroutine, one of these scenarios happens:

- If called from the main thread, the message is executed immediately; if an error occurs, `luaL_error` is directly called.

- If the thread state is `IDLE`, the message is passed to the thread. If an error will occur during the execution by the native thread, the error string is stored inside the message structure.

- When the thread state is `FINISHED`, the result is copied from the native thread. If an error has been stored in the message structure, `luaL_error` is called with that text error message.

- Otherwise, this means that a command is still in execution; the function yields again.

The synchronization between the native thread and the user functions uses two semaphores for each thread. The first one controls the start of command. It is signalled by the user function and waited by the thread. At the end of execution, the opposite is done: the thread signals a semaphore awaited by the user function. It also signals a shared semaphore that will be checked by `thread.wait`.

An important function is `thread.wait`. It is responsible to stop the execution of the main thread, without wasting CPU time, until one of the native threads has finished execution of their command. If the list of finished threads is not empty, it returns the first one. Otherwise, it waits on the shared semaphore signals by the threads and tries again.

Wget user function

The only slightly complex user function in the library is called `thread.wget` and is designed to perform an HTTP request to a web server. It can be used to build a simple Web browser or a robot. This implementation does not need LuaSocket library: it is completely written using simple C socket functions.

Typically, requesting several files in parallel takes less time to download than if they are retrieved one after the other. This function is an alternative to the example found in chapter 9.4 of "Programming in Lua", which uses the select function of LuaSocket library, with pure coroutine functions. If you have read that chapter, you will be able to compare both approaches.

Function `thread.wget` takes three parameters: the server host name, the file path to retrieve and the port number, defaulting to 80. Alternatively, the second parameter can also be the complete HTTP request header, if you need more control over the request.

The function just outputs the whole returned data into a single Lua string, containing both the HTTP response header and the file retrieved. It is easy to separate the header and the content parts in Lua language, using regular expressions:

```
header, content = data:match("(.-\n)\r?\n(.*)")
```

Error handling

As already mentioned, if an error occurs during a command execution, we cannot call lua_error directly, because the native thread has no access to the Lua interpreter object. Instead, it calls the local helper function error. This latter begins by closing opened resources: freeing the output string and closing the current socket, if available. Depending on whether or not it is called from a coroutine, it then calls luaL_error directly or stores the message for the caller. The return value is only a syntactic trick to enable the use of the idiom like this one inside the user functions:

```
return error(msg, "Some error occur");
```

This is also the reason for the existence of an unnecessary return value in user execute_* functions, although the return status could be used by the main thread function to determine whether or not the command succeeded (in order to perform logging, for example).

Example of Lua code

Scheduler

Besides the C implementation of this thread library, let's have a look of some Lua code using it. First, we need some form of scheduler function, which is a sort of operating system replacement. The simplest form of the scheduler is this one:

```
function thread.sched(threads)
  while next(threads) do
    local thr = thread.wait()
    if not thr then thr = next(threads) end
    if not coroutine.resume(thr, thread) then
      threads[thr] = nil
    end
  end
end
```

The argument is a table of coroutine objects. Repeatedly, while there are still active threads, it waits for the first thread that has finished a blocking command. It tries to resume it, passing the global table thread as argument to coroutine.resume, so that the loop of previous listing knows that it had yielded.

If the resume fails, this either means that the user script has normally finished its execution, or there was an error. On both cases, the thread object is removed from the table, and will be garbage collected some time later (provided there is no other reference to it). In the case of an error, it would be preferable to display the error message or log it to some file, depending on the environment, but this was just a simple example. Another limitation to this function is that it does not resume coroutines which have yielded for other reasons than inside the thread library (by calling coroutine.yield). When a coroutine is created, it is in the suspend state, so we have to resume it once before calling the scheduler function (alternatively, thread.sched may resume all threads before entering the while loop).

Interpreter

In a multithreaded Lua script, the main function is typically the scheduler function, which is called after the coroutine objects have been initialized. When called from the standalone Lua interpreter, this means that until the last thread has finished its job, no prompt is issued to the user. This can be annoying, since you might want to keep the control of what is going on. But it is easy to write a new interpreter in Lua, using the exported thread.gets function. Here is an implementation which mimics the behavior of the regular Lua interpreter:

```lua
function thread.shell()
  local line = ''
  local prompt = '--> '
  while true do
    io.write(prompt)
    prompt = '--> '
    line = line .. thread.gets(1000)
    if line == 'quit\n' then return end
    line = line:gsub('^=', 'return ')
    local fct, err = loadstring(line, '@stdin')
    if fct then
      local res = { pcall(fct) }
      if not res[1] or #res > 1 then
        print(unpack(res, 2, #res))
      end
      line = ''
    elseif err:sub(-7,-1) == "'<eof>'" then
      prompt = '-->> '
    else
      print(err)
      line = ''
    end
  end
end
```

The function is continuously issuing a prompt, slightly different from the default one of lua.c, so that you know you are in a multithreaded script, and reads a line with the blocking function thread.gets. Until you press the RETURN key, this script is suspended and other threads can execute other tasks. Like the regular interpreter, an equal sign at the beginning of the line is a shortcut for the return statement. The line is then compiled. If a compilation error occurs at the end of the block, this means a multiple line instruction is typed, and so a different prompt is issued, and the next read line is concatenated to the previous one. You can exit the function by issuing the command "quit" on its own.

Complete example

The web site contains a more complete example for running simple user scripts. All four user functions previously discussed are run in parallel. You may notice that they do not to worry about the underlying multithreading; the scheduler function with the help of the thread.wait function takes care about all low-level synchronization management.

25

Using Lua in Pascal

Jeremy Darling

Why Lua?

In the world of Pascal development there are plenty of native solutions for scripting an application. Most of these are built with the Pascal language itself and this only leads to limiting the user base for the scripting language in question. Utilizing a well known and commonly used scripting language within our applications only helps to expand our user base in the end.

There are other common scripting languages out there (JavaScript, Monkey, and VBA to name a few), but as of the time of this writing, Lua is the most robust and supported scripting language available. Due to the nature of how it is built, Lua allows for great flexibility within an application and it incorporates into Pascal applications seamlessly.

The basic needs

Before we start talking about how to use Lua within an application, we need to discuss what is needed to get Lua on your system and use it within your projects.

First, you will need a copy of the Lua interpreter, you can download that from `lua.org` easily enough. You will also need a copy of the Pascal headers for Lua: I personally recommend the version on my website called pLua. You can get it at `http://www.eonclash.com/` just look under "Projects/Pascal Wrappers". Make sure you download the latest version of pLua and not the Generic Pascal

Wrappers as many bugs have been fixed and new features introduced in pLua that haven't been applied to the Generic Wrappers.

Instead of focusing on the "common" implementation of Pascal (Delphi), I will be focusing on generic ANSI-ISO Pascal in its Object Oriented form. This will allow the same code to be executed within FreePascal, Lazarus, Delphi, Kylix, and most other implementations of Pascal.

We will also need a design problem to solve.

The problem

In order to provide the best walkthrough of integrating Lua into a Pascal application as possible, I'll present an application that would benefit well from Lua integration. The application is a game of sorts where the user is up against the HAL 9000 and must convince it to release control of the ship.

To keep with the ubiquitous first project ("Hello World"), our first implementation will load whatever script is passed in and execute it.

Project foundations (setting up the project)

The same process will be true for all projects here on out, so it will only be covered here once. Setting up a new project to use Lua within Lazarus requires that the compiler know where the libraries are and where to output the final application. (The same is true for Delphi, Kylix, or FPC.)

Open Lazarus and click on Project/New Project, click Program, then Create. You should be presented with a blank project and the basics of a console application. Now, click on Project/Compiler Options, select the Paths tab, and enter in the appropriate location (where you extracted the Lua wrappers to) into the "Other Unit Files (-Fu)" and "Other Sources (.pp/.pas, used only by IDE not compiler)" edit boxes:

[pic]

Click Ok to close the dialog. Then do a Save All.

This sets up the Lazarus environment so that it knows where our Lua source files are located (Other Sources edit box). The Other Unit Files edit box tells it where to find the Lua libraries when it compiles our source.

Next change the uses section to include the proper units that you will need access to (if you want to make sure that all units are available and compliable then include lua, LuaWrapper, LuaObject, Cutils, and LuaUtils).

Perform a build to test everything (Ctrl+F9) and you should get a message stating "Project *name* successfully built".

Defining HAL 9000

Before we can actually build anything we need to define exactly what we are going to build. As it's outside the scope of this document to explain project design and documentation, here is a basic idea showing what HAL 9000 will do:

```
Start Application
Check to see if game.lua file exists
   If so then load it
Else
   Throw an error
Setup the game and execute the script to prepare the environment
Player input and processing
```

Building HAL 9000

Our first iteration of HAL 9000 (H9K) will use lua.pas and the methods that it surfaces. While using LuaWrapper would make our lives easier, it would also hide knowledge of how Lua works under the hood. I'm a strong believer of show and tell, but to keep the article on track and not cluttered with code, please look at the different source files as you work though. For this first project notice the comments and how we are setting up Lua.

The source shows a very basic implementation of ReadLn being brought into Lua so that we can allow for some user interaction within our scripts.

To start with, we initialize a new instance of Lua by calling lua_open and storing the return value in the global L (L is a common name for the active instance of Lua; this comes more from historical background then anything and you could name your instance anything you wish).

Next we start a try–finally block to make sure that lua_close(L) gets called, as we must close any instances of Lua that we open (as with object creation, or memory allocation, we don't want to strand any memory on exit).

Now we test to see if the user passed in a default script to execute, making sure that the file exists. If the file does exist, we load it with a call to luaL_loadfile; in the case that it doesn't exist, we load our default script with luaL_loadbuffer.[1]

The call to luaL_openlibs loads the standard Lua libraries (base, table, io, os, string, math, and package) instead of having to make a call to load each library separately. If you need support for the debug library you will still need to call luaopen_debug.

We then register a custom method (all methods are functions in Lua and have a default return value assigned to them, whereas in Pascal we have procedures and functions) called readln. This is done via the call to lua_register by passing the Lua state to register to, the name of the method, and the address of the method. It is important to notice that the prototypes for methods that are to be exported for use in Lua must use the cdecl directive and must conform to the standard Lua Method Header: receive one argument (a pointer to a Lua State) and returning an integer (containing the number of items placed on the stack as return values).

---

[1]This is a good point to mention that the luaL* methods are not a standard part of the base Lua API, but instead are part of lauxlib (or Lua Auxiliary Library). Since they are built into the standard Lua binary release, they have been included in the lua.pas wrapper.

Finally, we call `lua_pcall` to execute the script that we loaded previously. This complies and executes the script, thus allowing us to use surfaced methods within the script at a later time.

The order that is presented above *must* be followed every time. If you try and open libraries before you load your script, you will receive exceptions stating that a particular method cannot be found due to the fact that the Lua instance has not been initialized. You can't register your private methods before you load the libraries, and you *must* execute the loaded source code before you can do anything with it (more on this later).

Read and writing variables

Having a scripting language integrated into your application is more than just loading a script and executing it. It is having the ability to read and write variables, objects, records, and other information to and from the script itself, thus allowing you to change the way that your application reacts or interacts with the user.

The next logical step in getting Lua integrated into your application is to setup global variables that can be modified and read inside the Lua script and inside your application. With this little bit of knowledge you could easily use Lua as a configuration storage device that will give you more flexibility than say .ini or registry files.

If you have read up on Lua outside of this article (and I hope you have), then you know that Lua works on a stack and uses different global spaces to store information. One of these spaces is LUA_GLOBALSINDEX, which is a table that is used to store global name/value pairs to be accessed by the current script.

Writing

To modify or create a new global value we need to do three things: first, we have to push the name or index associated with our value; second. we have to push the value itself onto the stack; finally, we have to tell Lua to set the value in the global table:

```
Lua_pushliteral(L, 'MyIdentifier');
Lua_pushstring(L, 'Some Value');
Lua_settable(L, LUA_GLOBALSINDEX);
```

As you can see in the code above (lua_pushstring), there are methods to read and write each variable type that we use (at least until we start using the variant type wrappers presented within the pLua unit). This should be nothing new if you have stored or retrieved information from a standard .ini or registry object.

We place our identifier onto the stack first with a call to lua_pushliteral; this could also be done with a call to any of the lua_push* methods. Lua uses a hash table lookup, so any type (except nil) can be used as a key within a Lua table. We then place the value that we want to associate with the name onto the stack using the proper `lua_push*` method. The final call is `lua_settable` with our Lua State Pointer as the first argument and the table identifier as the second (`LUA_GLOBALSINDEX` is a constant for the globals table). We can simplify this code by using methods from the pLua and variants libraries within Pascal. The variant library provides us a `VarIsType` function that we can use to see if the variant type is a string (`varString`). pLua provides us with a method called `plua_RegisterValue` that takes a Lua instance, value name, a value (quoted if the value is a string), and a table index (defaulted to `LUA_GLOBALSINDEX`) that performs the above actions for us. You will notice that this method is used quite a bit though the examples that accompany this article.

Reading

Retrieving the value back out of the table is almost as easy:

```
Lua_pushliteral(L, 'MyIdentifier');
Lua_rawget(L, LUA_GLOBALSINDEX);
If lua_isnil(L, 1) then
Else
   MyString := Lua_tostring(L, 'MyIdentifier');
```

We push the name of the variable that we want to retrieve onto the stack. We then call `lua_rawget` with our Lua state pointer and table index. Then we test for nil (`lua_isnil`). If the value on the top of the stack isn't nil, we get the value using the proper `lua_to*` method.

Just like writing a variable, there are some support methods provided by the pLua library that allow us to minimize our source code. The main one that we are interested in is `plua_tovariant`. This function takes the Lua state and the stack index that we wish to work with and returns a variant type that contains the value.

More on methods

Once we can read and write global variables, the next logical step is to move up to surfacing methods (procedures and functions) from our Pascal environment to our Lua environment. We will also need a way to call Lua methods (functions) from within our Pascal source code. We touched lightly on this before, but this time we will be looking at the specific needs of methods inside and out.

Differences between Lua and Pascal

One of the first things to keep note of is the difference between return values and arguments. In Pascal we can mark a method argument as a var arg, or input/output variable, out arg, and we can pass back a single value from any function. Procedures don't allow you to pass back any value, but can still contain var args.

This isn't true in Lua. All methods return a value (default is nil), and there is only one method type (a function). Parameters to a method are also static, and their values are cannot be marked as output of any kind. A method in Lua may return as many values as it wishes and the return types are not pre-defined.

Surfacing a method

The most basic of methods that you will need to call from a Lua script is the print function. While the standard Lua libraries surface print for us, there are some aspects of its implementation that may not be desirable. For instance, by default, print will only print to the standard output interface (console window). If we want to have our script print to another output (say a memo), then we will need to override the default print hander.

Remember that, since Lua is developed in C, we must always use the cdecl compiler flag to let the compiler know that we expect the method to follow C rules and not standard Pascal rules.

Our first call is to lua_gettop. This call will tell us how many arguments are being passed from Lua to our method. In some methods you can use this as a quick and dirty test to see if you are receiving the proper number of arguments. In most, you will also need to provide a type check along with the argument count check.

For our print implementation we will only be using this as a high for our counter. Next we create an empty string that we can place the passed in values into. We then iterate through all of the values passed in (notice that the Lua stack starts at a positive index of 1 instead of 0 like C and Pascal), placing each argument string representation into our container. We then add the combined string value to our memo.

The last step is to tell Lua that we didn't put anything back onto the stack (a return value) and thus that it should set the return value itself. Remember that Lua methods *always* have a return value.

Now that we have our method defined and ready within our application we need to surface it to the Lua virtual machine. We do this after we register the libraries that we want to make use of (in case we are overriding default behavior).

Our first call is to lua_pushliteral with the Lua instance and the name that we want scripters to use to call our method. This is followed by placing the pointer to the method onto the stack using lua_pushcfunction. We then make a call to lua_settable with the LUA_GLOBALSINDEX (that should now be becoming very familiar).

Getting something back

When we want to return a value from a method call we have to push it onto the Lua stack; we also have to tell the Lua virtual machine just exactly how many items we have placed on the stack. To demonstrate this, we will surface a method called `Size`, which will return the width and height of our applications main form.

Unlike `print`, we don't care how many arguments Lua is passing in; instead, we only care about returning values. In cases like this, it's a good idea not to waste time checking the number of input arguments and instead just place our values on the stack.

The two calls to `lua_pushinteger` place the width and then the height onto the stack and are followed by us setting the return value of the function to 2. This tells the Lua virtual machine that we returned two values. It's important to note the order that we pushed the return values, as when we use this method from within our script we will need to know what to expect first and last. I've stayed with the typical X-then-Y structure, but there is no good reason it couldn't be Y-then-X.

We register this method the same as any other method; in fact, this is a good place to introduce a procedure for registering methods. pLua has a wrapper to achieve this as well, and when you look at the source code you will find it using `plua_RegisterMethod` instead of all of the hand code.

Calling Lua methods

It's time to call Lua methods from Pascal. The code that is in place within the example of this section is more complex than what I am going to describe, but follows the same principles.

We have to tell Lua what method we would like to call, and then tell it what argument values we want the method called with. If appropriate, we then need to check for return values.

The first thing that we do is place the name of the method to be called onto the Lua stack. We then use `lua_rawget` to retrieve the method address (if it exists) and replace our name with it. It would be a good idea to perform a nil check at this point, but it's not necessary.

We need to loop through the values that we want to pass as arguments to the method and place them onto the stack. This is followed by a call to `lua_pcall` that makes the performs the actual call of the method within Lua.

After we have called the method, we then iterate all of the return values placing them into a return array. It's important to note that the return values are in reverse order, thus they should be placed as: item n into slot 0 with item 0 going into slot $n - 1$. The reason for the ordering is more apparent if you think about our `Size` example above: We placed the width and then the height onto the Lua stack. So width is at position 2 with height at position 1.

Using records and objects

Within Lua there is no object type defined. Yet, it would be very difficult to think of integrating a scripting language into an application without the ability to surface objects and records. No worries though, Lua has mechanisms in place to take care of object handling.

There are no hard and fast rules as to how you implement or handle objects within Lua. In fact, a quick search of the web will result in many different ways to handle objects. I'm going to present the one that I use and that I've found to work very well in the end this isn't the end all be all answer to objects. [CHECK!]

If you think that I forgot about records, you're mistaken. A record is nothing more than an object without methods. More accurately objects are just records with method pointers. Thus, if we can handle objects then records will fall in and work automatically.

Metatables

From the Lua manual (section 2.8): "Every value in Lua may have a metatable. This metatable is an ordinary Lua table that defines the behavior of the original value under certain special operations. You can change several aspects of the behavior of operations over a value by setting specific fields in its metatable. For instance, when a non-numeric value is the operand of an addition, Lua checks for a function in the field __add in its metatable. If it finds one, Lua calls this function to perform the addition."

Metatables make object types possible within Lua. It is outside of the scope of this article to cover all aspects of metatables, but we will need to at least understand them at their very basics in order to implement objects and records.

If you understand how exactly OO works, then the concept of a virtual method table (VMT) should not be alien at all. If you don't, then think of a VMT as an array of pointers that says what method address should be called when a particular method is called in the code. This way an object can contain only its private information (variables) and use a global method table (the VMT) along with its private address (object pointer) to save space and make its calls. This is the basis of polymorphic programming in general (OO). A metatable allows us to implement a VMT of our own. The primary difference is that the metatable doesn't only have to surface methods, it can surface values, alternate implementations (we won't cover this), and methods.

Garbage collection and the Lua registry

Lua has garbage collection; basically this means that Lua will collect and delete all types when they are no longer referenced. When it comes to objects this could be a very bad thing, if for instance we created a display manager that knows to draw all of the objects it contains every frame, we may not reference it again. According to Lua it would get garbage collected right after we finished using it.

The Lua registry is a table much like the globals table. It doesn't actually exist within the Lua stack or environment; instead, it's a virtual table that can be used much like the Windows Registry. As long as something is referenced in the Registry it won't be garbage collected. The Lua registry gives us another feature that we need: as long as our objects are referenced within it, they won't be optimized or moved within the Lua environment. This is another feature within Lua that lets it run faster, cleaner, better, but it could also destroy our objects.

We place items into the registry just like you would with any other table. Simply push the name of the value that you want to store then push the value itself. Call `lua_settable` or `lua_rawset` with `LUA_REGISTERINDEX` as the table to being place the value into the registry.

To retrieve a value you push the value name and then call `lua_gettable` or `lua_rawget` depending on your situation.

Finally introducing objects

It makes sense to look at how we can implement objects in Lua. Rather than completely re-invent the wheel, we will be using a piece of code that has already been developed within Lua as a reference. This code can be found in the Lua wiki at `http://lua-users.org/wiki/InheritanceTutorial` and I strongly suggest that you read it before continuing.

Back to the registry

In order for Lua to make use of Pascal objects we will need to make sure that Lua does not garbage collect its part of the object. The object will also need to retain a pointer back into Lua so that it can retrieve method pointers, variable values, and anything else that we choose to allow Lua to control.

This is where the Lua registry comes in. When we create a new object (either from a Lua script or from our application), we will need a way to let Lua know about it and let Lua know that we are managing it. The registry is the best place (note that's best and not only place) to do this.

Upon our objects instantiation we will need to request a registry entry. To do this, we will use the `pLuaObjects` unit and a few calls to `luaL_*` methods.

We also need a way to remove our reference when the object is destroyed so that Lua can garbage collect its part of the equation.

Hopefully the comments within the source will give good presence as to what is going on, but if they don't then please use your favorite search engine to learn more about the Lua registry and garbage collection.

Object properties

Lua tables have built-in meta-methods to allow developers to modify their default behavior. We will use this to our advantage to implement variables (read and write for the case of this document; read only or write only should be easy to figure out) and methods. For variables we will need to override the default `__index` and `__newindex` table entries to call our own getters and setters.

First we have to receive back a copy of the object that Lua is referencing. This is achieved with a call to a custom function that returns a Pascal Object from a Lua stack reference.

Within our TLuaObject descendant we will surface helper methods to read and write variable values. These methods are: GetPropValue, SetPropValue, GetPropObject, SetPropObject. They do exactly what they say: get a value, set a value, get a sub-object and set a sub-object.

If you choose to use the pLuaObjects unit then you will find that you can quickly and easily wrap existing objects. Take a look at the pLua demos folder for the pLuaObjects and pLuaObjects2 demos for more explanation.

Object methods

Methods are a bit trickier. We will need to tell Lua that the method exists and what class type the methods are tied to. We will then need to write a method handler that prepares the proper arguments and then passes them to the object instances actual method. We will need to check for results and out parameters and put them back on the Lua stack. The latter part is the same as when we covered methods above, the former is explained in the source code.

And the object

From everything above we can finally implement objects into our application and have them extended by Lua scripts with events, methods, and properties. H9K shows exactly how all of this comes together and allows you to create and extend Pascal objects from within Lua itself.

Records

While I know that I said if we supported objects that records would fall in automatically, but there is one caveat to records. You must use record pointers instead of actual record types. This is due to the way that records are passed and assigned within Pascal. If you assign an object instance to an object variable, the variable contains a pointer to the object instance. On the other hand, if you assign a record to a record variable then the entire contents of the record are copied over to the variable. If you can keep this in mind and use record pointers in all locations, then you will actually gain twofold. First, you will guarantee that your records will work properly, and second, you will notice that your application uses less memory.

Calling within a loop

There is a special case when it comes to Lua. That is calling a Lua script or method from within a loop. If you have jumped ahead and attempted to do this you might have noticed that you received access violations after the first call. This is because simply loading the Lua code does not compile the source and prepare the virtual machine (first part of the article).

Instead we need to load the source file, execute it once, and only then we can call our loop routine.

Final words

Everything that has been covered in this article has been wrapped up into a nice little package for you to work with. The files `LuaWrapper.pas`, `pLuaObjects.pas`, and `LuaObject.pas` have helper classes, functions, and base classes for you to extend and use. They have been built from experience and have quite a bit of testing going on with them all of the time. As with all libraries though, you should read and understand them as the author(s) are not responsible for any damage to your system.

26

Porting Lua to a Microcontroller

Ralph Hempel

The Lua language was designed from the beginning to be small in its memory footprint for both the developer and the target machine. The basic philosophy is to provide a concise and unambiguous syntax that the developer can use and depend upon.

The purpose of this gem is to outline some of the issues that come up when porting Lua to an extremely memory constrained target. I'll go over a basic introduction to the target, which is the LEGO MINDSTORMS NXT brick, talk a bit about how the run-time library is designed, and then introduce my compromise between 32-bit long integers and single-precision floating-point numbers, which I call "flongs".

The target processor – why use Lua to program LEGO?

I have been fascinated by little languages ever since I started programming embedded systems over 20 years ago. At the time, Forth was one of the few languages that could be ported to a microcontroller and provide a mechanism for compiling and interpreting right on the target hardware.

In late 1997, the original LEGO MINDSTORMS RCX system was released. It had an H8/300 microcontroller with 32K of OTP memory containing the basic firmware and about 32K of external RAM for applications. Again, at the time

Forth was about the only language I could imagine running right on the brick, and the result was pbForth.

In 2005, the new LEGO MINDSTORMS NXT was released. It has an ARM7 based micro with 256K of rewritable on-chip FLASH and 64K of RAM. I could have easily ported Forth to that device as well, but the syntax of Forth can make marginally sane programmers cross the line.

In searching for other small interpreted languages, I evaluated two additional options: Lisp and Lua. While very powerful, Lisp suffers from the same problems as Forth in terms of syntax. Since most programmers are very comfortable with infix notation, Lua provides a familiar syntax compared with Forth's postfix and Lisp's prefix notation.

I really wanted to try to port Lua to this device just to see if it could be done, and then realized that I would have a very powerful way of programming robots interactively. This might be useful for academic purposes when the limitations of the original GUI programming environment provided by LEGO are reached.

There are some special challenges to getting even a minimal Lua system working on a deeply embedded system. Besides the obvious one of putting together a toolchain that generates the code image, the more subtle problem is to figure out what can or should be removed in order to make a useful system.

Think before you get started

The porting project did not have any immediate urgency, which gave me lots of time to think about it before I ever got started. It also gave me time to read about Lua, poke around in the Lua mailing list archive, and write a few non-trivial programs in Lua. I was able to take the time to browse the Lua source at leisure, noting how the different layers were isolated into separate files, and generally getting the lay of the land.

Basically, I'm lazy. This forces me to work smart to get as much done as somebody that works hard. The weeks I spent getting the feel of the Lua code convinced me that any time I spent fiddling with the source code would be completely wasted. Eventually I had absorbed enough to put down these guidelines to get me started:

1. Use as much of the stock Lua source distribution as possible.

2. Only load the base, table, and string libraries initially.

3. Add target specific routines in their own library.

Being lazy has also made me dependent on make, which I use in all kinds of projects to make sure that I have to think and type as little as possible once I've figured out how to get a job done.

I have a standard framework that I set up for any embedded systems project, which I won't describe in detail here but is available in the pbLua distribution. In general terms, it starts with a directory that has the processor specific startup files and a few I/O routines that blink LEDs, make sounds, or read and write characters thought a serial port.

Once I have that framework set up and some minimal code compiled that will flash LEDs, make sounds, or read and write characters through a serial port I'm ready to move on. One other thing being lazy has taught me is that you will do a lot more work later if you don't start simple, gain confidence in your tools, and only then add complexity.

Add the Lua kernel code to the build system

The next step was to take Lua source code and put it in a subdirectory in my development tree. I then built a makefile that is compatible with my framework and built the Lua object files from source.

The Lua code subdirectory had the full Lua version number in the name, which was 5.1 when I first started. Since that time, I've upgraded the source to 5.1.2 (also in its own directory). The upgrade did not change any of the fundamental Lua operation, it is only a bug-fix release.

The upgrade was almost trivial because all I had to do was copy the old luaconf.h and the custom makefile to the new directory. All I had to change at the higher level was the name of the directory where the Lua source could be located.

But surely some things had to be changed to port even the basic Lua code to the ARM7 target? Yes, and thankfully all the changes were isolated to the luaconf.h file. When changing this file, it's generally not a good idea to actually make the changes all through the file.

The designers of Lua have thoughtfully provided a space at the end of the file where you can make all the changes you want and keep them in one place for easy reference by you and other programmers trying to figure out what you have done.

One thing most C compilers will complain about is redefining something that has already been #defined. For example, I had to change the LUA_MAXINPUT from 512 to 256 bytes to conserve as much RAM as possible. To prevent the compiler from complaining, make sure you #undef the value first, then #define it, like this:

```
#undef  LUA_MAXINPUT
#define LUA_MAXINPUT 256
```

The other major change in luaconf.h involved making the default number system of the first pass of the port long instead of double. Listing 1 shows those changes.

If you're reading closely, you'll see that luai_numpow() just returns 1 instead of the correct result. That's a side effect of my lazy programmer brain, which decided that I would deal with that problem later.

Getting the core Lua code to compile cleanly under my custom built gcc toolchain was very easy — it basically worked the first time. Linking was another story, and is the subject of the next section.

```
#undef LUA_NUMBER_DOUBLE
#undef LUA_NUMBER

#define LUA_NUMBER_LONG
#define LUA_NUMBER long

/*
@@ LUAI_UACNUMBER is the result of an 'usual argument conversion'
@* over a number.
*/

#undef  LUAI_UACNUMBER
#define LUAI_UACNUMBER long

/*
@@ LUA_NUMBER_FMT is the format for writing numbers.
@@ lua_number2str converts a number to a string.
@@ LUAI_MAXNUMBER2STR is maximum size of previous conversion.
@@ lua_str2number converts a string to a number.
*/
#undef LUA_NUMBER_FMT
#undef lua_number2str
#undef LUAI_MAXNUMBER2STR
#undef lua_str2number

#define LUA_NUMBER_FMT          "%li"
#define lua_number2str(s,n) sprintf((s), LUA_NUMBER_FMT, (n))
#define LUAI_MAXNUMBER2STR 32 /* 16 digits, sign, point, and \0 */
#define lua_str2number(s,p) strtol((s), (p), 10)

/*
@@ The luai_num* macros define the primitive operations over numbers.
*/
#if defined(LUA_CORE)
#include <math.h>
#undef luai_nummod
#undef luai_numpow

// Note, numpow() is just a placeholder until we get the real number
// system working...

#define luai_nummod(a,b) ((a)%(b))
#define luai_numpow(a,b) (1)
#endif
```

Listing 1.

Building a better run-time library

After building and linking a minimal Lua system, you're left with a lot of undefined symbols which are generally part of the run-time library (RTL). This is something that systems developers don't think too much about because the libraries are often part of the operating system distribution.

Embedded systems developers have a couple of choices in the matter. The first is to use the RTL that ships with your development system. In most cases this is fine, but sometimes it's a good idea to start from first principles and build your own RTL.

In the case of GNU gcc, the standard embedded RTL is newlib. It's a fine library that gets a lot of use, but for this project I felt it was a bit bloated especially in the IO section.

One reason to build your own RTL is that it can follow you around to other projects, and you'll have a better appreciation of some of the tradeoffs that different implementations will give you. This is especially true in the standard IO library.

Building your own RTL is not as hard as you might think if you break the job down into smaller pieces and are careful in choosing the base code for each part. Being lazy comes in handy again if you take the time to scour the web for libraries that are already written and tested. Look for code that's written to be portable and runs on a variety of hardware. If you're concerned about licensing, look for code with an MIT style license (like Lua) or maybe a BSD license (like FreeBSD). These give you the most flexibility in using the code but they do not require you to publish the changes or improvements you might make.

Thread-safe considerations

One of the buzzwords you'll hear in a discussion on embedded libraries is "thread-safe" or "re-entrant". In multi-tasking systems it is quite common for a routine called by a task to be interrupted at any time for a task switch. The new task may call the original routine as well. If the routine is thread safe, it won't get confused and return incorrect results to either task.

One of the first steps towards becoming thread safe is to not use global variables. As long as a routine allocates all of its variables on the calling task's stack, then chances are the routine is thread safe.

The ANSI C library

The ANSI C library is a set of basic routines that are used by almost every program you are likely to write, so it's a good idea to get the most complete one you can find.

The first and most obvious set of routines to get into the library are the string routines. These are often written in assembler, but modern compilers do such a good job of optimizing them that it's often more trouble than it's worth to do it in assembler. If you do find that the routines are too slow, then go ahead and rewrite them later. In the meantime you'll have code that works.

The basic string library that I settled on is based on the Minix project from Vrije Universiteit in Amsterdam. It's a well known project that has been in use for years, so I am confident that the library has had most bugs eliminated.

Besides the string routines, the Minix project source also yielded routines to handle character classification, memory operations, and basic error and locale handling:

memory	string		characters	locale
memchr.c	strcat.c	strncpy.c	isalnum.c	errlist.c
memcmp.c	strchr.c	strnlen.c	isalpha.c	locale.c
memcpy.c	strcmp.c	strpbrk.c	isascii.c	setlocale.c
memmove.c	strcoll.c	strrchr.c	iscntrl.c	strerror.c
memset.c	strcpy.c	strstr.c	isdigit.c	
	strcspn.c	strtoflong.c	isgraph.c	
	strerror.c	strtol.c	islower.c	
	strlen.c	tolower.c	isprint.c	
	strncat.c	toupper.c	ispunct.c	
	strncmp.c		isspace.c	
			isupper.c	
			isxdigit.c	
			chartab.c	

There are a few things I changed in order to save space, and the main one is in errlist.c where I set all errors to unknown except for the ones that are set by Lua and its libraries. Other than that I did not touch the code because it was unlikely that I'd be able to improve on it without breaking something.

The other place where I've taken some liberties is with the number conversion part of the string library. The routine that the Lua interpreter uses to convert strings to numbers is luaO_str2d. This routine operates as follows:

1. First, it tries to use the lua_str2number macro to read the string as a number. If it makes no forward progress in reading the string, then the conversion fails completely and luaO_str2d exits returning 0.

2. Next, it checks for a leading upper or lower case 'x', in which case it tries to convert the string as an unsigned hex number using the strtoul function.

3. Next, remove any trailing spaces and check if we've reached the end of the string we're trying to convert, and if so, luaO_str2d exits returning 1.

4. If we get here, we have illegal trailing characters after the end of the string we are trying to convert, so luaO_str2d exits returning 0.

I needed to make sure strtoul was available, and it's part of the strtol.c file. As you'll see later in the section on the math library, the trick was figuring out a way to get the interpreter to differentiate between floating point numbers and integers in a way that was not too complicated. The custom routine I came up with is called `strtoflong` and it's a fairly straightforward solution to the problem which is described in detail below, in section on "flongs".

That rounds out the basic RTL function needed for the project. I'll go over the I/O routines and math functions later.

Memory allocation library

Most programs written for desktop computers allocate memory from the heap, which is an area of memory set aside for objects that cannot be allocated at compile time. Embedded systems that I've worked on in the past never had a heap because it's generally bad practice to count on never running out of memory over the lifetime of your product. It's better to allocate the memory at compile time and then you know how much you can use now and in the future.

The Lua scripting language makes frequent use of the heap though, so I had to go looking for a tried and true memory allocation scheme that would be portable enough to run on the ARM7 microcontroller. The basic calls required are `malloc`, `realloc`, and `free`, just like on a big operating system.

Fortunately, Joerg Wunsch, the author of avr-libc has done a fantastic job of porting these key routines to the AVR series of microcontroller and in the process has pared the C code down to a bare minimum.

After reviewing a number of other implementations, including the one in newlib, I decided to go with the routines in avr-libc. One thing to note is that these routines are *not* thread-safe as they don't disable interrupts around critical sections and they use global variables. I decided that this was an acceptable trade-off in this case as Lua was the only user of the heap and there was only one instance of Lua running on the NXT.

The only change I had to implement was to ensure that the memory block was a multiple of a long-word (4 bytes) in size, so that the data is always aligned on long word boundaries. Without that change, the pointers to the next block of memory ended up on non-aligned addresses and caused the processor to throw a hardware exception.

Lua garbage collection and the heap

The other significant difference is that there is no extra space available when the system runs out of memory so the concept of `sbrk` is meaningless.

This leads to some interesting choices when deciding how to do garbage collection. The standard Lua interpreter runs garbage collection whenever the memory usage of the system doubles. In other words, suppose that the default memory usage of a Lua program is 8K. When the Lua machine determines that 16K is in use, a garbage collection cycle is started, and then the limit for the next cycle is set to twice the current limit, or 32K.

This is not too bad for desktop systems with lots of memory, but it's absolutely fatal for an embedded system with the kinds of resources that we have available. There are two places in `luaconf.h` that control the operation of the garbage

collection system. The one that needs to be changed is LUAI_GCPAUSE, which
defines the multiple of memory use that triggers a garbage collection cycle. The
default value of 200 (interpreted as a percentage) gives the operation described
above. By reducing the default value to 110 in the luaconf.h file, the pbLua
system forces a garbage collection cycle when the memory usage increases by
only 10%. Assuming that there is 32K available for dynamic memory allocation,
this means that the last garbage collection limit increase occurs when about 29K
of memory is in use.

File IO routines for systems without files

The other main difference between embedded and desktop libraries lies in the
file I/O implementation. On a desktop system, we routinely do operations on
files without thinking about how they are implemented underneath.

The pbLua system still needs to read input to get it to the parser and write
the output so that it can be viewed by a human or another computer. So it's clear
that we'll need some sort of I/O subsystem, but do we really need the complexity
of a full filesystem? It turns out that initially we do not, but it's still a good
idea to use the standard I/O system calls to implement the subset of operations
that we need. In this way we can ensure the maximum compatibility with the
Lua source code and at the same time leave room for expansion if we ever do
implement a more sophisticated filesystem.

The first step is to look for all the standard I/O calls made by Lua, and then
decide on which ones we actually need to implement. Once again, the work of
Joerg Wunsch makes my life easy by providing a minimal abstraction of the
standard I/O library that is suitable for microcontroller. I have seen similar
work before, but Joerg has documented his work very well, and once again I did
not have to change a single line of code to get it to compile or work.

There is no concept of actual files on the NXT. Instead the I/O library associates streams with devices at boot time. The first implementation used the
USB device port built into the NXT as a virtual serial port. All I had to do was
provide routines to send and receive individual characters from the serial port.
The addresses of these routines were placed in device description blocks, and
these blocks were in turn associated with the standard input, output and error
stream descriptors.

Once that was set up, the Lua interpreter was ready to receive characters
from stdin, send them to stdout, and if I did something stupid, an error message
was printed on stderr (which was the serial port too).

A second pass at the problem resulted in an implementation that allows the
user to choose either Bluetooth or USB as the standard console interface.

I still need to finish implementing a basic flat file storage system that uses
the internal FLASH and does not place undue stress on individual FLASH
blocks. My current thinking is a block of file descriptors that has a special GUID
or signature that can be distinguished at boot time will be simple to use and
allows the directory block to move around in FLASH.

A new kind of math using "flongs"

The standard Lua programming language is compiled to use double-precision floating-point math, which makes sense on a standard desktop or server class computer. Double-precision math has the advantage of being able to represent the full range of 32-bit integers exactly in addition to a very large dynamic range with about 14 digits of accuracy.

For small embedded systems, and certainly for the LEGO MINDSTORM NXT, double-precision math comes with a penalty. The ARM processor inside the NXT handles 32-bit integers very efficiently, but must do a lot of extra work to do floating-point calculations.

Fortunately, the designers of Lua thought about the speed-versus-precision tradeoff at a very fundamental level and came up with a clever macro based scheme to decouple the implementation of the arithmetic operations from the language. What this means for some applications is that we can specify the underlying numerical type for all of Lua's arithmetic operations. (Note that there is a distinction between arithmetic operations that are intrinsic operations like + and * in the Lua language, and the math operations such as sqrt and sin that are part of the math library.) The actual implementation is a section in luaconf.h that tells the compiler how you'd like to handle the numbers and was discussed in the section on adding the Lua kernel to the build system.

One part that I did not mention was that the Lua arithmetic operations were based on standard C operators and are defined as macros in luaconf.h In other words, the basic operators — addition, multiplication, modulo, etc. — all result in standard C expressions, and depending on the underlying type of the macro parameters, the compiler chooses either fixed or floating-point math.[1]

Trading speed for accuracy

In the process of thinking about how best to take advantage of the processor in the NXT, I decided to make long the default arithmetic type for Lua. Most of the routines in the NXT firmware source use long parameters. This includes timers, rotation counters, and many other fundamental structures. If we had to convert between float to long all the time we'd be wasting all kinds of CPU cycles in the process.

If doubles are too onerous, then what not use a single-precision float? The standard single-precision float has one disadvantage, and that's a significantly reduced range of precision when it comes to fixed-point numbers, and for that

---

[1]As an aside, one of the things I like to do when I'm evaluating a new programming language is to read and try to understand how it's implemented underneath. The first language I learned (besides assembler and C) was Forth. It had a wonderful structure that made it obvious how it worked. When I saw the Lua source code, I knew I was looking at something that had evolved over time and had some deep thought behind it. It looks obvious when you read the code that this is the "right way" but based on my experience, there were probably a few failed attempts before this... From the high level parser to the virtual machine, and the API that handles the interaction between C or assembler libraries and Lua itself, the Lua core is beautifully organized and a model of good code. I have much greater confidence that code is correct if it looks like it was carefully crafted.

reason it's not a good choice to be the single numerical representation of this implementation of Lua.

In addition to that, most of the time we're interested in doing fairly simple math when we're designing robots. While the overhead of converting all numbers to float is less than for doubles, it's still significant. Even simple operations like addition and subtraction become much more complicated with floats than with longs.

While these two tradeoffs competed against one another, I started to think about ways in which a compromise could be struck — and the result is a hybrid number type that uses standard representations for long and float while making maximum use of the benefits of both. I call it "flong".

The breakthrough came when I realized that the practical application of each of the number types is in several distinct domains — in other words you use one numeric type for the task at hand and avoid mixing them unless absolutely necessary.

I often get asked why I don't use standard or even light userdata for the new numerical type. The answer is quite simply speed. Light userdata values don't have metatables that we can use to override their operators, and standard userdata exacts a toll on the C API side.

Using flongs with the C math library

The compromise flong type gives us the speed to do the math operations that we do most often in long integer math, while giving us the ability to use an alternative representation for floats when we need them.

The disadvantage is that all floating-point operations, even basic arithmetic on floating-point values, is done through a series of API calls. One additional feature I implemented was the ability to automatically convert numbers in the input stream to long if they contain a decimal point. To use the new routine, we just change one line in luaconf.h like so:

```
#define lua_str2number(s,p) strtoflong((s), (p))
```

Once that decision was made, I just had to find a suitable single-precision floating-point library written in ANSI C. This was much harder to do than I thought because most implementations of this kind were done in assembler language, and were otherwise incomplete or incompatible with my hardware.

Essentially, the flong is a union of an unsigned long and float that looks like this:

```
union flong
{
    float f;
    long l;
};
```

Since I've compiled pbLua to use long as the default numerical type, the parameters to API functions are passed as longs too. The flong union provides a way to translate between the forms as needed without resorting to typecasts. Here's an example of how this is used in the sqrt function:

```
static int _sqrt(lua_State *L) {
    union flong fl;
    fl.l = luaL_optint(L, 1, 0);  /* 1st argument is sin */
    fl.f = sqrtf(fl.f);
    lua_pushinteger(L, fl.l );
    return(1);
}
```

Choosing a single-precision float library

Fortunately, the work of Jesus Calvino-Fraga for the SDCC (Small Device C compiler) project fit my needs almost exactly. His code is designed to be used with the SDCC system and has a very small number of minor code changes required to work with my build system. But the end result is wonderful. I now have a complete single-precision library upon which I can base the math routines I need.

One deviation from the standard C trig functions is that all input and output is in degrees, not radians. This is because I wanted the users of pbLua to be able to pick up the concepts quickly, and using degrees instead of radians makes that barrier much lower.

One additional function that is required is a way to convert between longs and floats, and these routines do just that:

```
f = tofloat( 45, 1 )   -- f = 45.000001
i,d = toint(f)         -- i = 45, d = 1
```

I set the precision of the floating-point portion of a flong to one part in 1,000,000 which is good enough for the kinds of math we're doing and the limit for single-precision floats anyways.

Conclusion

Building a complete Lua interpreter under Linux, BSD, OSX, or even Windows is relatively simple when you use the makefiles provided with the source code. Building Lua for use on a microcontroller with no underlying OS support requires more careful consideration of tradeoffs between speed, size, and accuracy.

Embedding Lua on a constrained micro forces the programmer to think hard about many things that are taken for granted on a desktop system. From math to memory, strings to stdio, almost everything is under the control of the designer, and knowing what the tradeoffs are can help you to make better decisions.

In the future, this project may take advantage of other work being done in the Lua world, including keeping some table information in non-volatile memory, and allowing pre-compiled code chunks to be stored and used later. I also plan on implementing a simple, flat, filesystem that can be used to log data and store raw or precompiled code.

In an ideal world, every university and high school would have a LEGO NXT lab where students could learn about programming by designing and building simple robots. I may have to settle for a bit less.

27

Writing C/C++ Modules for Lua

Ralph Steggink and Wim Couwenberg

We use Lua mostly as an embedded scripting environment in our software. Over the years we have developed many C and C++ libraries that integrate tightly with Lua code. Since one of us started to use Lua 4.0, a lot has changed in the newer releases of Lua. The changes that have impacted our way of binding C/C++ code the most are the introduction of metatables, environments, and a standard module system.

Even with the now default module system there are still lots of ways that modules can be written, both in Lua and in C. The module system is carefully designed to support different approaches to modules on different target platforms. It uses loaders to extend or modify the way in which modules are found and activated [1]. There really is no preferred way, by design, to write modules.

This gem presents our approach to writing C/C++ modules for Lua. It was adapted and tweaked over the last couple of years based on experience in several of our projects. We illustrate our method by wrapping an essential portion of the well known "libevent" library written by Niels Provos [2]. From its documentation: "Libevent is an event notification library [. . .]. The libevent API provides a mechanism to execute a callback function when a specific event occurs on a file descriptor or after a timeout has been reached."

Generic module layout

Compared to our approach in the Lua 4.0 days, one change that stands out in particular is the shift in focus from C code to Lua code in the implementation of C/C++ modules. Where for Lua 4.0 we tended to write a complete module in C, we now only do minimal coding in C to expose a library's API pretty much verbatim to Lua and then shape it into a scripting friendly module in Lua code.

A C module for Lua hence consists of two parts: a public Lua script containing the module's interface and a private C library that exposes the raw C API as literally as possible to the Lua script. Here "public" means that only the Lua script is ever required directly by client code.

The low-level API functions perform little to no argument checking since they are called only from the accompanying Lua script in a controlled and safe manner. Of course we must ensure that no low-level API function can "slip" out of our module and into the open since calling such a function in any other way than intended might lead to instant disaster.

Hence to make a C module for libevent we create `Event.lua` and a `C-Event.so` (or `C-Event.dll`) file. Requiring the "Event" module will in fact find, load, and run the `Event.lua` script. The `Event.lua` script will in turn require "C-Event" to load the private C part and properly setup the entire event module.

The distribution of responsibilities between the Lua and C part of a module is always roughly the same. The tables below list the typical content for both.

C part:

- Exposes C API to Lua part "as is".
- Provides garbage collection methods for the module's object types.
- Can define public constants.

Lua part:

- Defines structured Lua object methods around the low-level API calls.
- Sets up object meta tables.
- Exports object constructors in the module's namespace.
- Offers structured error handling.
- Checks preconditions on method parameters (correct types and values).

Note that in general the C part does not add any function definitions directly to the module's namespace. The public interface is taken care of by the Lua script. It is convenient to add public (numerical or string) constant to the module's namespace directly from the C part. This saves us from copy pasting their symbolic definition from a header file to the Lua script. The Event module defines its public constants in the C part.

A private communication channel between the Lua and C parts is setup by means of two local tables in the Lua script: A `prv` table that will hold the low level C API calls and an `aux` table that holds anything from the Lua script that must be available from within the C part. Being local, these tables are not accessible outside of the module. In particular, the `prv` table that holds dangerously low-level C calls is safely tucked away. (Similar to Lua Technical Note #7 [3].)

When the private C part is required from the Lua script it just returns an initialization function without any other side effects. This function is called with aux, prv, and the module table _M as parameters. The aux table is set as the environment of all low-level C API functions and this API is put in the prv table. Public constants are defined directly in the module table. For the libevent library, the script Event.lua would typically begin as follows (the exact script is presented at the end of this gem):

```
-- save global functions
local require = require
-- setup the module namespace
module "Event"
-- prepare auxiliary and prv tables
local aux, prv = {}, {}
-- load the C initialization function
local initialize = require "C-Event"
-- obtain the private functions and provide access to auxiliary data
-- and to the module namespace
initialize(aux, prv, _M)
```

The initialization function does three things: It defines public constants from event.h in the module's namespace. Then it replaces its own environment with the provided aux table such that it will be easily accessible to all API functions. Finally, it places all the low-level API functions in the prv table. Note that by pushing a C closure on the stack before storing it in "prv" it will automatically inherit aux as its environment table. The C part for libevent in Event.c would roughly look as follows (the exact source file is at the end of this gem):

```
/* module initialization with "aux", "prv" and module tables */
static int initialize(lua_State *L)
{
  < ... setup constants in module table (code omitted) ... >
  /* set "aux" table as environment. */
  lua_pushvalue(L, 1);
  lua_replace(L, LUA_ENVIRONINDEX);
  /* put low-level API functions in "prv" table. */
  lua_pushvalue(L, 2);
  luaL_register(L, NULL, prv_functions);
  return 0;
}


/* main entry point for C part. the "C-" prefix is stripped. */
EVENT_API int luaopen_Event(lua_State *L)
{
  /* just return the initialize function */
  lua_pushcfunction(L, initialize);
  return 1;
}
```

Notice that this C code is really minimalistic. Not even metatables are created and manipulated in C: All such interesting stuff will be left to the Lua script. Having established the generic setup of a module as a pair of a Lua script and a private C library we will now discuss how a module can organize an API in more scripting friendly objects.

Objects

Mostly a library's API is structured in an object-oriented way. This is obvious for C++ interfaces but is equally true for many C interfaces. For example, libevent really introduces an "event" object of which the event_set function is a constructor and the event_add function (among others) is a method. This object-oriented approach is really convenient from a scripting point of view, so we will want to structure the event module's interface in terms of objects.

An object is modeled as a combination of a Lua table and a full userdata. The userdata part represents an object from the C library while the Lua table is used to store additional information with this object. For libevent we reserve space for an event structure in a userdata. A Lua table is used to store the callback function for an event. The Lua table can be set as the environment of the userdata to make it easily obtainable from the userdata. Also, the userdata can be put in the Lua table (by assigning it to some "private" field __udata say), so that the userdata can be accessed from Lua.

The possibility to set an environment table for a userdata was introduced in Lua 5.1 and is a great help to associate Lua data with userdata. In Lua 5.0 we could only do this by maintaining a userdata-to-table mapping. Such a mapping can still be necessary for some other purposes even in Lua 5.1, as we will see in the libevent example, where we use it to retrieve a Lua object from a pointer-to-void callback argument.

When writing a module primarily in Lua we are confronted with the following restrictions of environments and metatables:

1. A userdata's metatable cannot be set in a Lua script.
2. A userdata's environment cannot be set or obtained in a lua script.

Restriction 1 means that the module's C code must have access to the metatable to construct a userdata object since it cannot be set by the Lua script later on. In our libevent example we put all metatables in the aux table (the environment of all C API functions) exactly for this reason.

Restriction 2 hinders the implementation of object methods in the following sense. We could simply implement an object as a userdata with a metatable and an environment to store associated data. In this case, each method receives a userdata instance as their first self parameter. If object methods are written in Lua (which we aim for), then a method cannot get at the environment table of self — an inconvenient situation. Even though we could work our way around this inconvenience (via a getenv function in the module's prv table), we implement objects differently.

An object is a plain Lua table that contains the userdata part as its `__udata` field. This field is considered "private" although we do not take extra measures to make it inaccessible. (It is private only by convention.) With this setup for objects we need two metatables for each object type: one to specify public methods and properties for an object and another one to specify a garbage collection function for its userdata part. (Remember that the `__gc` metamethod is never called for Lua tables.) The methods and properties metatable can be set on an object (a Lua table) in the Lua script itself. The userdata metatable must be set in the C part of the library when the userdata is created. Such metatables are placed in `aux` for easy access from C.

Boxing and packing

Objects from C/C++ can be put into a userdata in several ways. Common practices are to "box" or "pack" objects into userdata. Boxing an object in userdata means that only a pointer to the object is stored in the userdata. A `NULL` pointer can then be used to indicate that the object is no longer valid (e.g., it is explicitly discarded or got garbage collected). Lua's io library boxes a file pointer (`FILE*`) into a userdata and uses the `NULL` pointer to indicate that the file is closed.

Packing an object in userdata means that the storage space for the object is directly allocated in the userdata itself. Depending on the object type that is packed, you might need to reserve some extra space for a field that indicates the object's validity, much like the `NULL` pointer does for boxed objects. In our libevent example we chose to pack the event object instead of boxing it. Note that even a C++ class instance with a non-trivial constructor and destructor can be packed by using the placement operator `new` and an explicit destructor call. The example in Listing 1 shows how to properly pack an instance of class type `T`. (This example omits a "validity" flag.)

Note that Lua's garbage collector will free the actual space that was reserved for a userdata. Do not `delete` a packed object since the object is not allocated by operator new (the runtime library will most likely assert if you try).

Packing modules into a single library

During development of C modules for Lua it is practical to put each module in its own library. When deploying final code we find it convenient to distribute only a single library containing all needed C modules. It took us some time to realize that Lua 5.1 offers such a facility out of the box via what is called the "all-in-one loader". Requiring "distro.C-Event" will eventually try to locate a library called `distro.so` (or `distro.dll`) containing a function named `luaopen_Event`. Multiple modules can be contained in the single library `distro.so` in this way.

Moreover, providing a separate library `distro/C-Event.so` in a distro subdirectory will override module "C-Event" in `distro.so` since require will locate

```cpp
// for placement operator new
#include <new>
// create a userdata with a new packed instance of T
static int create_instance(lua_State *L)
{
  // reserve space
  void *space = lua_newuserdata(L, sizeof(T));
  // construct instance in userdata space
  // (this does NOT allocate memory)
  ::new(space) T;
  // set object metatable (stored in the environment)
  lua_getfield(L, LUA_ENVIRONINDEX, "meta_of_T");
  lua_setmetatable(L, -2);
  return 1;
}

// destroy a userdata with a packed instance of T
static int destroy_instance(lua_State *L)
{
  // assume userdata is first parameter and packed object is valid
  T *obj = static_cast<T*>(lua_touserdata(L, 1));
  // explicitly destruct object (this does NOT free memory)
  obj->~T();
  return 0;
}
```

Listing 1.

specific libraries before resorting to the all-in-one loader. This allows to "patch" selected modules from a distribution.

A libevent module

Finally, we present some of the techniques that we discussed to make a Lua module for the libevent library. The code below is fully functional but still intended as an example. Only a very small part of libevent's API is included, but enough to see that it is actually working. Of course, there is room for lots of improvements and variations. Function and method parameters could be checked for preconditions and error return codes translated into something more sensible. However, what this example aims to show is that such things are really easy to add simply in the module's Lua script.

First, a small example that uses the Event module to echo stdin with a timeout of 5 seconds:

Example.lua

```lua
require "Event"

local function callback(event, fd, event_type)
  if event_type == Event.EV_TIMEOUT then
    print("timeout")
  elseif event_type == Event.EV_READ then
    local s = io.read("*l")
    if s then
      print("you typed: " .. s)
      event:add(5)
    end
  end
end

event = Event.create(1, Event.EV_READ, callback)
event:add(5)
Event.dispatch()
```

Event.lua

```lua
-- save the used globals
local math, require, setmetatable, pcall =
      math, require, setmetatable, pcall

-- create the Event module
module "Event"

-- create the auxiliary and private C functions table
local aux, prv = {}, {}

-- open the C library, get the initialization function, and
-- call it with the aux, the prv and the module tables.
local initialize = require "C-Event"
initialize(aux, prv, _M)

-- create a weak table to map callback data to event objects
local events = setmetatable({}, {__mode = "v"})

-- metatable and garbage collector for Event object userdata
local umeta = {}
umeta.__gc = prv.del

-- metatable and method definitions for Event object
local Event = {}
```

```lua
Event.__index = Event

function Event:add(timeout)
  local sec, usec
  if timeout then
    sec = math.floor(timeout)
    usec = (timeout % 1)*1e9
  end
  return prv.add(self.__udata, sec, usec)
end

function Event:del()
  return prv.del(self.__udata)
end

-- global functions
function create(fd, event_type, handler)
  local udata, ptr = prv.create(fd, event_type)
  local event = setmetatable({}, Event)
  event.__udata = udata
  event.handler = handler
  events[ptr] = event
  return event
end

function dispatch()
  prv.dispatch()
end

-- dispatch event (called from C function)
function aux.handle_event(ptr, fd, event_type)
  local event = events[ptr]
  if event then
    pcall(event.handler, event, fd, event_type)
  end
end

-- Event userdata metatable (used by "create" C function)
aux.metatable = umeta
```

Event.c (compiled into C-Event.so)

```c
#include <sys/types.h>
#include <sys/time.h>
#include "event.h"
```

```c
#include "lua.h"
#include "lauxlib.h"

/* event wrapper to pack into userdata */
struct levent {
  struct event event;
  lua_State *L;
};

/* The libevent callback handler */
static void handler(int fd, short event_type, void *arg) {
  struct levent *ev = (struct levent *)arg;
  lua_getfield(ev->L, LUA_ENVIRONINDEX, "handle_event");
  lua_pushlightuserdata(ev->L, ev);
  lua_pushnumber(ev->L, fd);
  lua_pushnumber(ev->L, event_type);
  lua_call(ev->L, 3, 0);
}

/* Module-global dispatch */
static int dispatch(lua_State *L) {
  event_dispatch();
  return 0;
}

/* create an Event userdata */
static int create(lua_State *L) {
  /* Lua stack:  fd, event_mask */
  int fd = lua_tonumber(L, 1);
  int event_type = lua_tonumber(L, 2);

  /* pack levent structure in userdata */
  struct levent *ev = (struct levent *)lua_newuserdata(L, sizeof(*ev));
  ev->L = L;
  event_set(&ev->event, fd, event_type, handler, ev);

  /* set userdata metatable (from aux table) */
  lua_getfield(L, LUA_ENVIRONINDEX, "metatable");
  lua_setmetatable(L, -2);

  /* return userdata and address of levent (to index event objects) */
  lua_pushlightuserdata(L, ev);
  return 2;
}
```

```
/* bind the lua add function to the libevent add function */
static int add(lua_State *L) {
  /* Lua stack:  userdata [, seconds, useconds] */
  int res;
  struct timeval t, *pt = NULL;
  struct levent *ev = (struct levent *)lua_touserdata(L, 1);

  /* timeout specified? */
  if (lua_type(L, 2) == LUA_TNUMBER) {
    t.tv_sec = lua_tointeger(L, 2);
    t.tv_usec = lua_tointeger(L, 3);
    pt = &t;
  }

  res = event_add(&ev->event, pt);
  lua_pushinteger(L, res);
  return 1;
}

/* delete event.  doubles as garbage collection function */
static int del(lua_State *L) {
  /* Lua stack:  userdata */
  struct levent *ev = (struct levent*)lua_touserdata(L, 1);
  int res = event_del(&ev->event);
  lua_pushinteger(L, res);
  return 1;
}

/* definition of a constant name/value pair */
struct constant {
  const char * name;
  int value;
};

/* constants */
static const struct constant constants[] = {
  {"EV_TIMEOUT", EV_TIMEOUT},
  {"EV_READ", EV_READ},
  {"EV_WRITE", EV_WRITE},
  {"EV_SIGNAL", EV_SIGNAL},
  {"EV_PERSIST", EV_PERSIST},
  {NULL, 0}
};
```

```c
/* private functions */
static const luaL_Reg prv[] = {
  {"dispatch", dispatch},
  {"create", create},
  {"add", add},
  {"del", del},
  {NULL, NULL}
};

/* initialize the Event module */
static int initialize(lua_State *L) {
  /* Lua stack:  aux table, prv table, module table */

  /* define constants in module namespace */
  int index;
  for (index = 0; constants[index].name != NULL; ++index) {
    lua_pushinteger(L, constants[index].value);
    lua_setfield(L, 3, constants[index].name);
  }

  /* set the "aux" table as environment */
  lua_pushvalue(L, 1);
  lua_replace(L, LUA_ENVIRONINDEX);

  /* register prv functions */
  lua_pushvalue(L, 2);
  luaL_register(L, NULL, prv);

  /* initialize event library */
  event_init();

  return 0;
}

/* entry point for C-Event module */
EVENT_API int luaopen_Event(lua_State *L) {
  lua_pushcfunction(L, initialize);
  return 1;
}
```

References

[1] Roberto Ierusalimschy, Luiz Henrique de Figueiredo, Waldemar Celes, "Lua 5.1 Reference Manual", Lua.org, 2006.

[2] Niels Provos, "libevent – an event notification library".
http://www.monkey.org/~provos/libevent

[3] Roberto Ierusalimschy, "Technical Note 7 – Modules & Packages".
http://www.lua.org/notes/ltn007.html

28

Interpreted C Modules

Jérôme Vuarand

Lua 5.1 provides a flexible and powerful module mechanism. It can load two types of modules: Lua modules, which are written in Lua, and binary modules, which are written in any compilable language that can produce shared libraries. Through this mechanism it is possible extend Lua in many ways, making it a truly extensible language, for use as a general scripting tool.

However in certain circumstances these two extension mechanisms may not be enough. Hopefully, the Lua module mechanism has been carefully written and is itself extensible thanks to a searcher concept. The stock Lua interpreter comes with a few searchers that implement the Lua 5.1 module system. But it is possible to create additional searchers that will inject code inside the Lua interpreter state in whatever way may be needed.

In this article I will introduce a method to extend the Lua module mechanism to other kinds of modules. As an example, I will show how to support modules written in uncompiled C, with the help of a tiny embeddable C compiler, TCC (for Tiny C Compiler). This mechanism will allow us to load uncompiled C modules, and to compile them on the fly. I will first explain how the searcher mechanism of Lua works in detail, and how to hook into it. I will present TCC, and especially libtcc, which is a library that is able to compile C code and relocate it in the current executable for immediate use. We will finally see how to create a small binding library for TCC that injects its C compilation ability in the Lua module framework.

The Lua module system

The Lua module system is based on two global functions, require and module. Both use the package table to store information concerning already loaded modules and how to load additional modules. The basic usage of the module system consists in loading Lua files or shared libraries to expose a table containing functions to the script being executed. But these functions are much more powerful than that. require has been designed with flexibility in mind, and its behaviour can be totally configured. While module sticks closely to the module system and in fact defines it, require is just a wrapper around a searcher concept, and what exactly a searcher does is not limited. require existed before the Lua 5.1 module system was introduced, and it has been carefully redesigned to keep its old behaviour while allowing module to do its job.

require, searchers, and loaders

require defines a protocol to locate and execute external code. require is called with a single parameter, which usually represents the module name (*modname*). For the moment try to consider a module as an abstract concept; it may be any form of external code that can be executed. Actually, loading a module means executing the module loader. For Lua modules the loader is the module main chunk. For binary modules the loader is a function named luaopen_*modname*. For other types of modules it's up to the searcher designer to determine what the loader is.

require will first look in package.loaded to see if the module is already loaded. This allows modules to control whether they can be loaded twice or not. If a module loader sets package.loaded[*modname*] to a value resolving to true, the module won't be re-loadable. If it sets that entry to false or nil, the module can reloaded. Manually resetting that value allows to force a module reloading next time it is require'd.

If require determines that it must load the module, it will look for the module loader and execute it. To find a loader, require uses searchers. Searchers are located in the package.loaders array: they are functions. require will call each searcher, starting at index 1, with the module name as only parameter. A searcher can have three possible behaviours. If it doesn't find the module, it returns a string that will be displayed by require if no searcher finds the module. If it finds the module without any problem, it returns the module loader (a function). Finally, if the searcher finds the module but is not able to extract its loader, it can throw an error. This is the case for example when a Lua module contains syntax errors. This error will propagate outside require.

If require has found a loader, it executes it with the module name as single parameter, in an unprotected call. That way, if the loaders throws an error it is propagated outside of require, for example when a Lua module contains a runtime error. The first return value of the module loader is stored in package.loaded[*modname*]. If the module loader returns no value and has not set package.loaded[*modname*], true is used instead (that means that by default a module is considered non-re-loadable). Finally, whether the module was loaded or not, the content of package.loaded[*modname*] is returned by require.

In stock Lua there are four predefined searchers. The first one, preload, looks for loaders in the package.preload table, with the module name as a key. The second one, Lua, looks for Lua source files with the package.path string. If it finds a file it compiles it as a Lua chunk and that chunk is the loader. The third one, C, looks for shared libraries with the package.cpath string. If it finds one corresponding to the module name, it looks for a function called luaopen_*modname* in it, and that function is the loader. Finally, the last searcher, called Croot in Lua source code or the all-in-one searcher in the Lua manual, will also look for a shared library with the package.cpath string. But instead of using the module name to locate the shared library, it will only use the first component of it (everything before the first dot). To locate the loader inside the library, it uses the full module name. These searchers and their configuration strings (package.path and package.cpath) are documented in the Lua manual.

TCC

Tiny C Compiler

TCC is a C compiler targeted for x86 platforms written by Fabrice Bellard (of ffmpeg and QEMU fame). It is very small and very fast. It is so fast that it is used as a JIT compiler to interpret C programs, and that's precisely the feature we'll be using in this gem. Originally TCC was derived from OTCC, which is aimed to be the smallest self-compiling C compiler. OTCC was not capable of compiling full C99, only a subset of it, but that subset was C99 compliant and enough to build itself. TCC has kept that minimalistic approach while being much more usable in a production environment.

TCC is heading toward full ISO C99 compliance. It does have some extensions, but not as numerous as GCC's. It has almost no support for older versions of C not covered by C99. Also it has no support for C++, so C++ programmers used to GCC extensions must take care to program strictly in C. But past these little restrictions, TCC can compile most C code without any problem and very quickly (for example it can boot a typical Linux 2.4 from sources in less than 15 seconds on an average PC).

libtcc

TCC can be used as a standalone compiler, but it is internally built around a compiling library, libtcc. That library can be used from external projects, to compile and link C code. But libtcc is also able to relocate dynamically generated code into memory, and to return pointers to functions and other symbols in that relocated code. That's the way TCC is used as a C interpreter, and that's the feature we're going to use to create Lua modules at runtime from C source code.

Libtcc follows classic C compilation steps. First you can add include paths, library paths, and predefined symbols. Then each source file is compiled. All compiled files are finally linked between each other and with external libraries to produce the output binary. TCC can link to dynamic libraries too, but on some platforms it may require a specific import library (read the TCC manual for more information). The output binary can be saved into an executable file (ELF on Linux, PE on Windows), or it can stay in memory and be directly executed. In the latter approach, TCC can retrieve pointers to symbols in the binary and give them to the calling code. If the symbol is a function, it can be directly executed as a function pointer.

Special care must be taken when accessing symbols in the relocated binary. Libtcc has no way to ensure that the retrieved symbol is of a specified type, so you have to carefully handle the pointers returned and cast them to the proper type. This is especially important for functions pointers, since calling a function with an incorrect number of parameters or with the wrong calling convention can invalidate the stack pointer and lead to unpredictable results, among which the program crash is the least problematic. Here the fact that Lua uses a single function prototype almost everywhere will be very handy and will avoid many complications.

Another problem must be handled: data execution prevention hardware features. On some platforms, which includes modern x86 derivatives, there are safety mechanisms built in the memory hardware to separate code from data in memory. Libtcc output is considered as data (it is written by current process) and code (we want to execute it), so attempting to call functions in TCC relocated code is considered by the underlying hardware as a violation of the data/code separation and may interrupt the whole process. In your application you must make sure that this behaviour will be allowed (with its potential security implications). This is handled neither in libtcc nor in the libtcc binding presented here, since it's a very hardware and OS specific issue.

TCC binding

The TCC binding I'm going to expose here was originally based on the one written by Javier Guerra. It has been widely rewritten and extended to be used as a Lua searcher. This binding is split in two parts. The first part, the luatcc module presented in this section, is a simple binding to libtcc and allows to compile and execute C code. The second part, the luatcc.loader module, is a module searcher that locates C source files and compiles them as Lua modules.

The TCC binding is articulated around a context or state concept. A context is like an instance of the compiler. It has its own paths, you can add several source files, declare several libraries, and it can produce a single output binary. However, you can access several symbols in that binary. To create a context, just call the `luatcc.new` function. The module source code is not of much interest:

it's just a simple C library binding, so I won't explain it here; source files are self-explanatory. Here is a basic example that extracts a function called `hello` from a C source string:

```
local luatcc = require 'luatcc'
local context = luatcc.new()
context:compile([[
#include <lua.h>
int hello(lua_State* L)
{
    lua_pushstring(L, "Hello World!");
    return 1;
}
]])
context:relocate()
local hello = context:get_symbol("hello")
print(hello())
```

As you can see, you must call the methods `compile`, `relocate`, and `get_symbol` of the TCC context object. `compile` accepts as a second parameter the chunk name, which can be useful when you have several source files and an error occurs. Here we don't add include paths; TCC will use its predefined ones to locate `lua.h`. These predefined paths are defined at TCC compilation time.

TCC searcher

The TCC searcher is very simple. It mimics Lua and C searchers. We will examine its source code and comment each section.

The module header

```
module(..., package.seeall)
local luatcc = require("luatcc")
local function new_context()
    local context = luatcc.new()
    --context:add_include_path("some/path/to/header/files")
    --context:add_library_path("some/path/to/library/files")
    return context
end
local DIRSEP = '/'
```

We first declare the searcher module itself, with the name provided by `require`. We then require luatcc as a dependency, since we will use it to compile the interpreted C module. The `new_context` function is used to create a luatcc context. It exists primarily to ease addition of searcher-wide compilation parameters, such as standard include paths or library paths. `DIRSEP` is the directory separator. You may have to modify it to fit your OS.

The searcher function

The searcher itself is a function, which takes as its first and only parameter the module name.

```
local function search(modulename)
    -- Read source
    local filename
    local file
    local errmsg = ""
    for path in package.tccpath:gmatch"[^;]+" do
        filename = path:gsub("%?", (modulename:gsub("%.", DIRSEP)))
        file = io.open(filename)
        if file then
            break
        end
        errmsg = errmsg.."\n\tno file '"..filename.."'"
    end
    if not file then
        return errmsg
    end
```

The first action of the searcher will be to locate the C source file for the module we are trying to load. To do that we use the content of the package.tccpath variable in the same way that the Lua and C searchers use package.path and package.cpath respectively. Each tested path which doesn't match is added to an error message. If the module is not found, that filename list is returned to require in a string. The format is the same as the one used by the Lua and C searchers: each path is prefixed with a new line and a tab character.

```
    local source = assert(file:read"*a")
```

The content of the module source file is read entirely. That way we will be able to locate pragma directives inside the file (see below). It is not the most efficient way to load the file, especially if the source file is very big, but that is left as an optimization for future versions.

```
    -- Get luatcc pragma commands
    local commands = {}
    for command,argstr in source:gmatch"luatcc[%s]*([a-z_]*)%(((^)]*)%)"
    do
        commands[command] = commands[command] or {}
        local args = {}
        for arg in argstr:gmatch"[^,]+" do
            table.insert(args, arg)
        end
        table.insert(commands[command], args)
    end
```

Since we have no way to add compilation options specific to a module, the TCC searcher will read some pragma directives inside the module source file. An alternative method would have been to load a second file containing those parameters. With pragma directives we can keep the module configuration atomic. Also it does not prevent us from adding a second optional file containing other configuration parameters (for example if we need platform-specific parameters). Each directive has the form:

```
#pragma luatcc commandname(commandparameters)
```

The searcher will load all such found commands in the commands table. Each entry has the command name as key and a array as value. That array contains arrays, each containing the parameters of command. For example if you want to access the second parameter of the first foo command, you would access it through commands["foo"][1][2]. This system gives us an extensible way to add commands. All unused commands will be simply ignored. For the moment, the only command used is use_library, but we could add commands for each luatcc API function.

```
-- Interpret pragma commands
--- use_library
local libdeps = {}
if commands.use_library then
    for _,args in ipairs(commands.use_library) do
        local libdep = args[1]
        table.insert(libdeps, libdep)
    end
end
```

This section of the searcher is the interpretation of the pragma directives. As mentioned above, the only directive used at the moment is use_library. Here we simply build a list of libraries using the first parameter of each use_library command.

Next we create a luatcc context and allocate three local variables. Most luatcc functions return a boolean, success, and eventually an error message, errmsg, if the boolean is false. Also, for more safety, we will call these functions through pcall and the first return value of pcall, indicating the call success, will be stored in result.

```
local context = new_context()
-- Compile file
local result,success,errmsg =
                pcall(context.compile, context, source, filename)
if not result then
    error("error loading module '"..modulename.."' from file '"..
                filename.."':\n\t"..success, 0)
end
assert(success, errmsg)
```

The first step is the compilation of the file. We use `filename` as the chunk name passed to TCC since the source has been directly read from the file without modification. On error we will throw a Lua error. As mentioned before, when describing the searcher behaviours, a searcher has to return a string if it doesn't find a module, but it can throw an error if it finds the module but cannot load it. This is the behaviour used by the Lua and C searchers, and we simply mimic it here. Our first error case is when the `pcall` fails. In that case we throw a simple error message containing the `pcall` error message, stored in `pcall` second return value, here `success`. If the `pcall` went right but the compilation failed, the assert will throw the appropriate error message.

```
-- Add libraries
for _,libdep in ipairs(libdeps) do
    result,success,errmsg = pcall(context.add_library, context, libdep)
    if not result then
        error("error loading module '"..modulename.."' from file '"..
                    filename.."'":\n\t"..success, 0)
    end
    assert(success, errmsg)
end
```

This step is similar to compilation. We simply call `add_library` for each library declared in the module pragma directives. The error mechanism is the same as before.

```
-- Relocate binary code
result,success,errmsg = pcall(context.relocate, context)
if not result then
    error("error loading module '"..modulename.."' from file '"..
                filename.."'":\n\t"..success, 0)
end
assert(success, errmsg)
```

Here again we simply call the `relocate` method of the luatcc context, with the same error handling as before.

```
-- Extract symbol
local chunk
result,chunk,errmsg = pcall(context.get_symbol, context,
                "luaopen_"..string.gsub(modulename, "%.", "_"))
if not result then
    error("error loading module '"..modulename.."' from file '"..
                filename.."'":\n\t"..chunk, 0)
end
assert(chunk, errmsg)
return chunk
end
```

The last step of the loading mechanism is a bit different: instead of a success boolean value, `get_symbol` returns a function, which is the module loader. If all went well, the searcher simply returns the loader to `require`, which is responsible to execute it.

Installing the searcher

Finally, the searcher module contains two last parts.

```
local priority
if type(package.tccpriority)=='number' and package.tccpriority>=1 then
    priority = math.min(#package.loaders+1, package.tccpriority)
end
table.insert(package.loaders, search, priority)
```

The first one will add the interpreted C module searcher to the searcher list used by `require`: `package.loaders`. We simply use `table.insert` to add the searcher to the searcher list. You can specify the searcher priority through the global variable `package.tccpriority`. If you don't specify it, it will default to nil, letting `table.insert` add the searcher at the end of the list. This will give interpreted C modules the lowest priority when several modules of different type have the same name. To change that priority you can simply assign a positive integer value to `package.tccpriority` before loading the `tcc.loader` module (the integer 1 is the highest priority).

```
package.tccpath = "./?.c"
```

The last line is simply the initialization of the path parameter used by the searcher to locate the C source files. Here we look for modules in the current directory, but that path could be extended to include standard system-wide paths, just like `package.path` or `package.cpath`.

Conclusion

The main purpose of this gem was to show you how easy it is to add a completely new kind of module to Lua. With only a few tens of lines, you can convert an existing binding to some other form of programming into a module searcher. My example, which is able to load uncompiled C modules, is just an example. With the same principle, you could load Java classes or their .NET equivalents. You could access some web services, just by loading some interface definition file. You could load modules from Python, TCL, or Ruby.

There is also another field of development for more Lua searchers. With new module searchers, you could simply change the way the searcher locates the code. Instead of loading the modules from some directory according to `package.path`, you could look for the modules online, either in some company-specific intranet or in the wild internet. You could load the modules from a compressed form, just unzipping it before actual loading. You could locate the module in some big archive which contains all the data of your game. You could add a versioning scheme just like the smart one present in Ruby Gems. You could decrypt the module on the fly, or simply check it against a hash key before loading it.

The possibilities are endless. The Lua 5.1 module system is a mechanism that makes Lua module distribution and management much simpler and clearer, providing a standard. But that standard has been cleverly designed and it empowers programmers in such a way that it makes Lua interoperability with other computing systems much easier than it was before.

Lightning Source UK Ltd.
Milton Keynes UK
06 December 2010

163956UK00004B/8/P